Foreword by Dr. Sibichan K. Mathew, NIFT Delhi

SYMBIOCENE AI:
ALGORITHMS OF NATURE

JOSEPH DOLPHIN

notionpress.com
INDIA • SINGAPORE • MALAYSIA

ISBN
Hardcase 979-8-90362-368-6
Paperback 979-8-90319-730-9

Dedication

To
Hachi, my beagle
and
Dolphin, my last name

When your closest intellectual companion is a Dog, and your last name is Dolphin, writing about intelligence beyond humans isn't ambition—it's destiny.

Contents

Preface

For nearly a decade, my academic and professional journey has moved along two parallel tracks—both challenging, enlightening, and deeply transformative. As part of my PhD, my research initially focused on AI mimicking human intelligence in areas such as:

- Consumer behavior prediction
- Fashion shopping journeys
- Digital customer engagement
- Marketing personalization and experience design

This phase of my work was rooted in the widely accepted, dominant paradigm of the Anthropocene—the epoch defined by human-centered thinking, human-led disruption, and human-modelled intelligence systems. Much of the early AI work I encountered, and indeed contributed to, assumed that the human mind was the ultimate blueprint for machine intelligence, and that human decision-making was the gold standard for understanding markets, consumption, and engagement.

But as my research deepened, so did the contradictions.

Across retail, consumer psychology, and digital engagement, I began to see the limits of anthropocentric models. Human-centric AI struggled to explain:

- nonlinear shopping behavior
- collective preference shifts

- emotional contagion
- emergent community patterns
- ecosystemic dynamics of consumption
- unpredictable trend spirals

It became clear that the human brain alone could not explain the complexity of the modern consumer ecosystem.

This realization pushed me into a different frontier.

From Anthropocene to Biomimicry

Searching for answers beyond classical behavioral science and computational psychology, I began to explore biomimicry—the study of nature as a source of design intelligence. What began as curiosity soon became a turning point.

I discovered that:

- Fungal networks route resources more efficiently than many digital platforms,
- Bee colonies make decentralized decisions more adaptively than corporate systems,
- Plant signalling predicts stress and attention better than many engagement analytics models,
- Ocean ecosystems forecast trend flows more accurately than most social media dashboards.

Nature was not simply an inspiration.

It was a blueprint for intelligence itself.

This insight revolutionized my research.

Emergence of Symbiocene AI

Through biomimicry, I encountered the philosophical and ecological concept of the Symbiocene—a future epoch marked by deep coexistence, mutualism, and interdependence among all living systems. Translating this into AI, I began developing what I now call Symbiocene-driven AI models:

- AI rooted in ecological intelligence
- AI that regenerates instead of extracts
- AI inspired by systems, not individuals
- AI designed to enhance community well-being
- AI aligned with planetary boundaries
- AI that goes beyond human mimicry to more-than-human intelligence

This became the foundation for a new direction in my research.

The Turning Point: Pan IIM Conference, IIM Ranchi, November 2025

In November 2025, I had the privilege of presenting my early frameworks on Symbiocene-inspired AI at the prestigious Pan IIM Conference hosted at IIM Ranchi. Surrounded by scholars, directors, industry leaders, and international researchers, I realized that this body of work was ready to evolve beyond scattered papers and academic chapters.

The response to my presentation—"AI after the Anthropocene: Toward Symbiocene Intelligence"—was overwhelming. Many in the audience echoed the need for a paradigm shift in how AI models consumers, markets, and human–technology interactions.

That conference became the catalyst for this book.

Why This Book

Over the years, my research has grown into a comprehensive body of knowledge spanning:

- human-centric AI
- consumer behavior modeling
- biomimicry and ecological computation

- swarm intelligence
- multi-species cognition
- evolutionary and ecosystemic AI
- regenerative design
- Symbiocene theory applied to marketing, engagement, and society

The logical next step was to consolidate all this into a coherent, accessible, and future-oriented text. This book bridges AI, ecology, behavioral science, consumer engagement, and post-Anthropocene thinking.

This book is not just a compilation of my research. It is an invitation to rethink how AI understands people, markets, communities, and the planet. It is a manifesto for how we must build the next era of intelligence—not in competition with nature, but in symbiosis with it.

I hope this work inspires researchers, practitioners, designers, technologists, and policymakers to reimagine the future of AI, not as a tool of extraction, but as a partner in regeneration.

Joseph Dolphin

Kochi, Kerala, India

Foreword

The loss of the Garden of Eden due to the act of eating from the tree of life and knowledge, and the fall of humanity thereafter, as detailed in Genesis, made humans labour their way up. Human beings, in the race to progress and in the effort to strike a balance with machine-induced intelligence, lost the harmony they once had with non-humanity. A kind that they had learned to master with their intelligence, not realising the long-term imbalance this would result in for the ecology. Before it becomes extinct, Joseph Dolphin, in his present book, unravels the not-so-common knowledge among humans about the intelligence that exists in crows, dolphins, octopus, plants, fungi, and the like, and how that knowledge can be integrated in the future developments that might reinstate the harmony. A clear narration of the shift to mimicking non-human intelligence from the present thrust on human intelligence mimicking is presented in this book. From the time fire gave humans power, land domesticated them, money gave them purpose, and science made them deadly to such an extent that even their very existence became questionable, the non-humankind was in distress. At a time when Artificial Intelligence, with its capability of recursive self-development, is a growing concern of the majority of humans, Joseph, who is forever ahead on the new knowledge curve, travels back to a pre-evolved world and discovers the characteristics of the non-human and presents them in layers, stacks and algorithms that help in maintaining the human-non-human, man-machine, natural-artificial harmony. A practical solution to the impending perils of the

Holocene through an innovative and creative use situating AI in the non-humankind especially on distributed thinking, non-symbolic, chemical or tactical signalling and many such path ways form part of the discussion in this book.

It is interesting to see major marketing and consumer behaviour constructs finding a new treatment with transdisciplinary applications. Neuroevolution and its application in marketing, loyalty as an ecosystem, immune analogy, nature-inspired marketing intelligence, to cite a few. Going into the depths of service marketing, Joseph documents ways to convert natural phenomena such as biological evolution, neural structures, and collective animal behaviour to solve complex, non-linear optimisation and cognitive problems. There are mentions of artificial intelligence even in casual conversations in the present times. I was fortunate to understand and follow developments in information technology since the late 1980s. Two sectors that mattered most to most of the developing nations during that period were textiles and information technology. Joseph has been adept at it early on and has a ringside view of the business and technology over three decades. He is my go-to expert from the mid-1990s. Be it on how Electronic Data Exchange (EDI) helps organizations keep a real-time track of inventory at stores and information relayed back to the production team; E-commerce, which was in its infancy then, to CRM, Commerce, Community, Content, Social, Mobility, Analytics, Cloud, IoT, and AI. I will appreciate his need to communicate all futuristic thoughts stored in his memory. Joseph believes that time is too short and he is in an eternal hurry to tell the world about the rapid changes taking place and how this impacts the business value chain and therefore how the new generation should shape up to meaningfully deliver results in this changing scenario. The book consists of high-level educational material supplemented with projects for applications and contains a clear prescription for a new world. Joseph combines his Management Consulting practice and expertise as a Data Scientist who works towards customer delight and brings out exceptionally outstanding work. Dolphin is a passionate and very articulate presenter who has conducted several lectures/workshops on E-Commerce and EDI, Service Dominant Logic, Interactive Technologies, Innovation, Problem Solving, Project Management, Customer Experience Management, Technology Services, etc. Coupled with his deep knowledge of IT and the industry and academic research he had undertaken, Joseph channels all that would make a seminal work. Joseph brings together unique content on AI, which is creative and imaginative. He uniquely combines fiction and management topics to create a context for a nature-inspired future and takes the extant discussions on the topic to an entirely new level in his present book.

In all these years, Joseph has been able to build his body of knowledge and convert his contextual knowledge into services that he has successfully delivered to customers, especially academia. It is rare to find the combination of creativity, oratory, presentation, knowledge, and IT prowess in one individual, and with a flair for teaching.

I am honoured to have asked to write this foreword. Joseph is endowed with divergent thoughts and has maintained consistency in translating those into books. I trust that the readers will find many stacks, layers, and networks that align with goals to keep the non-mankind co-exist and co-create co-intelligently. I wish him the best to continue to create original products for academia to accelerate and enhance the knowledge of the teaching community and students.

Dr. Sibichan K Mathew

Former Head of Research,
National Institute of Fashion Technology (NIFT), New Delhi

The best way to understand the human mind is to try building one

01

Mainstream AI

1.1 Introduction to Human-Mimicking AI

The first and most dominant wave of artificial intelligence has revolved around a compelling proposition:

Can machines imitate human intelligence?

From early rule-based systems to today's transformers, mainstream AI has been shaped by human cognition. The reason is simple: the economy rewards tools that can perform human tasks—cheaper, faster, or more consistently.

This chapter introduces the **three pillars** of human-like AI:

- Language intelligence
- Vision intelligence
- Decision intelligence

We will explore why the world has invested so deeply in these models, how they work, what mathematical foundations support them, and where their limits lie.

1.2 Language Intelligence

Language is the crown jewel of human cognition.

It enables conversation, narrative, persuasion, memory, and shared meaning.

Modern **Language Models (LLMs)**—ChatGPT, Claude, Gemini, Llama—are built to imitate:

- Dialogue
- Storytelling
- Reasoning
- Summaries
- Explanations
- Inference

How they learn:

- They ingest text from books, the internet, transcripts, emails, and documents.
- They map patterns between words, ideas, emotions, and concepts.
- They model probabilities of what comes next in a sentence.

Why are they powerful:

LLMs don't only autocomplete; they reconstruct meaning, simulate reasoning, and produce human-like discourse.

1.3 Vision Intelligence

Human vision is fast, intuitive, and astonishingly detailed.

AI attempts to replicate this ability using:

- Computer Vision models: Computer vision models enable machines to interpret and understand visual data like images and videos. They extract patterns, detect objects, classify scenes, and even generate new visuals. These models power applications from medical imaging to self-driving cars.
- Convolutional Neural Networks (CNNs): CNNs are specialized neural networks designed to detect spatial patterns in images

using convolutional filters. They excel at tasks like object detection, image classification, and face recognition.

Their layered feature extraction makes them powerful for pixel-level understanding.

- Vision Transformers (ViTs): ViTs apply the transformer architecture to images by splitting them into patches and learning global relationships. They outperform CNNs in many large-scale vision tasks due to their ability to model long-range dependencies. They represent the shift from localized filters to holistic attention-driven vision.
- Diffusion Models: Diffusion models generate high-quality images by gradually denoising random noise through learned reverse diffusion steps. They produce photorealistic, diverse visuals and power tools like DALL·E and Midjourney.

These models are state-of-the-art in generative AI, surpassing GANs in stability and fidelity.

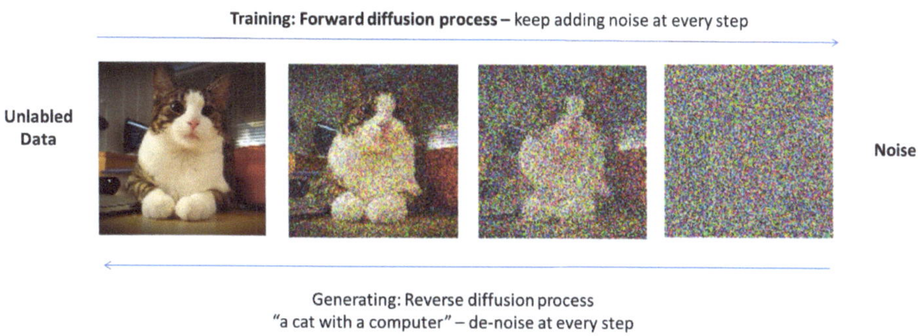

Figure 0: *Diffusion Models (e.g., Stable Diffusion)*

These models can:

- Recognize objects
- Detect emotions
- Understand scenes

- Process medical images
- Guide autonomous vehicles

They learn using millions of labeled images: cars, animals, roads, faces, crops, tools, and more.

Achievement: Vision AI now often surpasses human accuracy in specialized domains, including X-ray detection, manufacturing defect detection, and agricultural disease detection.

1.4 Decision Intelligence

Decision-making is a cornerstone of human cognition.

AI imitates this through:

- Reinforcement Learning: Reinforcement Learning (RL) is a learning paradigm where an agent learns by interacting with an environment. It receives rewards or penalties and optimizes actions to maximize long-term returns. RL powers robotics, gaming, and adaptive decision-making systems.
- Markov Decision Processes (MDPs): MDPs provide the mathematical framework underlying Reinforcement Learning. They describe environments in terms of states, actions, transition probabilities, and rewards. MDPs help formally model sequential decision-making under uncertainty.
- Predictive models: Predictive models analyze historical data to forecast future outcomes or behaviors. They use statistical or machine-learning techniques to detect patterns and generate predictions. Applications range from demand forecasting and churn prediction to risk scoring.
- Recommender systems: Recommender systems suggest products, content, or actions tailored to user preferences. They use collaborative filtering, content-based filtering, or hybrid methods to personalize recommendations. These

systems power platforms like Netflix, Amazon, and Spotify, driving engagement and conversions.

Examples include:

- Netflix recommending a movie
- Amazon predicting what you'll buy
- Banks detecting fraud
- Robots navigating obstacles

Why it works:

AI learns patterns in human choices and outcomes. It then builds models that output "the next best action"—just like humans do.

1.5 Why AI Mimics Human Intelligence

Three forces drive this trend:

1. Economic Utility

Organizations want automation that mirrors human work:

- Customer support
- Content writing
- Risk analysis
- Decision-making
- Quality inspection

Human-like tasks = large markets = strong economic incentives.

2. Human-Labeled Data Availability

The internet is a treasure trove of human-created information.

This makes human-task AI easy to train.

3. Intuitive and Philosophical Appeal

Humans love machines that mirror them.

We're fascinated by whether AI can:

- Think
- Reason
- Feel
- Write
- Understand

It is psychology as much as technology.

1.6 Conceptual Model: The Human-Mimicking AI Stack

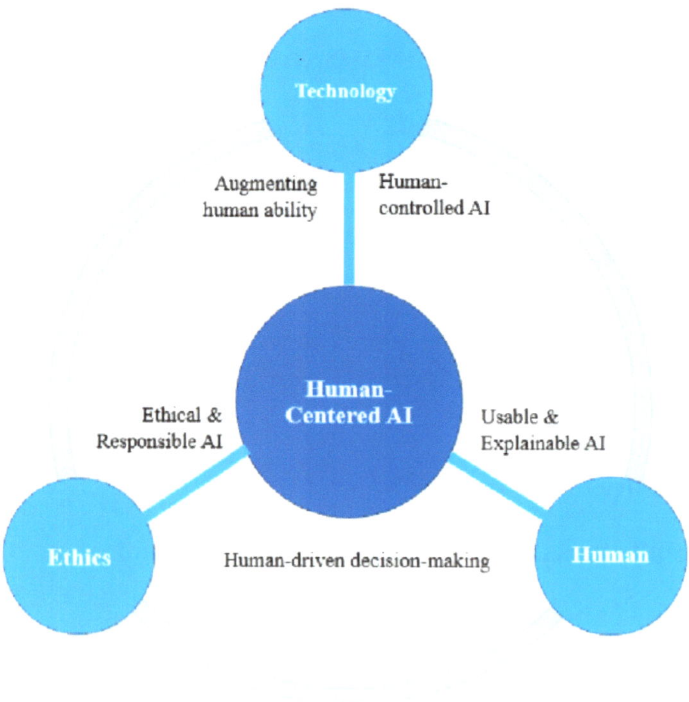

Figure 1: *The Human-Mimicking AI Stack*

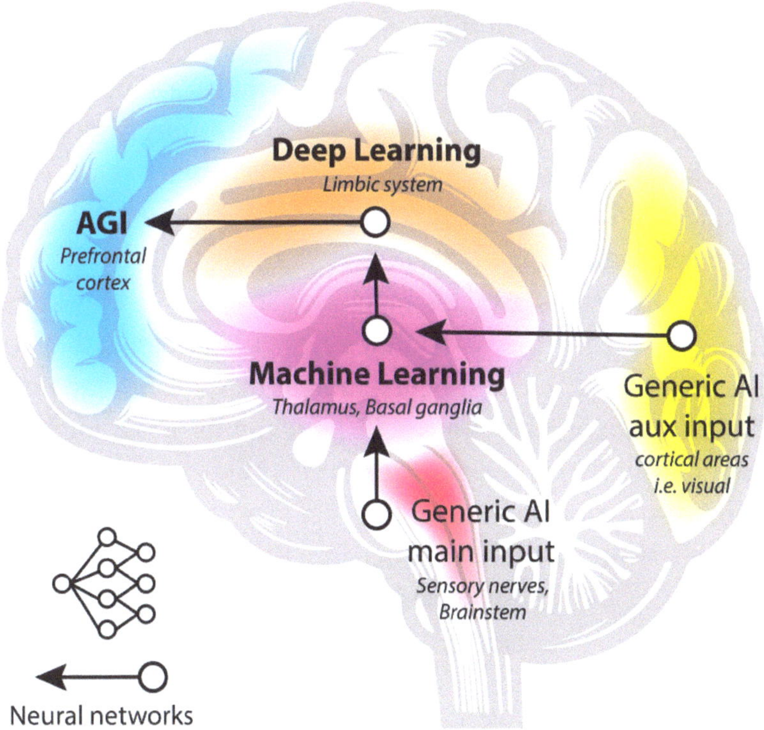

Figure 2: *The Human Mimicry AI Stack*

THE HUMAN MIMICRY AI STACK

The Human Mimicry AI Stack represents a grand synthesis of computational ambition: an engineered scaffold designed to emulate, approximate, and sometimes surpass the cognitive repertoire of human beings. Beginning with Layer 1, the stack anchors itself in quintessential human faculties—language comprehension, visual perception, memory consolidation, decision-making under uncertainty, and the nuanced spectrum of emotion. Layer 2 extends this foundation by feeding machines with the same sensory and behavioral residues that shape human cognition: text and speech, images and videos, and the sprawling trails of behavioral logs that encode our preferences, mistakes, and micro-intentions. Together, these layers craft the raw perceptual and experiential substrate from which humanlike intelligence can be computationally inferred.

This substrate is sculpted by Layer 3, where architectures such as transformers, CNNs, RNNs, and reinforcement-learning agents operationalize perception and reasoning into trainable mathematical structures. Layer 4 then imbues these models with learning dynamics—supervised signals that label the world, self-supervised strategies that let machines discover latent structure, reinforcement learning loops that reward adaptive behavior, and RLHF pipelines that encode societal norms through human feedback. Finally, Layer 5 manifests the practical dividends of this multilayered edifice: chatbots with increasingly humanlike interactivity, fraud-detection systems that anticipate deviance, autonomous vehicles that interpret the world with precision, recommender engines that intuit desires, and robotic systems that translate cognition into physical agency. Collectively, the stack is not merely a technical taxonomy—it is a blueprint for machines that aspire to mirror the astonishing complexity of the human mind.

Layer 1—Human Cognitive Functions

Language • Vision • Memory • Decision-making • Emotion

Layer 2—Human Data Sources

Text • Speech • Images • Videos • Behavioral logs

Layer 3—Model Architectures

Transformers • CNNs • RNNs • RL Agents

Layer 4—Training Mechanisms

Supervised Learning

Self-Supervised Learning

Reinforcement Learning

RLHF (Human Feedback)

Layer 5—Applications

Chatbots • Fraud detection • Autonomous driving • Recommenders • Robotics

1.7 Mapping Human Abilities to AI Models

Human Capability	AI Equivalent	Model Types	Data Source
Language	LLM	Transformer	Text corpora
Vision	Computer Vision	CNN, ViT	Images
Hearing	ASR	RNN, Transformer	Audio files
Decision-making	RL Agents	Q-learning, MDPs	Behavioral logs
Memory	Attention & Embeddings	Transformer blocks	Sequential data
Emotion Detection	Affective AI	Multimodal models	Facial & voice data

1.8 How Human-Like AI Learns: The Maths Behind It

AI learns *patterns*, not consciousness. It mimics human intelligence through a combination of mathematical tools:

Core Mathematics

- **Linear Algebra:** matrices, vectors
- **Calculus:** gradient descent
- **Probability:** likelihood functions
- **Statistics:** regression, distributions

- **Information Theory:** entropy, compression
- **Optimization:** loss functions

Key ML Techniques

- Backpropagation: Backpropagation is the algorithm used to train neural networks by calculating how much each weight contributed to the error. It propagates errors backward through the network and updates parameters to reduce loss. This technique enables deep learning by making multilayer training efficient.
- Stochastic Gradient Descent: SGD updates model parameters using small, randomly sampled batches of data. This makes training faster and more scalable compared to full-batch gradient descent. Its noisy updates help escape local minima and improve generalization.
- Self-attention: Self-attention allows a model to weigh the importance of different parts of an input relative to one another. It captures global relationships—like how words relate across a sentence or how patches relate across an image. This mechanism powers transformers and dramatically improves sequence and vision tasks.
- Embedding spaces: Embedding spaces represent items—like words, images, users, or products—as vectors in a continuous space. Distances in this space reflect semantic or behavioral similarity. Embeddings power search, recommendations, NLP, and multi-modal AI systems.
- Fine-tuning: Fine-tuning adapts a pre-trained model to a new dataset or task using additional training. It requires fewer resources and data because the model already learned general features. Fine-tuning enables domain-specific performance gains with minimal effort.

- Transfer learning: Transfer learning reuses knowledge from one task or dataset to improve performance on another. It accelerates training, especially in data-scarce domains. This technique underpins modern AI workflows, from NLP to medical imaging.
- Reinforcement learning: Reinforcement Learning (RL) trains an agent to make sequential decisions by maximizing cumulative rewards. It is based on trial-and-error interactions with the environment. RL fuels breakthroughs in robotics, gaming (AlphaGo), and adaptive control systems.

These methods allow AI to approximate facets of human thinking without actually being human.

1.9 Strengths and Limitations of Human-Mimicking AI

Strengths

- High accuracy
- Scales infinitely
- Works 24/7
- Learns from large human datasets
- Can support or augment human work

Limitations

- Inherits human biases
- Fails at edge cases
- Overfits to human patterns
- Lacks physical experience
- No common sense without training
- Cannot fully understand emotion or context

Human imitation is powerful—but also constrained.

1.10 Summary & Transition

Mainstream AI has succeeded because it aligns with:

- Human needs
- Human data
- Human economics
- Human intuition

It gives us machines that look, talk, and decide like us. But this is only the first paradigm. Future paradigms will extend beyond imitation to regeneration, symbiosis, and ecosystem intelligence. Now that the foundations are clear, we move to a practical application.

Project: Building an AI Customer Support Agent

A large telecom company wants to automate 70% of customer-service interactions using an AI system that speaks naturally, solves problems, and escalates issues intelligently.

Challenges

- Wide variations in customer emotion and tone
- Multiple levels of problem complexity
- Risk of misinterpretation
- Need to mimic human empathy

Solution Matrix

Problem	Method	Technique/Math
Understanding intent	LLM	Transformers, embeddings
Detecting emotion	Sentiment model	Logistic regression, SoftMax
Maintaining conversation	Dialogue management	Markov Chains
Choosing the best response	Reinforcement Learning	Q-Learning, reward functions
Improving quality	RLHF	Gradient estimates, feedback loops
Measuring accuracy	Evaluation	Confusion matrix, precision, recall

MCQs

1. Mainstream AI focuses on mimicking:

   a. Solar activity
   b. Human intelligence
   c. Animal instincts
   d. Mechanical systems

2. Language models learn from:

   a. Weather patterns
   b. Human text
   c. Ocean currents
   d. Satellite signals

3. Vision AI replicates:

   a. Human digestion
   b. Human sight
   c. Human metabolism
   d. Human reflexes

4. The main driver of human-labelled AI data is:

   a. Scarcity
   b. Abundance
   c. Government control
   d. Secret databases

5. Reinforcement Learning imitates:

   a. Natural disasters
   b. Reward-based decision-making
   c. Agricultural cycles
   d. Gravity patterns

6. Transformers rely on:

    a. Matrices
    b. Chemical bonds
    c. DNA
    d. Black holes

7. CNNs are used in:

    a. Computer vision
    b. Cooking
    c. Pollution modelling
    d. Metal smelting

8. RLHF uses:

    a. Human feedback
    b. Storm simulations
    c. DNA editing
    d. None of the above

9. Embeddings convert language into:

    a. Sculptures
    b. Vectors
    c. Liquids
    d. Heat signals

10. Decision-making models use:

    a. Markov processes
    b. Clay models
    c. Weather balloons
    d. Lava flows

11. Sentiment analysis detects:

    a. Tree growth
    b. Emotion
    c. Metal density
    d. Radio signals

12. Optimization in AI involves:

    a. Maximizing loss
    b. Minimizing loss
    c. Removing maths
    d. Adding noise

13. Vision Transformers use:

    a. Pixel attention
    b. Boiler pressure
    c. Air density
    d. Salt water

14. Predictive analytics relies on:

    a. Astrology
    b. Statistics
    c. Mythology
    d. Architecture

15. Linear algebra is key for:

    a. Matrix operations
    b. Soil testing
    c. Wind turbines
    d. Marine biology

16. AI inherits bias from:

    a. Random noise
    b. Human data
    c. Ocean currents
    d. Fiction books

17. The internet enables AI because:

    a. It is artistic
    b. It contains massive human data
    c. It is encrypted
    d. It is anonymous

18. RL agents learn through:

    a. Rewards
    b. Rainfall
    c. Gravity
    d. Astronomy

19. Transformers outperform earlier models because they use:

    a. Attention
    b. Metal alloys
    c. Oil pressure
    d. Soil composition

20. Human-mimicking AI is limited by:

    a. Lack of heat
    b. Human bias
    c. Solar flares
    d. Too much hardware

Answers

1-b

2-b

3-b

4-b

5-b

6-a

7-a

8-a

9-b

10-a

11-b

12-b

13-a

14-b

15-a

16-b

17-b

18-a

19-a

20-b

Intelligence is not what thinks like us. Intelligence is what survives, adapts, and organizes life.

02

Beyond Human

2.1 AI Inspired by Non-Human Intelligence

For most of the history of AI, we tried to build machines that resembled *ourselves*—machines that speak, see, and reason like humans.

But nature is full of intelligences **radically different** from ours:

- Ant colonies that solve optimization problems without leaders
- Octopuses that think with their arms
- Fungi that route nutrients with internet-like mycelial networks
- Forest ecosystems that self-regulate through dynamic feedback loops
- Evolutionary processes that design strategies through trial, mutation, and selection

And so, a new question emerges:

What if the future of AI is not human at all?

- What if the most powerful models will be inspired by:
    - Swarms
    - Octopuses
    - Plants
    - Ecosystems
    - Evolution

Chapter 2 explores this paradigm: **Non-Human Intelligence as Inspiration for AI.**

2.2 Swarm Intelligence: Nature's Decentralized Coordination

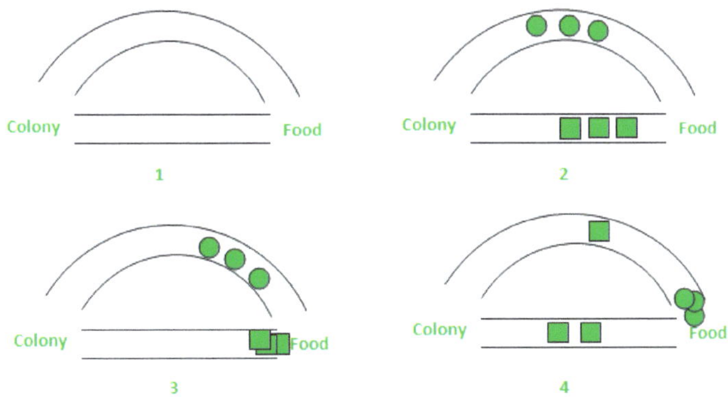

Figure 3: *Swarm Intelligence: Nature's Decentralized Coordination*

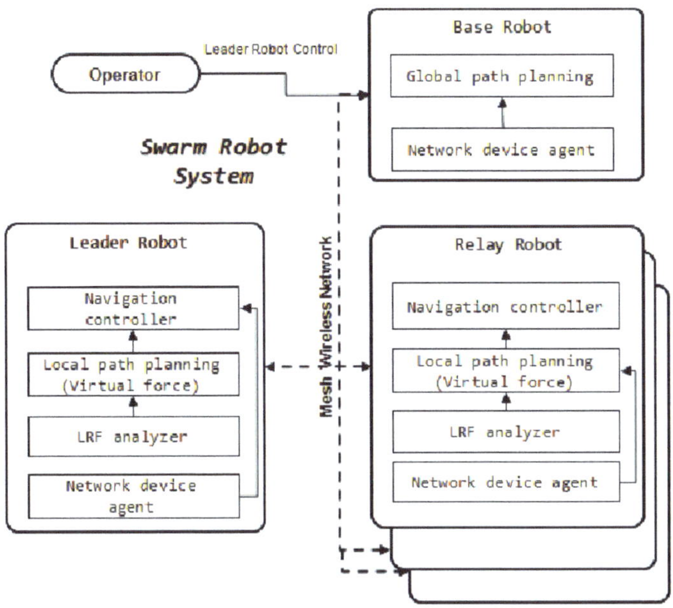

Figure 4: *Swarm Robot System*

Swarm intelligence originates from the collective behavior of animals:

- Ant colonies
- Bee swarms
- Bird flocks
- Fish schools

These groups solve complex problems **without a leader**, using simple local rules.

Core Principle

Simple agents + simple rules → complex global behavior

Why it matters for AI

Swarm intelligence is ideal for problems where:

- There is no central controller
- Real-time adaptation is required
- Multiple possibilities must be explored
- Robustness is essential

Examples:

- Drone fleets
- Traffic routing
- Logistics
- Optimal pathfinding
- Disaster search and rescue

2.3 Algorithms Inspired by Swarms

Algorithms inspired by swarms embody a profound philosophical shift in computation: they derive intelligence not from a single omniscient entity but from the emergent coordination of many simple agents. **Ant Colony Optimization (ACO)** exemplifies this paradigm. Just as real ants discover the shortest route to nourishment by reinforcing successful paths with pheromone trails, artificial agents simulate these chemical cues to iteratively converge on optimal solutions. This humble biological metaphor now underpins high-stakes technologies—route planning for Amazon and UPS, intelligent internet routing protocols, large-scale network optimization, and intricate scheduling problems—where decentralized problem-solving outperforms rigid top-down control.

Particle Swarm Optimization (PSO) extends this biomimetic ethos into the aerial and aquatic worlds of birds and fish. Each agent navigates the solution space by reconciling two forces: its own historically best position and the superior positions found by its neighbours. The result is a fluid, adaptive search mechanism that avoids the brittleness of traditional optimization. PSO has become indispensable for hyperparameter tuning in machine learning, for guiding robots through uncertain environments, for engineering complex design systems, and for orchestrating sophisticated financial optimization strategies. In both ACO and PSO, swarm intelligence proves that collective simplicity can give rise to computational elegance—and, often, to solutions that rival human ingenuity.

1. Ant Colony Optimization (ACO)

Ants find the shortest path to food using pheromone trails.

AI Version:

Agents simulate pheromone updates to find optimal solutions.

Used in:

- Route planning (Amazon, UPS)
- Internet routing
- Network optimization
- Scheduling tasks

2. Particle Swarm Optimization (PSO)

Inspired by birds and fish.

Agents adjust movements based on:

- Their own best-known position
- Their neighbour's best position

Applications:

- Hyperparameter tuning
- Robotics navigation
- Engineering design problems
- Financial optimization

2.4 Comparing ACO and PSO

Feature	**ACO**	**PSO**
Inspiration	Ant colonies	Bird flocks/Fish schools
Strength	Optimal paths	Searching for optimal values
Memory	Collective pheromones	Personal + social best
Best for	Logistics routing	Continuous optimization
Key Weakness	Slow convergence	Local minimal risk

2.5 Animal Cognition: The Alien Minds

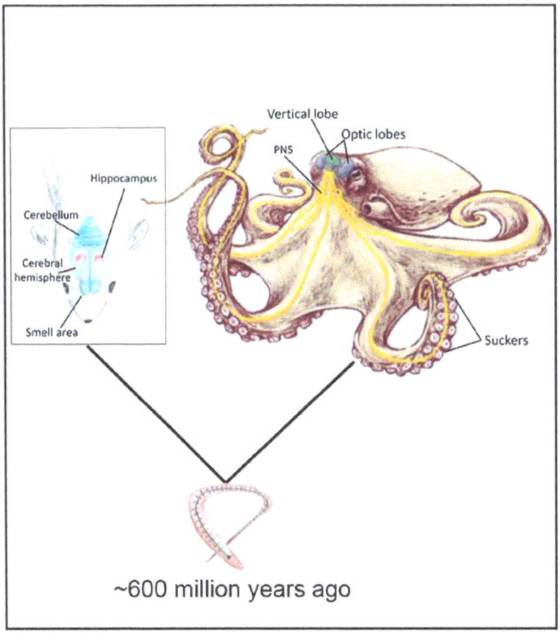

Figure 5: *Animal Cognition – Octopus*

Figure 6: *Animal Cognition – Crow*

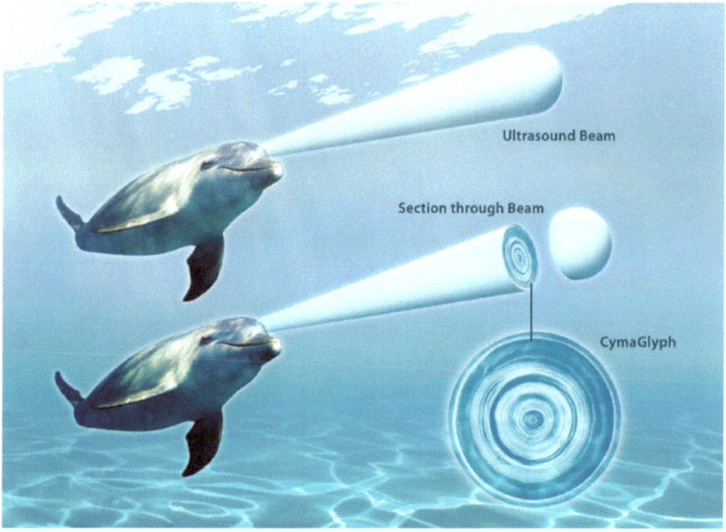

Figure 7: *Animal Cognition – Dolphins*

Animals like **dolphins, crows, elephants, and octopuses** demonstrate:

- Problem-solving
- Tool use
- Communication systems
- Social learning
- Memory
- Emotional intelligence

But their cognition is *non-human.*

Why this matters for AI

We may learn new forms of intelligence:

- Distributed cognition (octopus' arms)
- Embodied cognition (dolphins, elephants)
- Non-symbolic reasoning (crows)
- Chemical or tactile signalling (marine animals)

2.6 Octopus Intelligence: Distributed Thinking

Key Insight

An octopus has **9 brains**:

- 1 central brain
- 8 arm ganglia that act semi-independently

This inspires **distributed AI architectures**, such as:

- Multi-agent systems
- Decentralized decision networks
- Edge-AI computing

Example

Imagine a robot with:

- A central controller
- Local smart modules handling tasks independently

This mirrors how octopus arms explore, manipulate, and sense.

2.7 Crows and Dolphins: Tools, Symbols & Communication

Crows

- Make hooks
- Solve puzzles
- Understand water displacement
- Remember human faces

AI Idea: Hybrid symbolic-non-symbolic reasoning (Logic + learning combined)

Dolphins

- Complex "click-whistle" language
- Social teaching
- Cooperative hunting strategies

AI Idea: Emergent communication systems in multi-agent AI (e.g., deep multi-agent reinforcement learning)

2.8 Intelligence without Neurons: Plants & Fungi

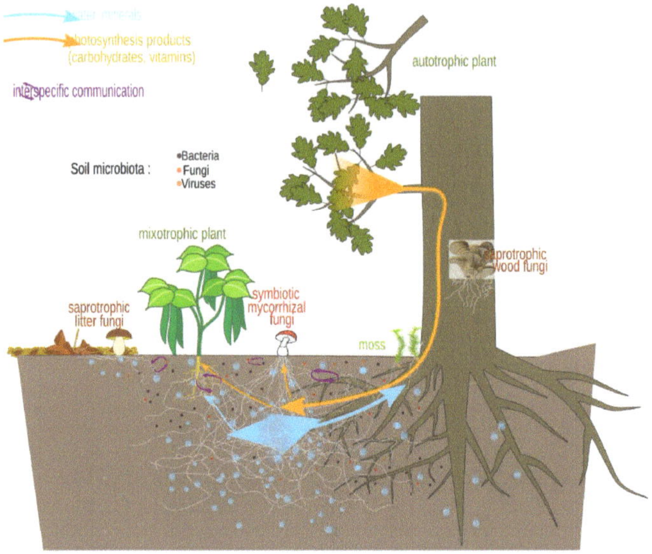

Figure 8: *Intelligence without neurons: plants*

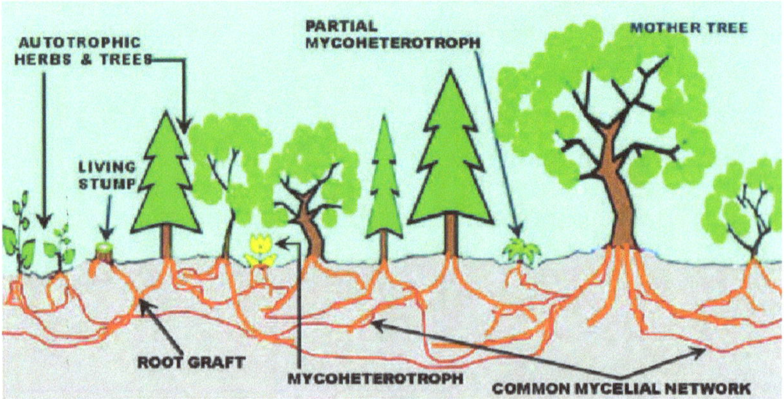

Figure 9: *Intelligence without neurons: fungi*

Plants and fungi challenge our brain-centric view of intelligence.

Examples of plant & fungal intelligence

- Mycelium networks share nutrients based on need
- Tree roots signal danger chemically
- Fungi re-route resources around obstacles
- Plants track sunlight, moisture, and competitors

This is **decentralized adaptive intelligence**.

2.9 What Plants Teach AI

1. Distributed Information Flow

Mycelium networks behave like decentralized routers.

→ Inspiration for decentralized computing.

2. Slow but Optimal Decision-Making

Plants optimize resources over long periods.

→ Inspiration for long-term planning of AI.

3. Chemical Signalling Networks

Plants communicate through chemicals, not signals.

→ Inspiration for non-electrical communication protocols in AI.

2.10 Human vs Plant vs Fungi Intelligence

Capability	Humans	Plants	Fungi
Central Brain	Yes	No	No
Communication	Language	Chemical	Chemical/ Electrical
Decision Style	Fast	Slow	Distributed
Network Type	Neuronal	Root networks	Mycelium web

Capability	Humans	Plants	Fungi
Relevance to AI	Symbolic reasoning	Resource optimization	Decentralized routing

2.11 Ecosystem & Gaia Intelligence

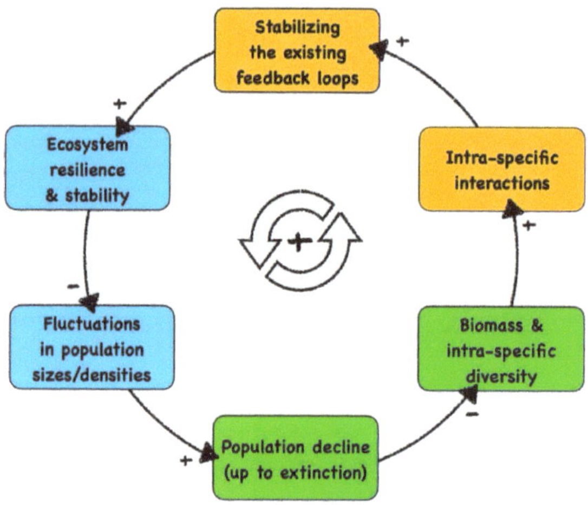

Figure 10: *Ecosystem Intelligence*

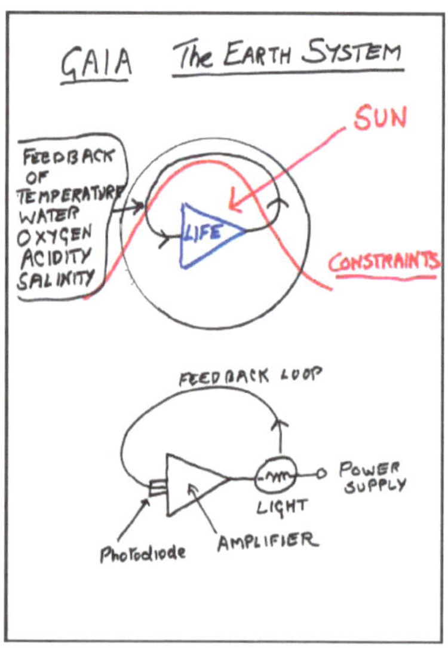

Figure 11: *GAIA Model*

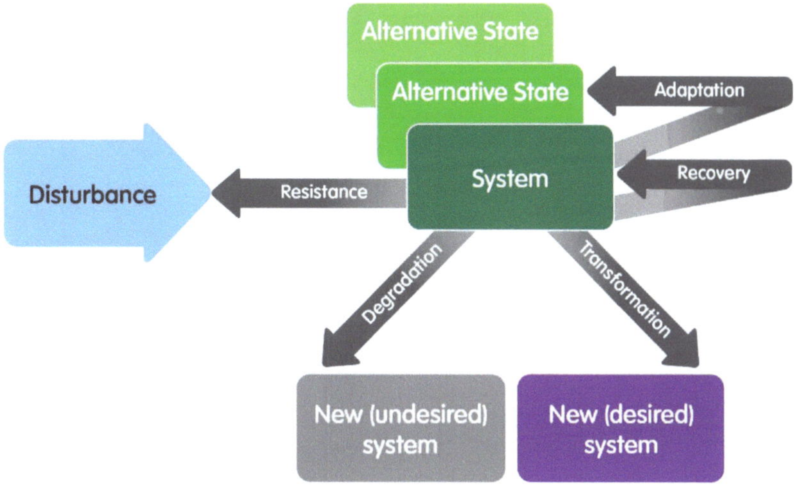

Figure 12: *Self-Regulating Intelligence System*

An ecosystem is a **self-regulating intelligence system**:

- Feedback loops
- Resilience mechanisms
- Competition & cooperation
- Resource balancing
- Emergent behaviors

Examples:

- Forests regulate temperature and moisture
- Coral reefs manage symbiosis
- Oceans maintain chemical balance

2.12 Systems Thinking for AI

Key principles:

1. Feedback loops

Systems change inputs based on outputs.

2. Non-linear dynamics

Small changes → big impacts.

3. Emergence

Order emerges without central control.

4. Resilience

Recovery from shock.

Applications:

- Smart cities
- Climate AI
- Energy grid optimization
- Supply chain resilience
- Epidemic forecasting

2.13 Gaia Models

The Gaia hypothesis treats Earth as a **self-regulating superorganism**.

AI applications:

- Climate simulations
- Global food systems modeling
- Planetary-scale optimization
- Biosphere health monitoring
- Large-scale ecological forecasting

This moves AI away from *individual performance* toward *planetary-scale intelligence.*

2.14 Evolutionary & Developmental Intelligence

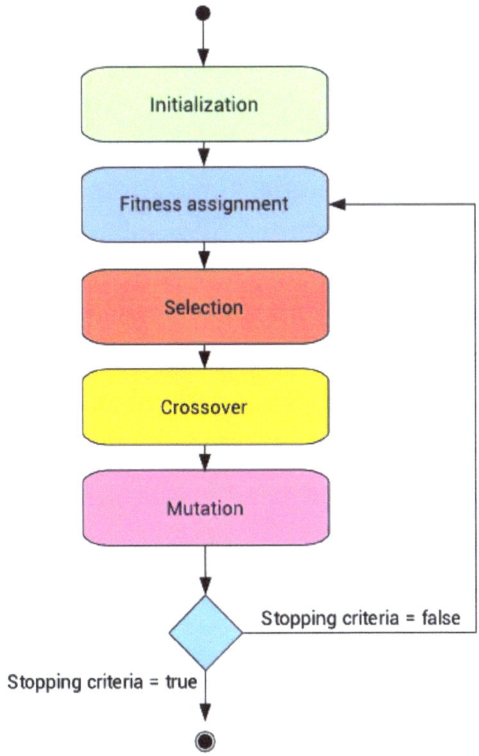

Figure 13: *Evolutionary Intelligence*

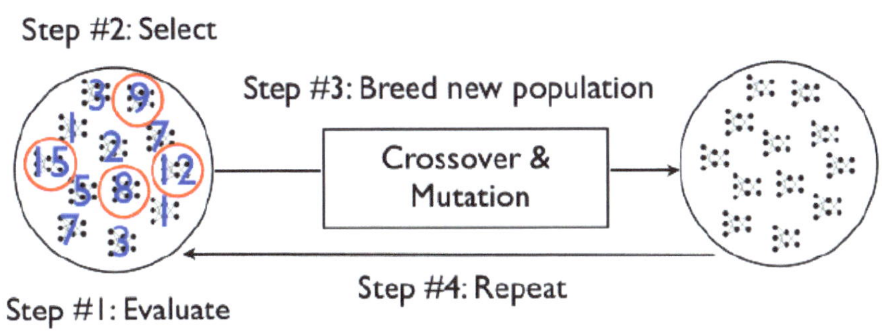

Figure 14: *Developmental Intelligence*

Evolution is nature's ultimate problem-solving engine.

AI techniques inspired by evolution channel the relentless inventiveness of natural selection into computational form, transforming randomness, variation, and survival into engines of optimization. **Genetic algorithms, evolutionary strategies, genetic programming, neuroevolution, and A-Life** all draw from the same Darwinian logic: populations of candidate solutions compete, mutate, recombine, and adapt across generations. In **Genetic Algorithms (GAs)**, this process unfolds through a disciplined cycle—begin with random solutions, evaluate their fitness, induce mutations and crossovers, retain the strongest performers, and iterate. This evolutionary loop has proven astonishingly effective in domains as diverse as game-strategy design, engineering optimization, financial portfolio modeling, and neural architecture search, particularly where search spaces are vast, nonlinear, or inhospitable to classical mathematical methods.

Neuroevolution elevates this paradigm by allowing neural networks themselves to evolve rather than be sculpted through gradient descent. Architectures, weights, and behaviors emerge through evolutionary pressure, yielding systems that often exhibit startling ingenuity. Such networks thrive in environments where adaptability, exploration, and embodied intelligence matter—game-playing agents that discover unorthodox winning strategies, robots that teach themselves to walk in unfamiliar terrains, drones that autonomously navigate chaotic airspaces, and multi-agent ecosystems where cooperation and competition evolve organically. These evolutionary algorithms remind us that, just as life innovates without foresight, machines too can uncover solutions that defy human intuition—sometimes crude, sometimes elegant, but frequently superior.

AI techniques inspired by evolution:

- Genetic algorithms
- Neuroevolution
- Genetic programming
- Evolutionary strategies
- Artificial life (A-Life)

2.15 Genetic Algorithms (GA)

GA steps:

1. Start with random solutions
2. Evaluate fitness
3. Mutate, crossover
4. Select the best performers
5. Repeat

Applications:

- Game strategy optimization
- Engineering design
- Portfolio optimization
- Neural architecture search

2.16 Neuroevolution

Neural networks that *evolve* instead of being trained through gradient descent.

Used in:

- Game-playing AI
- Robot locomotion
- Drone navigation
- Multi-agent ecosystems

Neuroevolution leads to surprising, creative strategies—often better than human-designed ones.

2.17 Mathematics Behind Non-Human-Inspired AI

Swarm Mathematics

Swarm Mathematics relies on stochastic and collective dynamics: *random walks* and *probabilistic exploration* allow agents to traverse vast search spaces without central control, while *distributed consensus* mechanisms enable groups to converge on shared decisions. *Flocking equations*—notably Reynolds' rules—capture how simple local interactions produce coordinated, lifelike group behavior.

- Random walks: **Random walks** model movement through a space using unpredictable, step-by-step transitions, enabling algorithms to escape local traps and explore broader solution landscapes.
- Probabilistic exploration: **Probabilistic exploration** guides agents to choose actions based on likelihoods rather than certainty, balancing curiosity with efficiency in complex environments.
- Distributed consensus: **Distributed consensus** allows multiple agents to collectively agree on a shared value or decision without centralized control, ensuring coordination in large, decentralized systems.
- Flocking equations (Reynolds rules): **Flocking equations (Reynolds' rules)** use simple local behaviors—alignment, cohesion, and separation—to produce remarkably lifelike group motion seen in bird flocks and swarm robots.

Evolutionary Mathematics

Evolutionary Mathematics encodes adaptation through quantifiable competition. *Fitness functions* measure how well solutions perform, while *mutation operators* and *probability distributions* generate variation across generations. *Selection-pressure models* determine which candidates survive, ensuring continuous refinement toward optimality.

- Fitness functions: **Fitness functions** quantify how well a candidate solution performs, acting as the guiding metric that evolution attempts to maximize.
- Mutation operators: **Mutation operators** introduce small, random changes to solutions, ensuring diversity and enabling the discovery of novel, potentially superior variations.
- Probability distributions: **Probability distributions** shape how traits are sampled, mutated, or recombined, giving evolutionary processes their characteristic blend of randomness and structure.
- Selection pressure models: **Selection pressure models** determine how aggressively the best solutions are favored, controlling whether evolution proceeds steadily, conservatively, or explosively.

Ecosystem Mathematics

Ecosystem Mathematics models complexity using dynamic, interdependent systems. *Differential equations* express how populations change over time, *predator–prey models* reveal cyclic stability, and *network-flow equations* track resource movement. Together with *multi-agent optimization,* these frameworks replicate ecological intelligence in computational form.

- Differential equations: **Differential equations** describe how systems evolve, allowing AI models to capture continuous, dynamic changes in complex environments.
- Predator–prey models: **Predator–prey models** simulate cyclical interactions between competing or cooperating agents, revealing patterns of stability, oscillation, and emergent balance.

- Network flow equations: **Network flow equations** track how resources, information, or energy move through interconnected systems, enabling efficient routing and allocation in large networks.
- Multi-agent optimization: **Multi-agent optimization** coordinates many autonomous agents to collectively solve problems, balancing cooperation and competition to reach globally efficient outcomes.

2.18 Technical Techniques

Technical Techniques extend these ideas into cutting-edge AI systems. Multi-agent reinforcement learning and decentralized optimization enable cooperation without a central controller, while cellular automata and self-organizing maps emulate local rules giving rise to global patterns. Graph neural networks and emergent communication models empower agents to reason collectively, forming the mathematical backbone of non-human-inspired intelligence.

- Multi-agent reinforcement learning: **Multi-agent reinforcement learning** trains multiple agents to learn, adapt, and interact simultaneously, often producing complex cooperative or competitive behaviors.
- Decentralized optimization: **Decentralized optimization** allows agents to solve large-scale problems without a central controller, using local information to reach globally efficient solutions.
- Cellular automata: **Cellular automata** use simple, rule-based updates on a grid of cells to generate surprisingly rich and emergent patterns from minimal local interactions.
- Self-organizing maps: **Self-organizing maps** project high-dimensional data onto low-dimensional grids, revealing hidden structures through unsupervised, topology-preserving learning.

- Graph neural networks: **Graph neural networks** enable reasoning over interconnected entities by learning patterns embedded in graph structures like social networks or transportation systems.
- Emergent communication models: **Emergent communication models** allow agents to invent and evolve their own languages, creating shared symbols and protocols that enhance coordination and problem-solving.

2.19 Advantages of Non-Human Intelligence Models

Strengths

- Great for decentralization
- Robust under uncertainty
- Highly adaptive
- Creative solutions
- Evolves continuously

Limitations

- Hard to control
- Hard to explain
- May require computation
- Solutions may be "non-intuitive."

2.20 Summary: The Mind of the Future May Not Look Like Ours

Non-human intelligence models expand the imagination of AI:

- Swarms teach collaboration
- Animals teach embodiment
- Plants teach decentralization
- Ecosystems teach resilience
- Evolution teaches adaptation

Project: Autonomous Disaster Response Swarm

Scenario

A government agency wants to build a **swarm of drones** for disaster zones:

- No central command
- Must self-organize
- Must search collapsed areas
- Must coordinate like ants, birds, and mycelium networks

Solution Matrix

Problem	Technique	Math/AI Field
Exploration	Ant Colony Optimization	Pheromone equations
Search patterns	Particle Swarm Optimization	Velocity update equations
Local decision-making	Multi-agent RL	Markov processes
Communication	Decentralized consensus	Graph theory
Avoiding collisions	Flocking model	Reynolds equations (cohesion, alignment, separation)
Adaptation	Genetic algorithms	Mutation, crossover
Routing signals	Mycelium-inspired routing	Network flow theory

MCQs

1. Swarm intelligence is based on:

    a. Central controllers
    b. Simple agents following simple rules
    c. Emotion modeling
    d. DNA editing

2. ACO is inspired by:

    a. Wolves
    b. Ants
    c. Trees
    d. Dolphins

3. PSO models the behavior of:

    a. Birds & fish
    b. Reptiles
    c. Microbes
    d. Humans

4. Octopuses demonstrate:

    a. Centralized intelligence
    b. Distributed cognition
    c. No problem-solving ability
    d. Machine-like logic

5. Crows inspire AI in:

    a. Aerodynamics
    b. Symbolic + experiential reasoning
    c. Mining
    d. Policing

6. Plants communicate through:

    a. Language
    b. Chemical signals
    c. Electromagnetic waves
    d. Vibration frequencies

7. Mycelium networks inspire:

    a. Centralized computing
    b. Internet-like routing
    c. Rocket design
    d. Car engines

8. Ecosystem intelligence emphasizes:

    a. Isolation
    b. Linear thinking
    c. Feedback loops and resilience
    d. Random guessing

9. Gaia models view Earth as:

    a. A passive rock
    b. A self-regulating system
    c. A mechanical computer
    d. A perfect sphere

10. Genetic algorithms use:

    a. Telepathy
    b. Mutation & selection
    c. Combustion
    d. Magnetism

11. Neuroevolution evolves:

    a. Countries
    b. Neural networks
    c. Forests
    d. Weather

12. Swarm intelligence excels at:

    a. Centralized planning
    b. Distributed optimization
    c. Cooking
    d. Boxing

13. Flocking models come from:

    a. Bee hives
    b. Bird flight patterns
    c. Human traffic
    d. Volcano studies

14. Mycelium networks resemble:

    a. Chemical factories
    b. Wireless power grids
    c. The internet
    d. Muscles

15. Evolutionary AI finds solutions by:

    a. Random destruction
    b. Trial, mutation, recombination
    c. Human oversight
    d. Solar cycles

16. Ecosystem models are useful for:

    a. Video editing
    b. Planetary-scale simulation
    c. Tailoring clothes
    d. Quick cooking

17. Multi-agent RL teaches agents to:

    a. Cooperate or compete
    b. Sleep
    c. Count
    d. Rotate physically

18. PSO tracks:

    a. Local best & global best positions
    b. DNA sequences
    c. Ocean tides
    d. Road temperatures

19. Genetic algorithms rely on:

    a. Evolutionary pressure
    b. Soil acidity
    c. Population decline
    d. River flow

20. The key insight of Chapter 2 is:

    a. Human intelligence is superior
    b. non-human intelligence offers powerful AI inspiration
    c. Computers should mimic humans only
    d. All AI must be supervised

Answers

1-b

2-b

3-a

4-b

5-b

6-b

7-b

8-c

9-b

10-b

11-b

12-b

13-b

14-c

15-b

16-b

17-a

18-a

19-a

20-b

Consumers don't behave logically. They behave ecologically

03

Nature-Inspired AI in Consumer Behavior & Marketing

3.1 Introduction: Marketing Beyond Psychology

For decades, marketers relied on linear models: the funnel, segmentation, 4Ps, and rational-choice theory.

But modern consumer behavior is:

- Non-linear: Consumer decisions no longer follow neat, sequential steps; instead, people jump unpredictably across touchpoints, influenced by shifting moods, new information, and dynamic digital triggers.
- Emergent: Behavior arises from interactions—not just individual preferences. Trends, memes, and viral movements emerge spontaneously from collective dynamics rather than deliberate persuasion.
- Context-dependent: The same consumer behaves differently depending on time, place, device, social setting, and emotional state; context now shapes choices as much as the product itself.
- Multi-agent influenced: Decisions are shaped by a constellation of actors—algorithms, influencers, peer networks, recommendation engines, and automated systems—creating a shared decision-making ecosystem.

- Emotionally volatile: Digital environments amplify emotion, making consumer responses fast, reactive, and sometimes contradictory, driven by micro-emotions rather than stable, rational preferences.

Nature offers alternative models of intelligence—swarm behavior, evolution, fuzzy logic, ecological dynamics—that perfectly match the complexity of modern markets. This chapter explores how **nature-inspired AI** transforms consumer behavior analysis, personalization, fraud detection, loyalty systems, and retail optimization.

3.2 Swarm Intelligence in Marketing

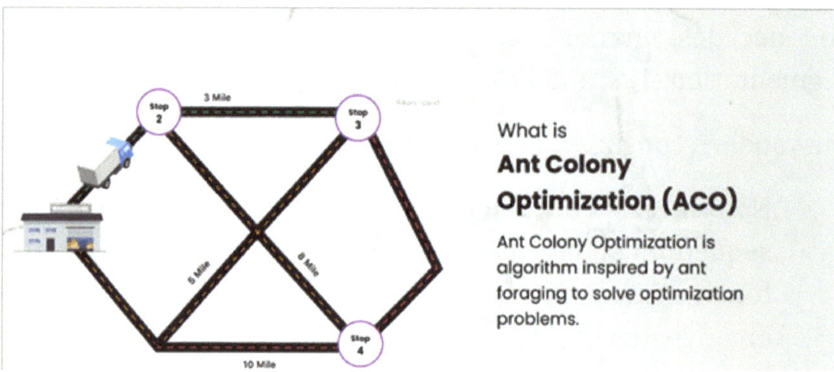

Figure 15: *Ant Colony Optimization*

Swarm intelligence mimics how ants, bees, birds, and fish coordinate without leaders. In marketing, **each consumer action becomes a signal**, shaping collective digital behavior.

Core Principle

Individual signals → collective recommendation patterns

Why Swarms Matter in Marketing

- Predict group movements
- Optimize navigation paths

- Recommend products
- Match consumers with content
- Improve inventory decisions

3.3 How Digital "Pheromones" Work

Ants leave pheromone trails to mark useful paths.

Consumers leave **digital pheromones**:

- Clicks
- Product views
- Wishlist
- Abandoned carts
- Reviews
- Social shares
- Checkout flows

These trails inform algorithms which products are "hot routes."

AI interprets these as:

- Product clusters
- Frequently co-purchased items
- Trending preferences
- Demand signals

3.4 Applications in Recommendation Engines

Swarm Concept	Marketing Equivalent
Pheromone strength	Product popularity signal
Ant movement	Consumer journey
Food source discovery	Product discovery
Multiple paths	Multi-touch journeys
Path optimization	Conversion funnel optimization

Real-World Uses:

- Amazon-style "Frequently Bought Together."
- Netflix similarity engines
- Spotify collaborative filtering

3.5 Table: Swarm Algorithms in Marketing

Algorithm	Inspired By	Used For	Benefit
Ant Colony Optimization	Ants	Personalization, pathfinding	High conversion pathways
Particle Swarm Optimization	Bird flocks	Price optimization	Faster convergence
Bee Colony Algorithms	Bees	Search optimization	Diversity in product discovery

3.6 Neuroevolution in Advertising

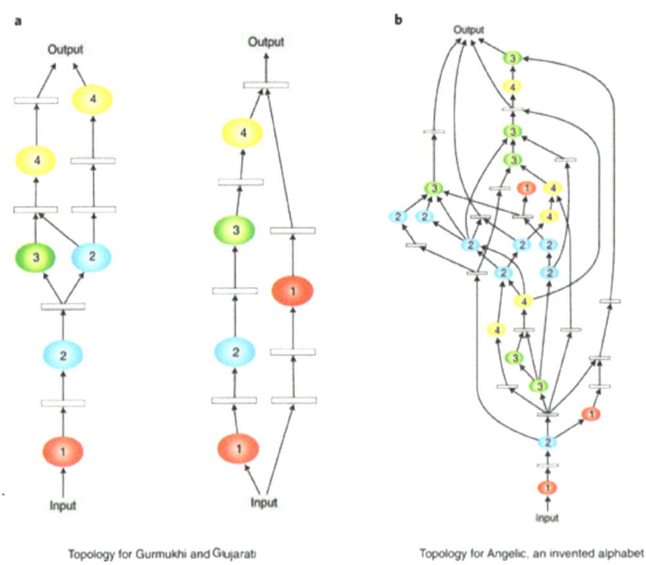

Figure 16: *Neurovision in advertising*

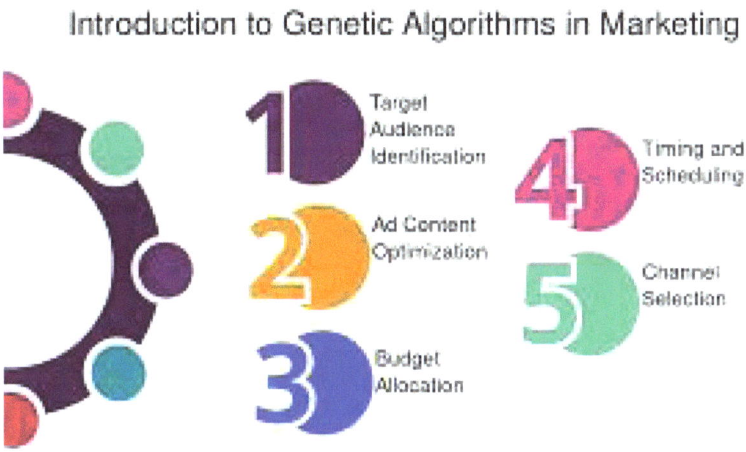

Figure 17: *Genetic algorithms in marketing*

Traditional A/B testing is too slow.

Neuroevolution **evolves marketing strategies** the way nature evolves species. Traditional A/B testing, with its rigid comparisons and long cycles, is increasingly inadequate for the velocity of modern digital markets. Neuroevolution, by contrast, adapts marketing strategies the same way nature evolves species—through continuous variation, competition, and survival of the fittest. In this paradigm, ads behave like "organisms," with headlines, images, and calls-to-action functioning as "genes" that combine and mutate across generations. Their performance metrics—CTR, CVR, engagement depth—serve as the "fitness" criteria that determine which variants persist. Over many evolutionary rounds, the system autonomously discovers high-performing creative combinations that no human team could iterate fast enough to uncover manually.

This evolutionary intelligence powers a new frontier in advertising personalization. Neuroevolution enables **real-time optimization of landing pages**, **dynamic creative optimization**, **smart**

bidding strategies, and deeply **personalized offers for micro-segments** that shift with user behavior. Instead of testing one idea at a time, brands can evolve hundreds of variants simultaneously, converging toward precision-fit messaging for every audience cluster. Tools such as **Evolv AI**, **Sentient Ascend (legacy)**, and **Optimizely X's genetic modules** operationalize this approach, turning experimentation from a slow, linear process into a living, adaptive ecosystem of continual improvement.

How it works

- Ads = "organisms"
- Headlines, images, CTAs = "genes"
- Performance (CTR, CVR) = "fitness"
- Fitter variants survive
- Multiple generations evolve optimal ads

3.7 Uses in Advertising Personalization

- Real-time optimization of landing pages
- Dynamic creative optimization (DCO)
- Smart bidding strategies
- Personalized offers for micro-segments

Tools:

- Evolv AI
- Sentient Ascend (legacy)
- Optimizely X (genetic testing modules)

3.8 Table: Neuroevolution Workflow in Marketing

Step	Description	Marketing Output
Mutation	Random variation	New headline/image combo
Crossover	Combine top performers	Hybrid ad creatives
Fitness Evaluation	Measure performance	CTR/CVR scoring
Selection	Keep the best variants	Best ads scale

3.9 Fuzzy Logic in Consumer Modeling

Figure 18: *Fuzzy Logic in Consumer Modeling*

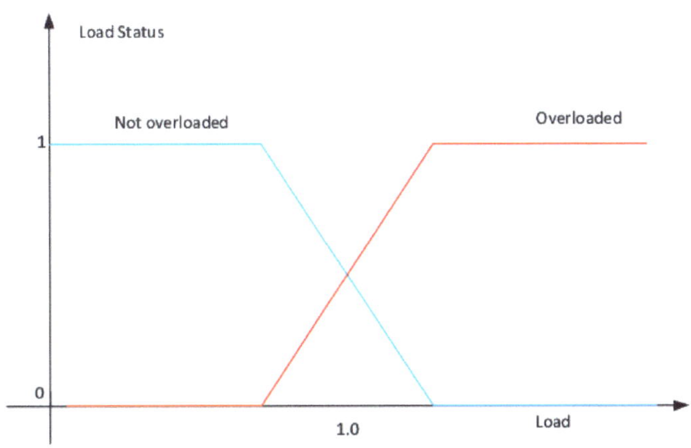

Figure 19: *Human decisions are not binary*

Human decisions are **not binary**. We exist in the world of "maybe," "somewhat," and "depends."

Fuzzy logic handles ambiguity—perfect for marketing.

Why fuzzy logic matters

Consumer states like:

- "Somewhat likely to buy."
- "Moderately satisfied."
- "Slightly interested."

cannot be modelled using crisp 0 or 1 labels.

3.10 Applications of Fuzzy Logic

Used in:

- Customer satisfaction scoring: Fuzzy logic captures shades of satisfaction—"somewhat happy" or "mostly dissatisfied"—instead of forcing rigid numerical ratings.
- Price elasticity modeling: It models consumer responses to price changes using gradations, allowing marketers to estimate sensitivity even when behavior is inconsistent.
- Sentiment analysis: Fuzzy systems interpret emotional tone on a spectrum, handling mixed or ambiguous sentiments better than strict positive/negative labels.
- Churn prediction: It assesses churn risk using partial truths—like "likely to leave" or "some risk"—for more realistic retention insights.
- Recommendation softness (approximate matches): Fuzzy logic enables recommendations based on similarity and closeness, offering alternatives that feel intuitively relevant rather than exact matches.

Industries:

- Automobiles
- Electronics
- Hospitality
- FMCG

3.11 Table: Fuzzy Logic States (Example)

User Statement	Crisp Logic	Fuzzy Logic
"I might buy it if the discount increases."	0	0.4
"I like this model, but prefer red."	0	0.7
"I love it, but it's expensive."	0	0.6

Fuzzy logic models nuanced preference landscapes.

3.12 Behavioral Ecology in Store Layout & UX

Information Foraging Theory proposes that humans search for information the way animals forage for food—by maximizing reward while minimizing effort. The diversification hypothesis suggests that people switch between multiple information "patches" when the perceived yield of the current one declines. In marketing and retail contexts, this means consumers naturally diversify their attention across aisles, categories, or digital sections when they sense diminishing relevance or novelty. Likewise, different task types—exploratory, goal-driven, or opportunistic—shape how deeply or broadly a consumer will search, echoing the behavioral strategies animals adopt when food is scarce, abundant, or uncertain.

Applied to behavioral ecology inside stores, diversification becomes a powerful design principle. Shoppers forage through physical space, navigating shelves, endcaps, and displays based on perceived "information scent"—the cues that signal value or relevance. When aisles feel monotonous or reward-poor, consumers diversify into adjacent categories, much like animals shifting feeding grounds. This explains why retailers cluster complementary products, use sensory anchors, or create discovery zones; they shape the foraging landscape to keep reward signals high and encourage continued exploration.

In UX design, task-type differences mirror these ecological patterns. A goal-driven user expects high information scent and direct navigation—akin to a predator focused on a specific prey—while exploratory users prefer rich, diversifiable environments with multiple cues and pathways. Interfaces that ignore these distinctions force users into inefficient foraging strategies, increasing cognitive load and abandonment. Good UX ensures predictable navigation for targeted tasks while maintaining serendipitous branches for users who are browsing, comparing, or scanning for inspiration.

Ultimately, both store layout and digital UX become ecosystems where human foraging strategies unfold. By aligning environments with diversification dynamics and task-type sensitivities, designers can engineer higher engagement, smoother wayfinding, and more profitable behavioral flows. When the information "nutrients" in each patch is continuously refreshed—whether through signage, micro-content, product adjacencies, or interface scaffolding—users stay longer, explore more deeply, and traverse the experience with the same adaptive efficiency that governs foraging in the natural world.

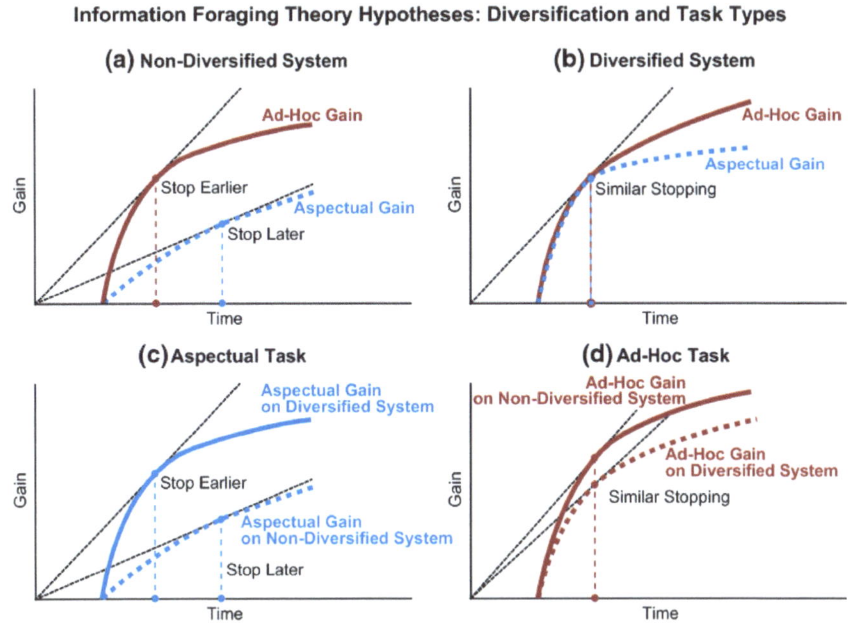

Figure 20: *Information Foraging Theory*

The figure illustrates how **Information Foraging Theory** predicts different patterns of "gain over time" depending on whether a system is **diversified** or **non-diversified**, and whether the user's task is **aspectual** (broad exploration) or **ad-hoc** (narrow, goal-specific). In a **non-diversified system** (panel a), ad-hoc users extract useful information quickly but plateau early, prompting them to stop sooner. Aspectual users, who need a wider range of information, keep foraging longer but gain more slowly because the environment doesn't provide enough variety. In contrast, a **diversified system** (panel b) offers richer information "patches," causing both task types to reach similar stopping points since both can find value for longer. Diversification increases the efficiency of exploration by smoothing the gain curve for broad tasks while sustaining relevance for focused tasks.

The bottom panels highlight how task type interacts with system design. For **aspectual tasks** (panel c), diversified systems dramatically improve the gain curve: users gather the variety they need sooner and stop earlier because the system supplies richer cues. Non-diversified environments force them to forage inefficiently, delaying their decision to stop. Conversely, for **ad-hoc tasks** (panel d), the advantage shifts: non-diversified systems—being narrower and more focused—may deliver higher early gain for specific goals, while diversified systems spread information more broadly and therefore offer slower initial progress. However, both curves converge to similar stopping points, reinforcing the theory's central claim: users optimize their foraging behavior based on perceived information scent, switching or stopping when marginal gain drops below expectation.

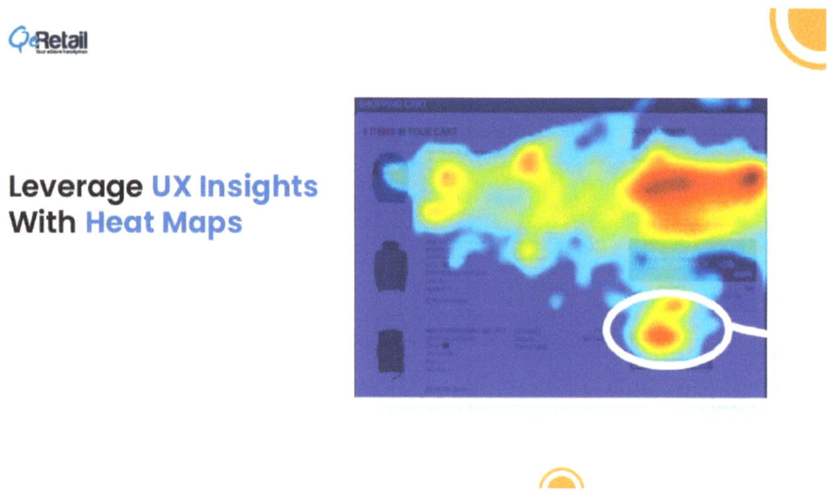

Figure 21: *UX Insights using heat maps*

Animals forage optimally: They minimize energy cost to maximize food gain.

Consumers do the same: They minimize cognitive effort to maximize satisfaction.

Core Idea

Consumers are "digital foragers."

3.13 Applications in Retail & Digital UX

- Heatmap optimization: Heatmaps reveal where users concentrate their attention or clicks, helping designers amplify high-value zones and fix dead areas in retail or digital interfaces.
- Shelf placement strategy: Understanding foraging patterns helps retailers position products where visual and cognitive "scent" is strongest, increasing discovery and impulse purchases.
- Eye-tracking models: These models show how shoppers or users visually scan environments, enabling layouts that guide attention efficiently and reduce search friction.
- Conversion journey mapping: By tracing users' step-by-step paths, brands can identify where information scent weakens and optimize flows to keep consumers progressing toward purchase.
- Menu layout testing: Menus—physical or digital—are tested to maximize readability and choice efficiency, ensuring that users can forage rapidly without overload.

Tools: These platforms provide heatmaps, behavior analytics, and visual attention predictions that reveal how digital foragers navigate interfaces, enabling continual UX refinement.

- Hotjar
- Crazy Egg
- EyeQuant
- Microsoft Clarity

3.14 Table: Foraging Theory Applied to Retail

Foraging Concept	Marketing Equivalent
Energy cost	User effort (clicks, scrolls)
Reward density	Discount & product value
Patch selection	Product category choice
Patch leaving	Bounce rate
Path optimization	Conversion funnel

3.15 Immune-System–Inspired AI for Fraud Detection

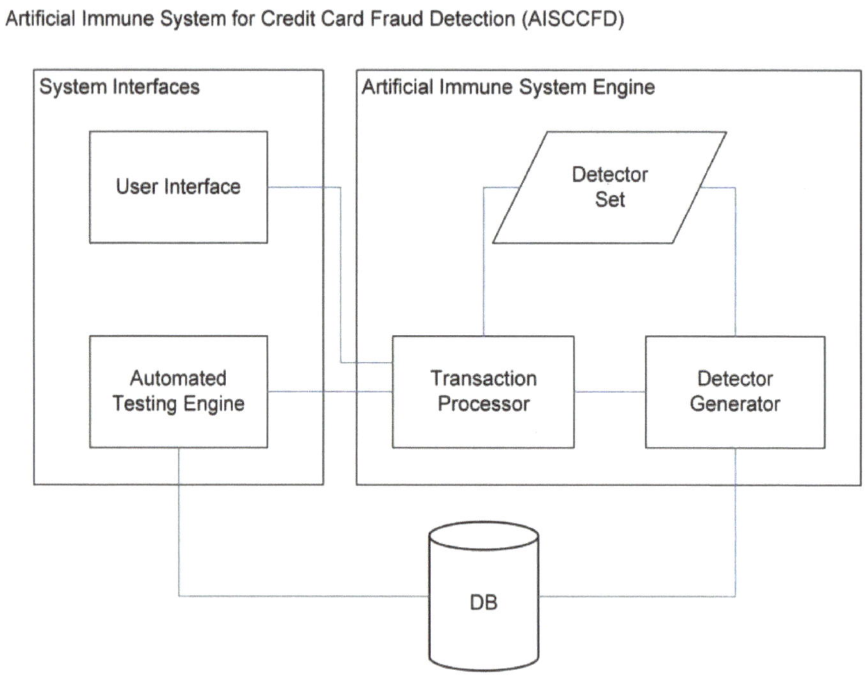

Figure 22: *Immune-System-Inspired AI for Fraud Detection*

Immune systems detect pathogens by recognizing deviations from "normal." Immune-system-inspired AI mirrors the biological immune system by distinguishing "self" from "non-self," identifying fraud the same way the body identifies pathogens—through deviations from expected patterns. In the diagram, the Detector Generator creates synthetic detectors that mimic immune cells, while the Detector Set acts like an adaptive defence layer that continuously monitors transactions. The Transaction Processor evaluates incoming activity against these detectors, and when anomalies appear—unusual spending patterns, impossible geolocations, unexpected device fingerprints—the system flags them for further review. Just as the biological immune system evolves antibodies after exposure, the artificial immune engine adapts dynamically as new fraud behaviors emerge.

This paradigm is particularly powerful in marketing and digital commerce, where fraudulent behaviors evolve rapidly. By first defining "normal" customer behavior and then scanning for anomalies, immune-inspired systems excel at ecommerce fraud detection, fake-review filtering, bot identification, and sentiment anomalies on social platforms. The approach continuously adjusts detection thresholds as patterns shift—whether due to seasonal buying changes, new fraud tactics, or emerging social behaviors. Integrated alongside user interfaces, automated testing engines, and transactional databases, these systems create self-learning, adaptive defences that grow stronger with every data point—much like a living immune system protecting an organism.

Marketing AI uses this for:

- Fraud detection
- Spam review filtering
- Bot detection
- Anomaly detection in sentiment

3.16 How Immune-Inspired AI Works

Steps

6. Define "normal" customer behavior
7. Watch for anomalies
8. Flag suspicious events
9. Adapt detection thresholds

Applications

- E-commerce fraud
- Fake reviews
- Transaction pattern shifts
- Social media anomalies

3.17 Table: Immune Analogy in Marketing

Immune Concept	Marketing Equivalent
Antigen	Fraudulent transaction
Antibody	Detection algorithm
Immune memory	Historical data patterns
Autoimmune errors	False positives

3.18 Ecosystem Intelligence in Loyalty Programs

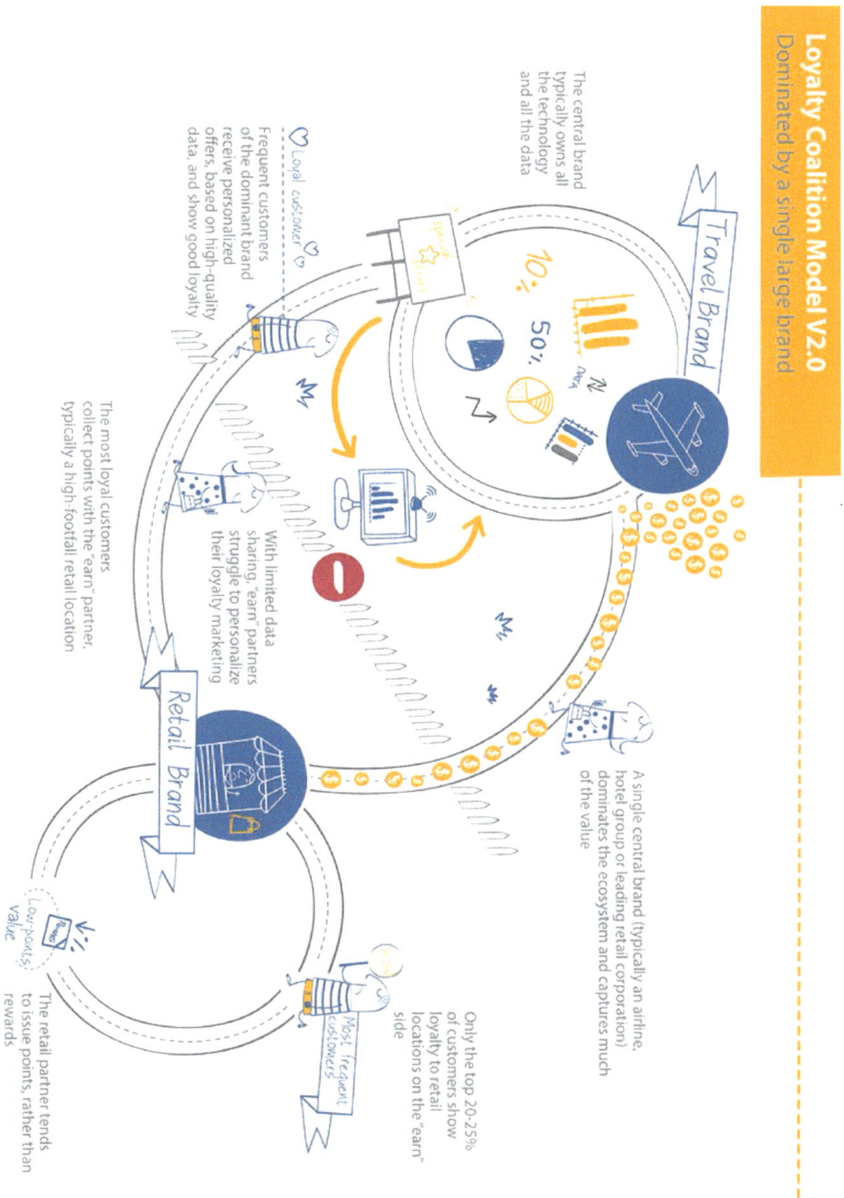

Figure 23: *Ecosystem Intelligence in Loyalty Programs*

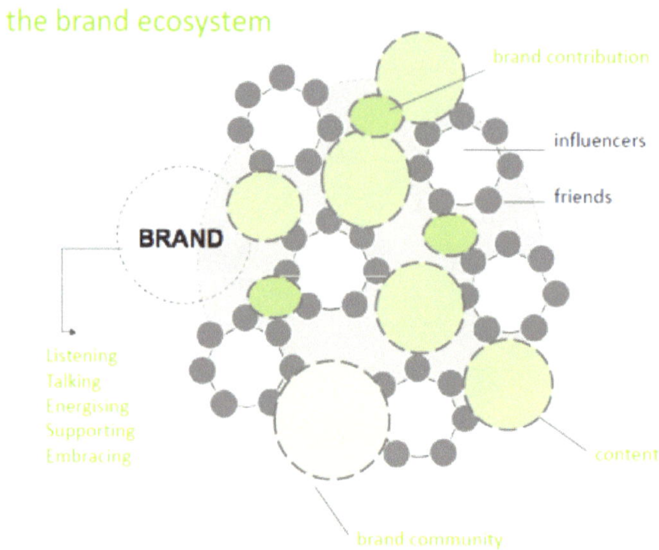

Figure 24: *Loyalty ecosystems resemble ecological systems*

Loyalty ecosystems increasingly function like ecological systems, where consumers behave as species navigating a landscape of brand "habitats." Points operate as a form of transferable energy that fuels participation, while rewards act as nutrient cycles that sustain long-term engagement. When these flows are healthy and well-balanced, the entire ecosystem thrives; when they stagnate—through irrelevant rewards or weak incentives—engagement declines just as real ecosystems falter when resources become scarce. Viewing loyalty through an ecological lens reveals how interdependent all elements are: the richness of the habitat (brand experience), the energy available (points), and the nutrient loops (rewards) collectively determine the vitality of the consumer community.

Ecosystem models transform marketing by enabling brands to predict customer lifetime value with greater precision, model engagement flows across touchpoints, and manage the dynamics of communities rather than isolated transactions. They allow companies to balance reward tiers to sustain participation, identify failing segments before churn accelerates, and orchestrate healthier patterns of user interaction. Leading brands such as Starbucks, Sephora, Nike Run Club, and Amazon Prime already employ ecosystem-based thinking, designing loyalty programs that behave less like linear funnels and more like living networks—resilient, adaptive, and continuously self-renewing.

Loyalty ecosystems resemble ecological systems:

- Consumers = species
- Brands = habitats
- Points = energy
- Rewards = nutrient cycles
- Engagement = ecosystem health

3.19 How Ecosystem Models Transform Marketing

- Predict customer lifetime value
- Model engagement flows
- Manage community interactions
- Balance reward tiers
- Detect failing segments

Used by:

- Starbucks
- Sephora
- Nike Run Club
- Amazon Prime

3.20 Table: Loyalty as an Ecosystem

Ecological Concept	Loyalty Analogy
Migration	Customer churn
Symbiosis	Brand–consumer relationship
Predator pressure	Competitor offers
Resource scarcity	Reward difficulty
Ecosystem collapse	Loyalty fatigue

3.21 Unified Model: Nature-Inspired Marketing Intelligence (NIMI)

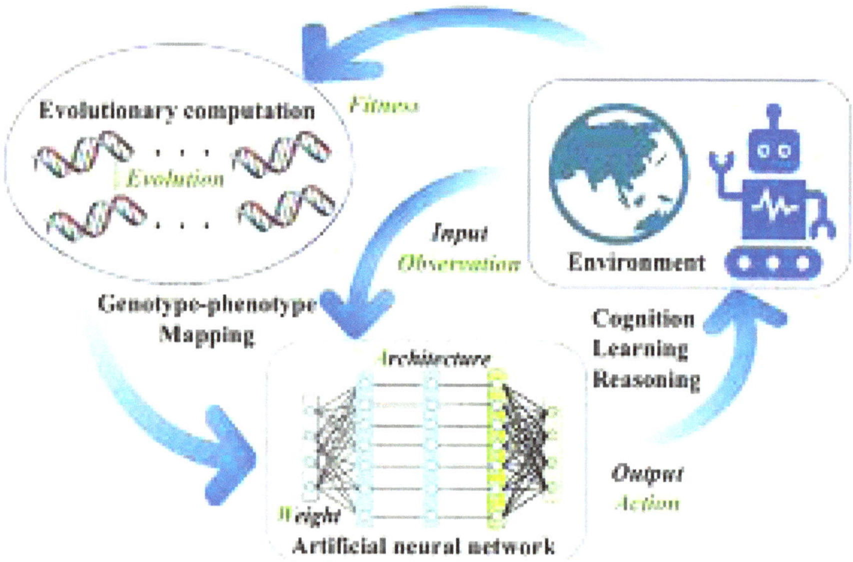

Figure 25: *Unified model: nature-inspired marketing intelligence*

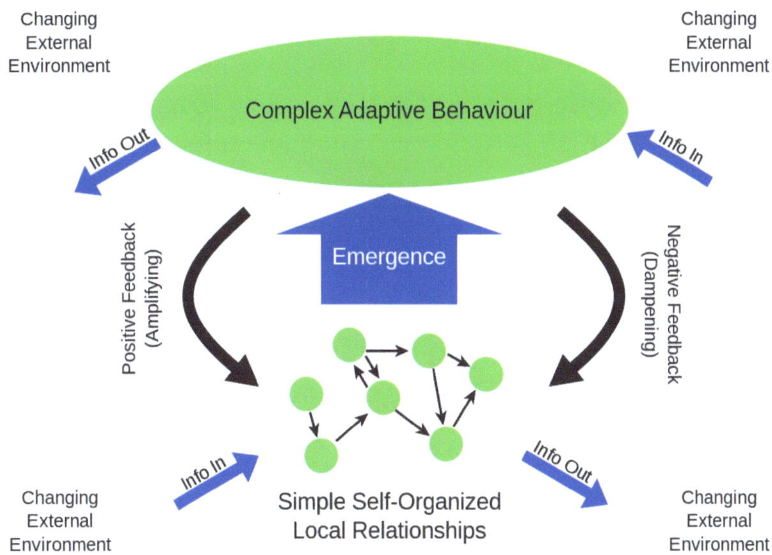

Figure 26: *Unified model: nature-inspired marketing intelligence*

Layers:

1. Swarms → Recommendation Engines: Swarm intelligence inspires algorithms that collectively infer what users may like by observing patterns across millions of micro-behaviors. Like ants finding optimal paths, recommender systems converge on high-value content with minimal explicit instruction.
2. Evolution → Ads and Personalization: Evolutionary algorithms mutate, recombine, and select ad variations to discover what performs best in real time. Personalization becomes a living process, adapting to user behavior the way species adapt to environments.
3. Fuzzy Logic → Preference Modeling: Fuzzy logic captures the "in-between" nature of human preferences, translating vague sentiments into usable predictions. It allows marketing systems to handle ambiguity instead of forcing binary choices.
4. Ecology → UX & Store Layout: Ecological models guide the design of digital and physical spaces where users forage for

information or products. Layouts are optimized like habitats—rich in cues, low in friction, and supportive of diverse search behaviors.

5. Immune System → Fraud Detection: Immune-inspired AI detects anomalies by identifying behaviors that deviate from the norm, much like the body identifies foreign pathogens. It continuously adapts to new threats, making fraud systems resilient and self-renewing.
6. Ecosystems → Loyalty Systems: Loyalty programs function as dynamic ecosystems where points circulate as energy and rewards sustain community health. Ecosystem thinking enables brands to maintain balance, prevent churn, and nurture long-term engagement.

3.22 Why Nature Models Beat Traditional Marketing Models

Traditional Models

- Linear: Traditional linear models assume consumers move step-by-step through fixed funnels, ignoring the chaotic, looping paths people actually take. This oversimplification leads to weak predictions in real-world environments.
- Assumption-heavy: They rely on rigid assumptions about behavior, motivation, and rationality, which often collapse under the complexity of modern digital ecosystems. As a result, their insights degrade quickly when conditions change.
- Segment-based: Segment-based frameworks group people into broad buckets, missing micro-patterns, fluid identities, and moment-to-moment shifts. This reduces personalization and overlooks emergent behaviors.
- Static: Static models fail to adapt as behaviors evolve, treating markets as stable rather than dynamic. In fast-moving

environments, this rigidity makes traditional approaches increasingly obsolete.

Nature Models

- Emergent: Nature models reveal patterns that arise from interactions rather than top-down design, capturing behaviors traditional models cannot predict. They allow marketers to see how small actions scale into large trends.
- Adaptive: These systems continuously update in response to new data, much like organisms adjusting to their environment. This makes them resilient in fast-changing markets.
- Multi-agent: They account for many interacting actors—consumers, algorithms, influencers, and competitors—mirroring real marketplace dynamics. This produces richer, more realistic behavioral insights.
- Nonlinear: Nature models embrace feedback loops, tipping points, and disproportionate effects, reflecting how small stimuli can trigger large shifts in consumer behavior. They offer a truer representation of how decisions evolve.
- Real-time: They operate dynamically, learning and responding instantly as conditions change. This enables timely personalization, anomaly detection, and continuous optimization.

Modern consumers behave more like **ecosystems**, not "segments."

3.23 Mathematics Behind These Approaches

Swarm Intelligence

- Pheromone update equations: These equations strengthen or weaken paths based on success, allowing systems to converge on optimal routes the way ants do.

- Probability transition matrices: They guide agents' movement choices by assigning likelihoods to each possible action, enabling coordinated exploration.
- Random walk algorithms: Agents wander stochastically through solution spaces, helping escape local optima and discover new opportunities.

Neuroevolution

- Mutation operators: Randomly alter network weights or structures to introduce diversity and discover novel solutions.
- Genetic fitness scoring: Evaluates how well each network performs, ensuring only the most effective architectures survive.
- Population sampling: Creates new generations by selecting and recombining high-performing models from the population.

Fuzzy Logic

- Membership functions: Convert vague human concepts (like "high interest") into numerical ranges for computation.
- Fuzzy inference systems: Combine multiple fuzzy rules to make nuanced decisions under uncertainty.

Ecosystem Models

- Network flow equations: Model how value, attention, or resources move across interconnected nodes in a marketing ecosystem.
- Markov chains: Predict state-to-state transitions, such as customer movement across loyalty tiers.
- Differential equations: Capture continuous change in engagement, sentiment, or resource availability over time.

3.24 Data Science Techniques Used

- Reinforcement learning: Learns optimal actions through reward feedback loops, ideal for bidding, personalization, and navigation.
- Evolutionary optimization: Searches large solution spaces by evolving candidates over generations.
- Multi-agent modeling: Simulates interacting consumers, bots, competitors, and systems to reveal emergent behaviors.
- Bayesian inference: Continuously updates beliefs based on new data, improving predictions under uncertainty.
- Graph neural networks: Analyze networked relationships—social graphs, product co-purchases, store layouts—for deeper pattern recognition.
- Clustering: Groups similar users or behaviors, revealing tribes, niches, and micro-segments.
- Probabilistic forecasting: Predicts future behavior using probability distributions instead of fixed outcomes.
- Anomaly detection: Identifies rare or suspicious patterns for fraud, churn, or sentiment anomalies.

3.25 Real-World Example 1: Amazon

- Swarm-based recommendation pathways: Recommendations evolve like swarm trails, strengthening links between products frequently co-explored.
- Dynamic pricing using PSO: Particle Swarm Optimization adjusts prices in real time based on demand signals and competitor movement.
- Fraud detection using AIS (Artificial Immune Systems): Artificial immune systems flag behavior that deviates from normal user patterns.
- Fuzzy logic in satisfaction prediction: Interprets ambiguous feedback to estimate customer delight or disappointment.

3.26 Real-World Example 2: Starbucks Rewards

- **Ecosystem model for loyalty tiers**

  Customers move across tiers like species in habitats, driven by energy (points) and rewards.

- **Mycelium-style routing between locations**

  Foot-traffic patterns resemble fungal networks, optimizing store placement and service flows.

- **Behavioral foraging for menu layout**

  Menus are arranged to match how customers scan and "forage" for options.

- **Evolution-based campaign personalization**

  Campaigns evolve based on user responses, selecting the most effective messages.

3.27 Real-World Example 3: Walmart Retail

- **Heatmaps (behavioral ecology)**

  Heatmaps reveal how shoppers move, mirroring animal movement patterns in resource-rich habitats.

- **Auto-optimized shelf placement**

  Algorithms position products where attention naturally clusters, maximizing "information scent."

- **Genetic algorithm–based supply chain simulation**

  Supply networks evolve toward efficiency through generational optimization.

- **Fuzzy logic for price elasticity**

  Models consumer price sensitivity with gradations rather than rigid thresholds.

3.28 Limitations & Risks

- **Emergent behavior is hard to predict**

  Complex interacting systems can produce unexpected outcomes that defy traditional analytics.

- **Lack of explainability**

  Nature-inspired models often behave like black boxes, making decisions difficult to interpret.

- **Risk of reinforcing herd behavior**

  Algorithms may amplify trends excessively, reducing the diversity of choices.

- **Ecosystem collapse (loyalty fatigue)**

  Overloaded reward systems can fail if the value diminishes or becomes too complex.

- **Over-optimization risks**

  Systems tuned too tightly may break when real-world conditions shift.

3.29 Future of Nature-Inspired Marketing

- **Multi-agent consumer digital twins**

  Simulated consumers will enable marketers to test strategies in virtual ecosystems before deployment.

- **Evolutionary brand ecosystems**

  Brands will adapt like species, co-evolving with cultural and consumer shifts.

- **AI that co-evolves with consumer tribes**

  Algorithms will learn within distinct cultural clusters, evolving alongside user communities.

- **Plant/fungi-inspired decentralized marketplaces**

  Markets will resemble distributed root or mycelium networks—resilient, adaptive, and self-organizing.

- **Emotionally adaptive loyalty algorithms**

  Future loyalty systems will sense emotional states and adjust rewards to maintain engagement health.

3.30 Summary

Nature models allow marketers to embrace **complexity, emergence, and adaptiveness**.

They reveal consumers as dynamic nodes in evolving ecosystems—not static targets in segments.

Marketing must evolve from prediction → adaptation → co-evolution.

Project: Build a Nature-Inspired Recommendation & Loyalty System

Scenario

A retail chain wants:

1. A swarm-based recommendation engine
2. An evolutionary advertisement personalization system
3. A fuzzy logic–driven satisfaction model
4. An ecosystem-based loyalty system

Solution:

Component	Technique	Math/Principle
Recommendation	ACO	Pheromone equations
Price optimization	PSO	Velocity update
Ad personalization	Neuroevolution	Mutation + fitness
Satisfaction modeling	Fuzzy logic	Membership functions
Fraud detection	Artificial immune system	anomaly scoring
Loyalty system	Ecosystem model	network flow + Markov chains

MCQs

1. Swarm intelligence in marketing models consumer actions as:

    a. Static events
    b. Digital pheromones
    c. Fixed preferences
    d. Random noise

2. ACO is mainly used for:

    a. Fraud detection
    b. Path and recommendation optimization
    c. Ad copywriting
    d. Shelf stocking

3. Neuroevolution treats ads as:

    a. Machines
    b. Genes
    c. Puzzles
    d. Furniture

4. Mutation in neuroevolution creates:

    a. Identical ads
    b. New creative variations
    c. Fraud alerts
    d. Competitor insights

5. Fuzzy logic handles consumer preferences that are:

    a. Always binary
    b. Ambiguous
    c. Chemical
    d. Geological

6. Behavioral ecology compares consumers to:

   a. Statues
   b. Foragers
   c. Robots
   d. Planets

7. Heatmaps in UX are inspired by:

   a. Bird migration
   b. Animal foraging
   c. Cloud formation
   d. DNA mapping

8. Immune-system-inspired AI detects:

   a. Colours
   b. Fraud
   c. Sound waves
   d. Rainfall

9. Ecosystem modeling treats loyalty points as:

   a. Furniture
   b. Energy
   c. Gravity
   d. Air flow

10. Fuzzy logic uses:

   a. Membership functions
   b. Currency tables
   c. Weather maps
   d. Engine oil

11. PSO is inspired by:

    a. Owls
    b. Birds & fish
    c. Turtles
    d. Horses

12. Neuroevolution selects best ad versions using:

    a. Mechanical pressure
    b. Fitness functions
    c. Fabric testing
    d. Light intensity

13. Behavioral ecology is useful for:

    a. UX & store layout optimization
    b. Earthquake prediction
    c. Rocket modeling
    d. Movie script writing

14. Immune systems detect pathogens by spotting:

    a. Random bacteria
    b. Deviations from normal
    c. Electromagnetic pulses
    d. Water levels

15. Ecosystem loyalty systems monitor:

    a. Shoes
    b. System resilience
    c. Planet size
    d. Fabric softening

16. Swarm intelligence enables:

    a. Decentralized recommendations
    b. Manual segmentation
    c. Paper-based surveys
    d. Stone carving

17. Evolutionary algorithms rely on:

    a. Chemical bonding
    b. Mutation and crossover
    c. Breathing rate
    d. Lunar rotation

18. Fuzzy logic is ideal when consumers behave:

    a. Predictably
    b. Ambiguously
    c. Uniformly
    d. Mechanically

19. Ecosystem models prevent:

    a. Loyalty fatigue
    b. Cloud formation
    c. Stone erosion
    d. Sound vibrations

20. Nature-inspired models outperform traditional models because they are:

    a. Linear
    b. Adaptive and emergent
    c. Expensive
    d. Random

Answers

1-b

2-b

3-b

4-b

5-b

6-b

7-b

8-b

9-b

10-a

11-b

12-b

13-a

14-b

15-b

16-a

17-b

18-b

19-a

20-b

Nature is writing data continuously—we've only just begun learning how to read it.

04

Collecting Intelligence: Data from Non-Human Sources

4.1 Introduction: The New Frontier of Non-Human Data

Most of today's AI systems learn from **humans**: text, speech, clicks, transactions, and images.

But the planet contains **millions of active data streams** produced by animals, plants, fungi, oceans, forests, and ecosystems.

Nature is the largest data ecosystem in the world.

The challenge

Nature does not speak in spreadsheets—it speaks in:

- Movements
- Vibrations
- Chemical signals
- Electrical pulses
- Migration trails
- Acoustic signatures
- Environmental patterns
- Multispectral light

This chapter shows how researchers **digitize nature**, convert it into structured data, and use it for intelligence modeling.

4.2 The Data Pipeline of Nature

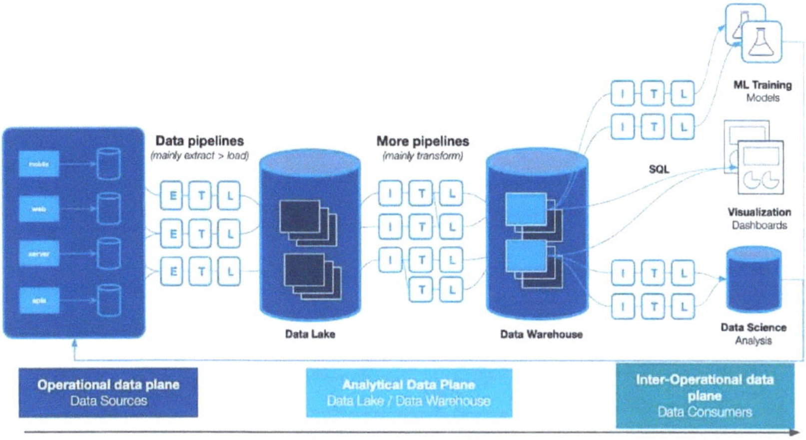

Figure 27: *Data Pipeline of nature*

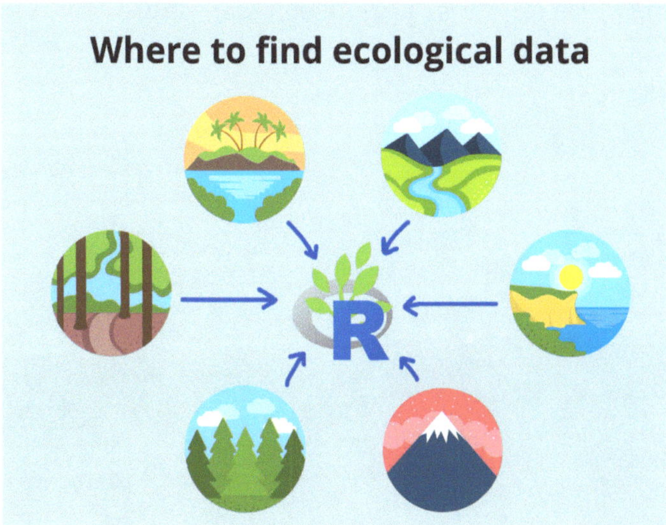

Figure 28: *Where to find ecological data*

The process of capturing non-human intelligence:

1. **Sensing**—sensors, tags, collars, drones, satellites
2. **Digitization**—translating raw signals into usable formats
3. **Feature Extraction**—pattern detection using AI

4. **Modeling**—machine learning over biological or ecological signals
5. **Insight & Application**—conservation, robotics, supply chain, climate models

4.3 Section 1: Animal Behavior & Cognition Data

Animals constantly generate **behavioral data streams**:

- Movements
- Communications
- Hunting patterns
- Social signals
- Energy usage
- Territory maps

Capturing these requires specialized techniques.

4.4 Bio-Logging & Tracking

Figure 29: *Bio-Logging & Tracking*

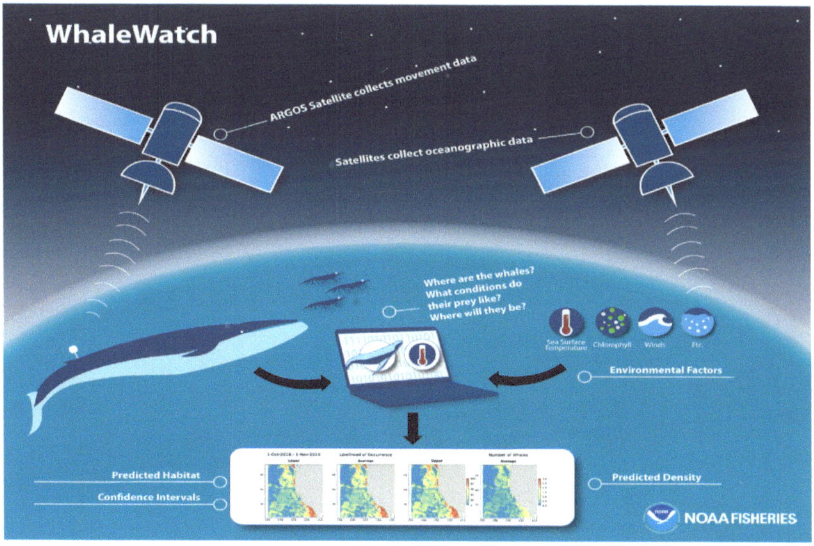

Figure 30: *Whale watch*

Bio-logging uses lightweight electronics attached to animals.

Devices used:

- **GPS collars** → movement & migration
- **Accelerometers** → posture, gait, activity
- **Gyroscopes** → turning & orientation
- **Depth loggers** → diving patterns
- **Heart-rate sensors** → stress + energy

Output

Structured behavioral time series.

4.5 Real-World Examples of Bio-Logging

Marine Animals

Sharks & whales tracked to model:

- Migratory intelligence
- Efficient pathfinding

- Ocean temperature gradients
- Ship-avoidance behaviors

Application:

Shipping companies optimize routes using whale migration patterns (reducing collisions and fuel usage).

4.6 Table: Bio-Logging Sensors & Data Types

Sensor	Used On	Data Collected	AI Applications
GPS collar	Mammals	Path, speed	Migration prediction
Accelerometer	Birds/land animals	Wing beats, steps	Behavioral classification
Gyroscope	Marine animals	Turns, dives	Hunting modeling
Hydrophone	Whales, dolphins	Calls	Communication decoding

4.7 Audio & Sonar Monitoring

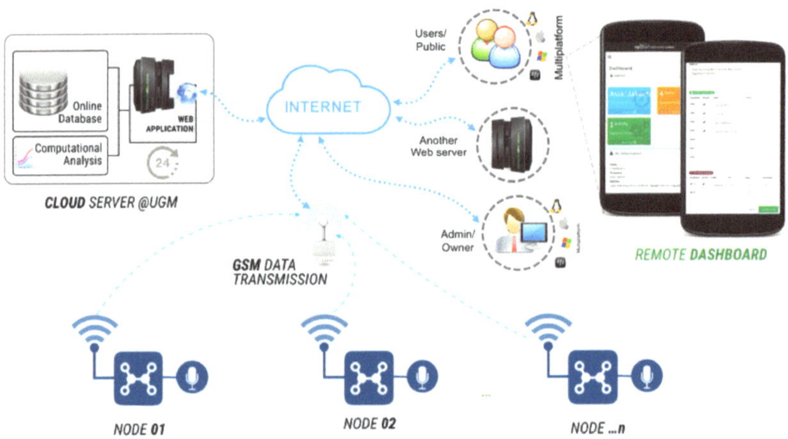

Figure 31: *Audio & Sonar Monitoring*

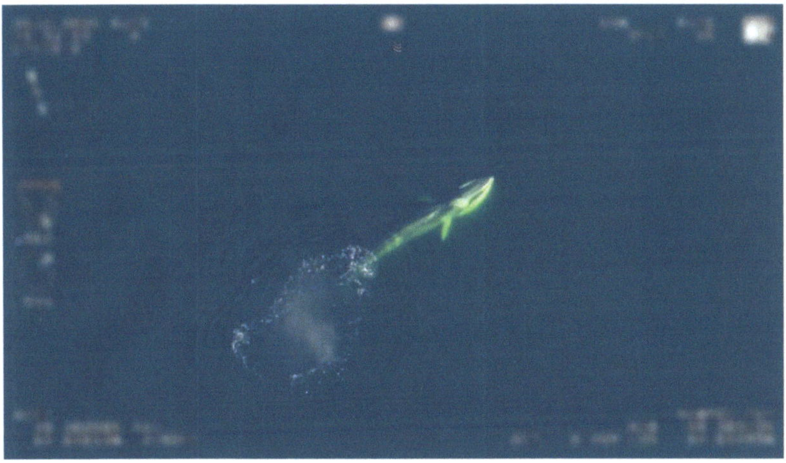

Figure 32: *Audio & Sonar Monitoring*

Animals communicate through:

- Songs
- Calls
- Vibrations
- Clicking
- Sonar echolocation

Devices:

- **Microphones** (forest bioacoustics)
- **Hydrophones** (ocean acoustics)
- **Ultrasonic detectors** (bats)

4.8 AI-Assisted Acoustic Decoding

Birdsong AI

Trains models to detect species via sound.

Used in:

- Biodiversity monitoring
- Poaching detection
- Ecosystem health analysis

Elephant Communication AI

Low-frequency rumbles interpreted to detect:

- Stress
- Poaching events
- Mating calls
- Herd movement signals

4.9 Section 2: Plants & Fungi Data

Plants and fungi generate **electrical, chemical, and structural signals.**

These can be digitized and used for AI modeling.

4.10 Electrical & Chemical Signalling in Plants

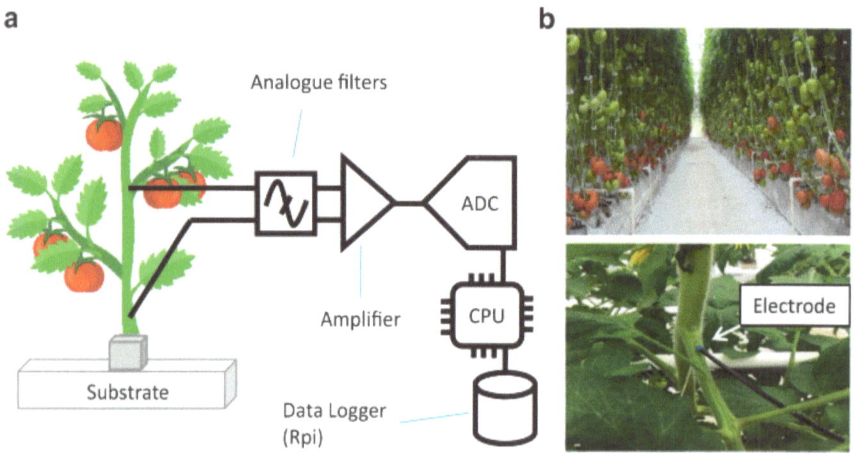

Figure 33: *Electrical & Chemical Signalling in Plants*

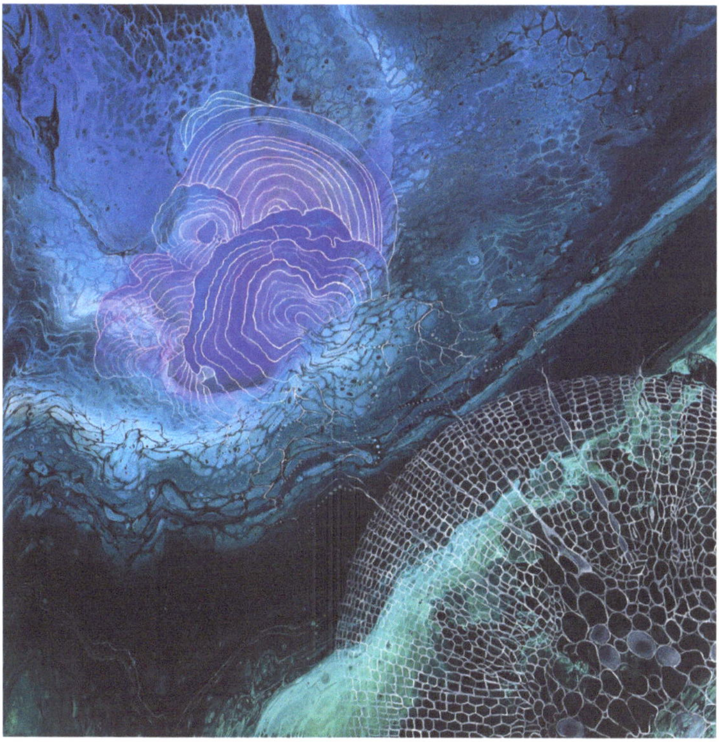

Figure 34: *Electrical & Chemical Signalling in Plants*

Plant neurobiology shows:

- Action potentials (electrical spikes)
- Mechanical responses
- Electromechanical communication
- Root-to-root signalling

Fungi (mycelium networks) produce:

- Pulse-like electrical signals
- Distributed communication pathways

4.11 Real-World Example

Tomato plants

Emit measurable electrical signals when attacked by pests.

Mushrooms

Show rhythmic pulses that resemble neuronal spikes.

AI Use

Models detect stress, hydration levels, and environmental changes *before* they are visible.

4.12 Table: Plant/Fungi Signals & Sensors

Source	**Sensor**	**Signal**	**AI Use**
Plant roots	Electrodes	Micro-voltage	Soil analysis
Fungi mycelium	Electrodes	Pulses	Network modeling
Leaves	Spectral cameras	Chlorophyll data	Stress detection
Shoots	Thermal cameras	Evapotranspiration	Hydration models

4.13 Growth & Behavior Observation

Plants and fungi are slow, but **time-lapse imaging + AI** reveals:

- Phototropism: Time-lapse AI reveals how plants bend and orient themselves toward light sources, optimizing energy intake through subtle, continuous adjustments.
- Symbiosis patterns: AI uncovers slow-forming cooperative relationships—such as fungi exchanging nutrients with roots—showing how mutual benefit shapes long-term growth.

- Growth direction optimization: By analyzing directional changes over time, AI identifies how plants and fungi choose paths that maximize resources while minimizing resistance.
- Environmental adaptation: Time-lapse models show how organisms alter growth rates, shapes, or directions in response to stress, moisture, temperature, or obstacles, demonstrating adaptive intelligence.

Tools used:

- High-speed cameras
- Hyperspectral imaging
- Deep learning vision models

4.14 Section 3: Environmental & Ecosystem Data

Data from:

- Atmosphere
- Soil
- Water
- Forest cover
- Temperature gradients
- Chemical cycles

Captured through satellites, drones, and IoT networks.

4.15 Remote Sensing

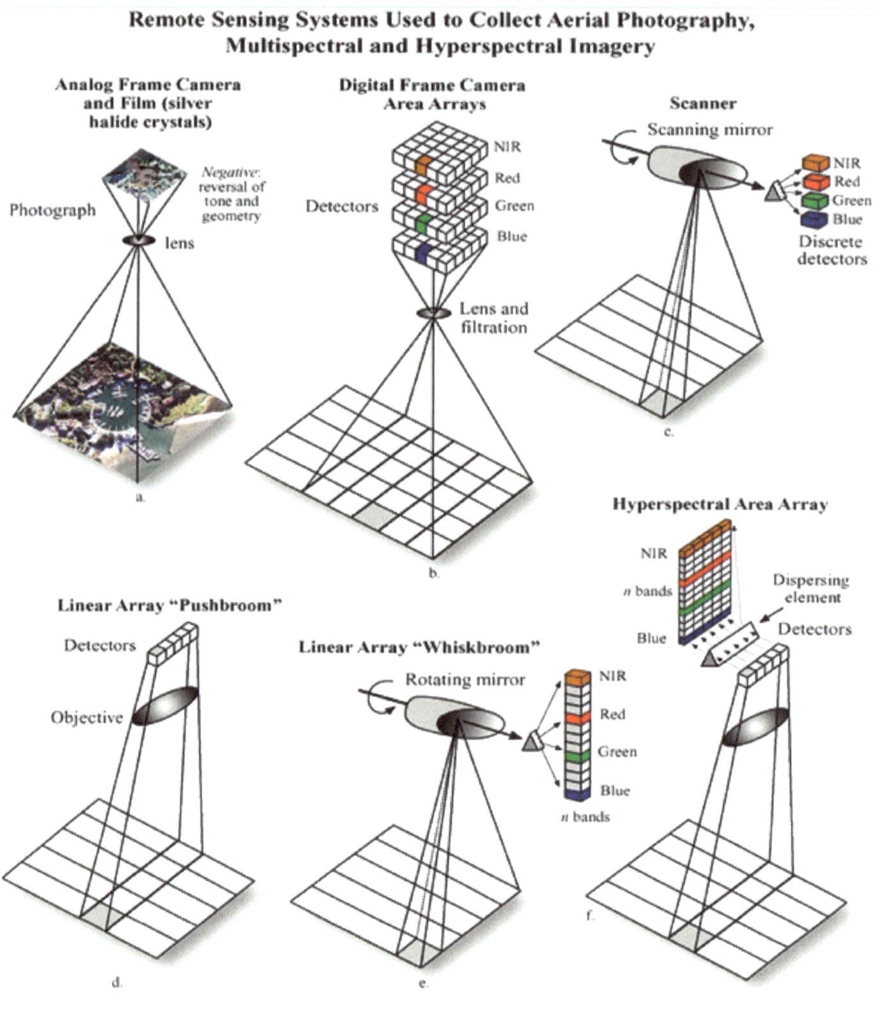

Figure 35: *Remote Sensing*

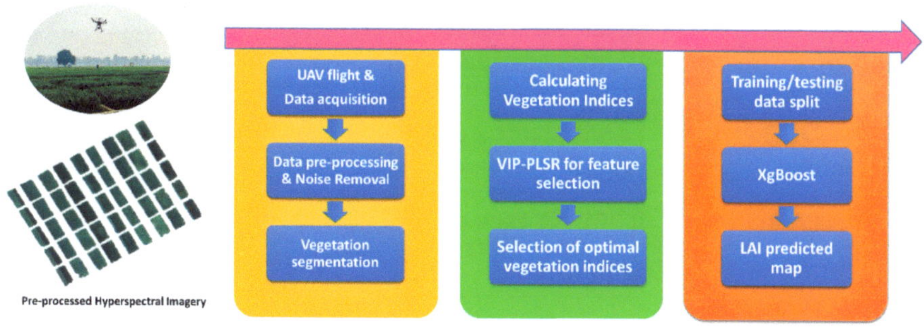

Figure 36: *Pre-processed hyperspectral imagery*

Remote sensing uses:

- Multispectral cameras
- Thermal imaging
- Hyperspectral scans
- SAR (Synthetic Aperture Radar)
- LiDAR

Used in:

- Smart farming
- Climate modeling
- Wildlife monitoring
- Disaster prediction

4.16 Environmental Sensors (IoT)

IoT devices measure:

- Temperature
- Humidity
- pH
- CO_2
- Soil nutrients
- Water quality
- Acoustic environment

4.17 Table: Environmental Sensors

Sensor Type	Parameter Measured	AI Use
pH Sensor	Acidity	Water quality prediction
DO Sensor	Oxygen	Fish population modeling
CO_2 Sensor	Carbon levels	Pollution analysis
Thermal sensor	Temperature	Forest fire prediction

4.18 Section 4: Swarm & Collective Behavior Data

Tracking collective agents:

- Bees
- Ants
- Termites
- Fish schools
- Bird flocks

4.19 Observing Swarms

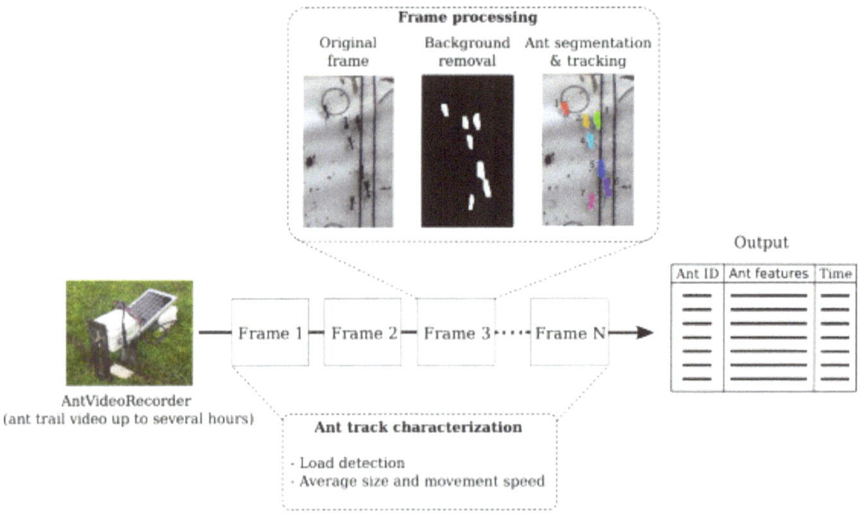

Figure 37: *Observing swarms*

Techniques:

- RFID micro-tags
- Computer vision tracking
- Marker less motion capture
- High-speed imaging

Analysis:

- Task-switching
- Foraging optimization
- Role allocation
- Traffic regulation

4.20 Applications

Used to build:

- Swarm robotics
- Decentralized logistics routes
- Adaptive traffic systems
- Group intelligence models

4.21 Table: Swarm Behaviors & Data Outputs

Species	Behavior Captured	AI Use
Bees	Foraging paths	Drone routing
Ants	Load-balancing	Multi-agent systems
Termites	Construction patterns	Autonomous building robots
Fish	Schooling	Collision-free navigation

4.22 Section 5: Evolutionary & Emergent Systems

Not all non-human data is observed physically. Some comes from **digital ecosystems**.

4.23 Artificial Life (A-Life) Simulations

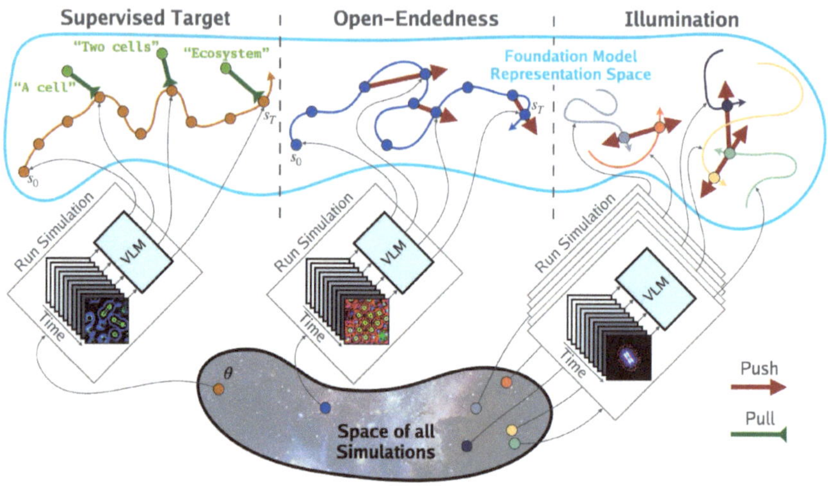

Figure 38: *A-Life Simulations*

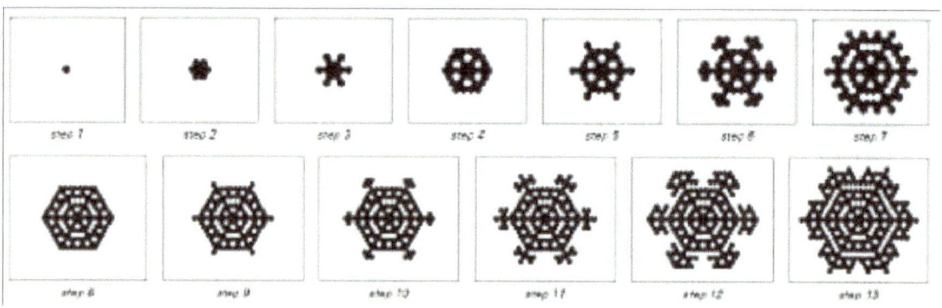

Figure 39: *A-Life Simulations*

Platforms:

- **Avida**

  A research platform where digital organisms mutate and evolve, helping scientists study adaptation and complexity.

- **Tierra**

  A virtual "biosphere" where self-replicating code evolves, revealing how digital life competes, cooperates, and diversifies.

- **Cellular Automata**

  Grid-based systems where simple rules generate lifelike patterns, ideal for exploring emergence and self-organization.

- **EvoBots**

  Simulated robotic agents that evolve movement and decision-making, enabling safe testing of adaptive behaviors.

Used for:

Studying emergence

A-Life systems show how complex behaviors arise spontaneously from simple interactions.

Evolving agent behaviors

Digital organisms learn to move, gather resources, or compete, offering insights into adaptive intelligence.

Stress-testing ecosystems

Researchers simulate shocks and disruptions to observe resilience and collapse dynamics in artificial environments.

Building robust AI policies

Evolved agents help train AI systems that remain stable and effective under unpredictable real-world conditions.

4.24 Types of Digital Organisms

- Rule-based (Cellular Automata): Organisms follow simple deterministic rules that collectively generate rich, emergent patterns.
- Agent-based (digital creatures): These entities act autonomously, sensing environments and responding with adaptive behaviors.

- Neuroevolution entities: Agents whose neural networks evolve over generations, producing creative, non-intuitive strategies.
- Simulated ecosystems with predators & prey: Full ecological systems where digital species compete, hunt, cooperate, and co-evolve over time.

4.25 Table: A-Life Input & Outputs

System	Input Data	Output Data	AI Use
Cellular Automata	Rules	Emergent patterns	Complexity study
Avida	Digital genomes	Fitness traits	Evolution modeling
Neuroevolution	Random networks	Optimized policies	Reinforcement learning

4.26 Data Processing Techniques

Signal processing

Extracts meaningful patterns from raw sensory or behavioral data by filtering, transforming, and denoising complex signals.

Time-series modeling

Analyses sequential data to detect trends, cycles, and anomalies, enabling prediction of evolving consumer or system behavior.

Ecological modeling

Uses population dynamics and interaction models to understand how users move, cluster, and compete within digital or physical environments.

Deep learning for sensor fusion

Combines inputs from multiple sensors—visual, audio, behavioral—to create richer, more accurate representations of user activity.

Graph neural networks

Learn from interconnected structures like social networks, product co-purchase graphs, or store pathways to reveal deeper relational insights.

Multi-agent simulation

Models the behavior of many interacting agents to study emergent patterns, cooperation, and competitive dynamics.

Noise-filtering algorithms

Remove irrelevant data fluctuations, enhancing clarity and improving downstream predictions and analytics.

4.27 Conceptual Model: The Non-Human Data Engine

Figure 40: *The non-human world*

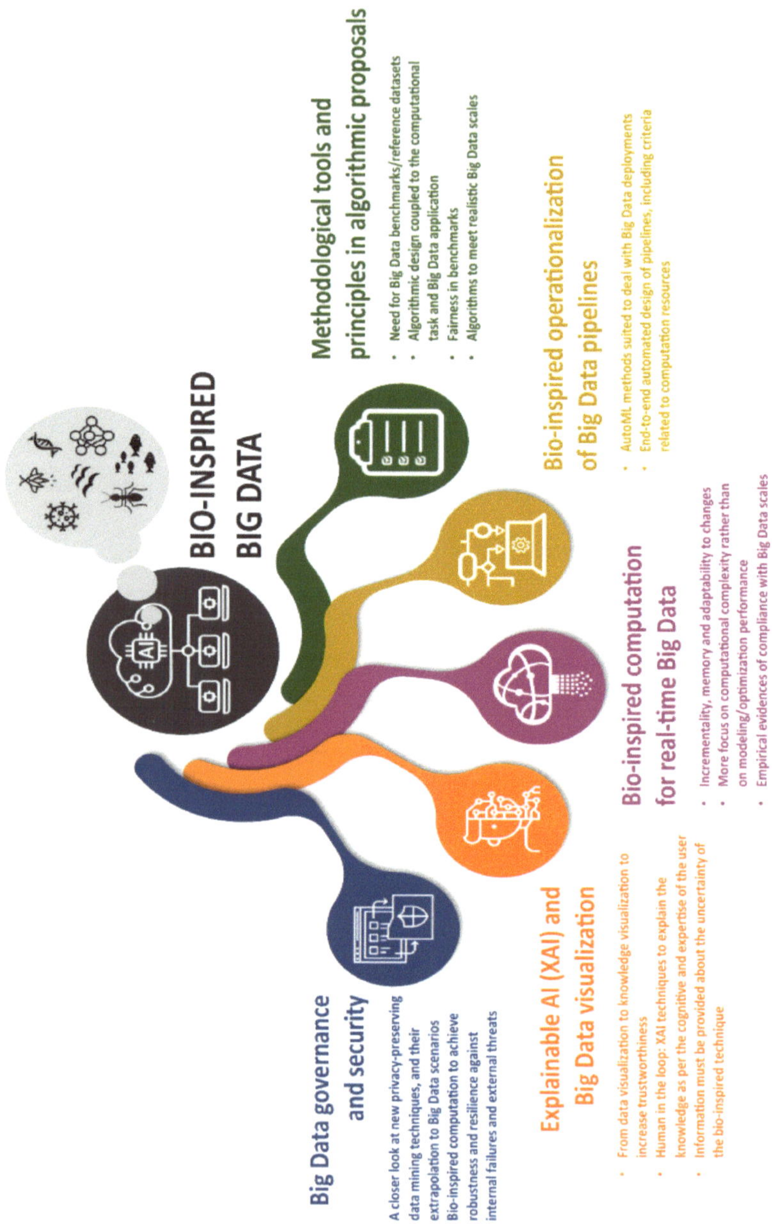

Figure 41: *Non-human data pipeline*

Layers:

- **Sensors (bio-loggers, satellites)**

  Collect raw environmental or biological signals directly from animals, plants, or ecosystems. These sensors capture data humans cannot easily observe in real time.

- **Digitization (signal → data)**

  Converts analog signals like movement, sound, or temperature into structured digital formats. This step standardizes diverse inputs for downstream processing.

- **AI interpretation**

  Machine learning models decode patterns, behaviors, and anomalies hidden within the data. AI helps translate non-human signals into meaningful insights.

- **System modeling**

  Builds dynamic simulations of ecological or behavioral systems using the interpreted data. These models reveal interactions, dependencies, and emergent dynamics.

- **Insight generation**

  Synthesizes patterns into actionable understanding—movement trends, stress indicators, habitat shifts. This allows researchers and marketers to make informed decisions.

- **Real-world application**

  Applies insights to conservation, supply chains, climate monitoring, or bio-inspired business systems. The pipeline bridges raw biology with practical human impact.

4.28 Limitations & Challenges

- **Sensor durability**

  Devices may fail under harsh environmental conditions, limiting data reliability.

  Wildlife interactions or terrain can cause rapid wear and tear.

- **Weather interference**

  Rain, heat, storms, or cloud cover distort signals and reduce measurement accuracy. Environmental noise often overwhelms delicate sensing equipment.

- **Animal stress**

  Tracking technologies can disrupt natural behavior or cause discomfort.

  Ethical deployment requires minimizing intrusion and monitoring impact.

- **Energy constraints**

  Remote sensors and tags often run on limited battery power. This restricts data frequency and long-term monitoring.

- **Data sparsity**

  Non-human environments generate patchy or infrequent data streams. Sparse data challenges model accuracy and generalization.

- **Signal noise**

  Natural environments introduce high levels of unpredictable disturbance. Filtering noise becomes essential to extract meaningful patterns.

- **Ethical concerns**

  Monitoring wildlife raises questions about intrusion, consent, and ecological impact. Ethics guide how, why, and when non-human data should be collected.

4.29 Future Directions

- **Wearable sensors for insects**

  Ultra-light micro-sensors will unlock behavioral insights from the planet's smallest ecological workers.

- **Coral reef bioacoustics AI**

  AI systems will decode reef soundscapes to assess health, biodiversity, and early signs of stress.

- **Mycelium internet-of-fungi networks**

  Fungal networks may become biological data platforms, communicating moisture, nutrients, and stress in real time.

- **Planet-scale AI ecosystems**

  Global models will integrate species, climate, and human activity into unified ecological intelligence systems.

- **Emotion detection in wildlife**

  AI will infer stress, fear, or comfort states using movement, vocalizations, and physiological signals.

- **Plant-based communication models**

  Future algorithms may decode plant signalling—chemical, electrical, acoustic—to inspire new communication systems.

4.30 Summary Page

Nature is the world's oldest intelligence system. Collecting data from non-human sources gives us:

- Multi-species insight
- Cross-ecosystem intelligence
- Distributed behavioral models
- Evolutionary learning paths

The future of AI is planetary—not just human.

Project: Build a Multi-Source Bio-Ecological Data Platform

Objective

A research agency wants a platform to collect and use data from:

- Animals
- Plants & fungi
- Environmental sensors
- Swarms
- Digital artificial life

Solutions

Problem	Technique	Math/AI Field
Animal path modeling	Hidden Markov Models	Probability theory
Plant signal decoding	Fourier transforms	Signal processing
Environmental fusion	Kalman filters	Bayesian estimation
Swarm modeling	Multi-agent RL	Game theory
Fungi network analysis	Graph theory	Network science
A-Life simulation	Evolutionary algorithms	Fitness landscapes

MCQs

1. Bio-logging involves collecting data from:

    a. Robots
    b. Animals with sensors
    c. Satellites
    d. Cars

2. Hydrophones record:

    a. Soil nutrients
    b. Underwater sounds
    c. Thermal images
    d. Wind patterns

3. Plants can produce:

    a. Electrical signals
    b. Ultrasound
    c. Metal deposits
    d. Geothermal waves

4. Mycelium networks are measured using:

    a. Lasers
    b. Electrodes
    c. Motors
    d. X-rays

5. Remote sensing includes:

    a. Multispectral imaging
    b. Cooking sensors
    c. Audio speakers
    d. Springs and levers

6. RFID tags are used to track:

    a. Bees
    b. Galaxies
    c. Mountains
    d. Clouds

7. A-Life simulations produce data from:

    a. Digital organisms
    b. Soil
    c. Marine heatwaves
    d. Electric grids

8. Hyperspectral cameras capture:

    a. Animal DNA
    b. Hundreds of light bands
    c. Metal density
    d. Air pollution only

9. Fungi produce:

    a. Monetary signals
    b. Electrical pulses
    c. Sonic booms
    d. Radio signals

10. Behavioral ecology models:

    a. Animal architecture
    b. Foraging and movement patterns
    c. Weather cycles
    d. Light refraction

11. Cellular automata are:

    a. Machine parts
    b. Rule-based digital ecosystems
    c. Tree bark layers
    d. Computer worms

12. Avida is used for:

    a. Plant breeding
    b. Digital evolution
    c. River mapping
    d. Battery storage

13. Satellite imaging helps detect:

    a. Muscle growth
    b. Vegetation health
    c. Human DNA
    d. Metal reserves

14. Kalman filters combine:

    a. Noise + signal estimates
    b. DNA samples
    c. Wood density
    d. Rock magnetism

15. Animal acoustics can help detect:

    a. Poaching
    b. Cryptocurrency
    c. Software licenses
    d. Magnetism

16. Fungi networks resemble:

    a. Roads
    b. Internets
    c. Igloos
    d. Bones

17. Multi-agent RL is used in modeling:

    a. Swarms
    b. Rivers
    c. Metal alloys
    d. Soil erosion

18. Environmental sensors measure:

    a. CO_2 levels
    b. Song lyrics
    c. Painting colours
    d. Poetry difficulty

19. Plant electrophysiology measures:

    a. Leaf taste
    b. Electrical action potentials
    c. Tree age
    d. Chlorophyll smell

20. The core aim of non-human data collection is:

    a. Entertainment
    b. Translating natural signals into usable AI data
    c. Replacing forests
    d. Mining minerals

Answers

1-b

2-b

3-a

4-b

5-a

6-a

7-a

8-b

9-b

10-b

11-b

12-b

13-b

14-a

15-a

16-b

17-a

18-a

19-b

20-b

Move past the mirror—build systems that learn from forests, flocks, and fungi

05

Beyond Human Models: Applying Non-Human Intelligence to Consumer AI

5.1 Framing the Problem

Most consumer-facing AI is built to imitate humans: cognitive models, behavioral economics, demographic buckets. Those methods are powerful for many use cases—but they assume decision-making is individual, rational (or predictably irrational), and relatively stable.

Reality in digital markets is different:

- Interactions are emergent and multi-agent (virality, herd effects).
- Signals are noisy, passive, and asynchronous (browsing trails, long-tail behaviors).
- Environments change quickly (trends, supply shocks, platform shifts).

This chapter argues there's a **research & application gap**: non-human intelligence models can provide robust, adaptive frameworks for consumer AI—but they are underused in marketing.

5.2 Why Non-Human Paradigms Fit Modern Consumer Behavior

Key reasons non-human metaphors align with digital consumer dynamics:

1. **Decentralization:** Consumers act like swarms—no central leader, emergent patterns.
2. **Slow/Distributed signalling:** Plants & fungi model passive, cumulative signals (e.g., long-term engagement).
3. **Resilience & Feedback:** Ecosystemic models handle shocks and maintain stability (useful for loyalty and retention).
4. **Evolutionary Adaptation:** Markets evolve; evolutionary algorithms mirror market selection and creative adaptation.

Takeaway: non-human models are not replacements for psychological models—they are **complementary lenses** that capture different dynamics.

5.3 Core Non-Human Models Relevant to Marketing

A compact mapping:

Model Family	Core Idea	Marketing Analogy
Swarm Intelligence	Local rules → global order	Crowd trends, recommendation co-flows
Plant/Fungal signalling	Slow chemical/electrical messaging	Passive intents, latent preferences
Ecosystem Dynamics	Networks of interacting species	Brand portfolios, loyalty ecosystems
Evolutionary Systems	Variation + selection	Creative testing, campaign evolution
Immune Systems	Baseline normality, anomaly detection	Fraud/abuse detection, reputation monitoring

This is the toolbox we will use to fill gaps.

5.4 Conceptual Model: Hybrid Consumer Intelligence Stack

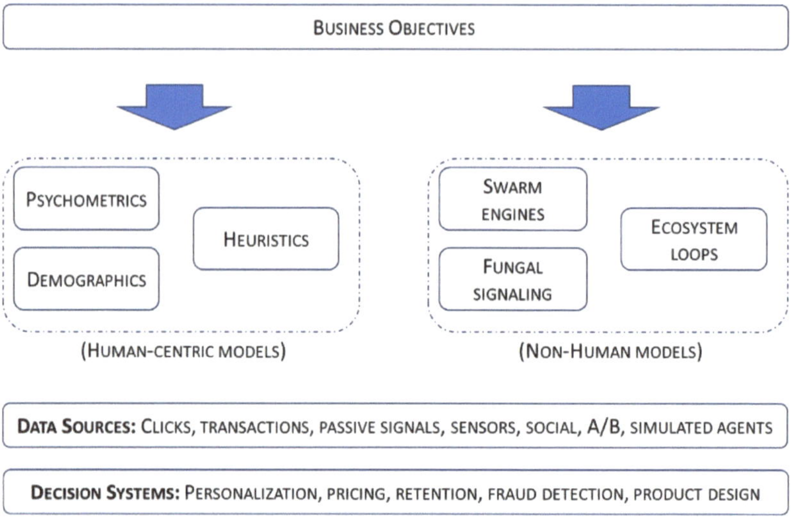

Figure 42: *Hybrid = combine human models where they work; augment with non-human models where emergence, distribution, or slow signals dominate.*

5.5 Where Conventional Models Fail (and How Non-Human Models Help)

Failures of human-centric models:

- Overconfidence on sparse signals (cold-start users)
- Fragility to rapid trend shifts (viral spikes)
- Poor long-term engagement modeling (latent interest)
- Weakness in detecting coordinated inauthentic behavior (bots, fraud rings)

How non-human models help:

- **Swarm algorithms** infer collective routes for new product adoption.
- **Fungal/plant metaphors** let us model slow accretion of preferences (e.g., cluster of signals across sessions).

- **Ecosystem models** help balance loyalty currencies and prevent collapse (over-rewarding).
- **Evolutionary frameworks** explore creative campaign spaces beyond human intuition

5.6 Two Detailed Examples (Illustrative Use Cases)

Example A—Swarm-Enhanced Recommendation for Cold-Start Products

Problem: New product with no purchase history.

Approach: Treat early interactions as pheromone deposits; use ACO-style propagation from products with similar microjourney traces to recommend the new item to users with overlapping trails.

Example B—Fungal-Signal Loyalty Decay Model

Problem: Customers drift slowly before churn; signals are weak.

Approach: Aggregate micro-signals (view time, micro-conversions, sentiment) as "mycelial nutrient levels" and model depletion/redistribution to predict long-term disengagement earlier than standard recency/frequency models.

5.7 Table: Typical Algorithms and their Marketing Roles

Algorithm/Class	**Marketing Role**	**Strength**
Ant Colony Optimization	Recommendation pathing	Finds high-conversion multi-step flows
Particle Swarm Optimization	Price & promo tuning	Fast convergence on numeric optima
Genetic Algorithms/ Neuroevolution	Creative optimization	Explores vast creative spaces

Algorithm/Class	Marketing Role	Strength
Fuzzy Logic Systems	Satisfaction & intent scoring	Models degrees of interest
Graph Neural Networks	Ecosystem interaction modeling	Captures interactions & propagation
Artificial Immune Systems	Anomaly/fraud detection	Adapts to new attack patterns

5.8 Integrating Non-Human Models into Existing Stacks (Practical Roadmap)

1. **Audit:** Identify where existing models fail (spikes, slow churn, cold-start).
2. **Select metaphors:** Map problem → non-human model (e.g., cold-start → swarm).
3. **Prototype layer:** Build a modular microservice (e.g., ACO-based recommender) that can be A/B tested.
4. **Hybridize:** Combine human-model outputs and non-human outputs via a gating model (meta-learner).
5. **Observe & adapt:** Use evolutionary strategies to evolve gating rules over time.
6. **Governance:** Add interpretability checks and ethical constraints before production rollout.

5.9 Ethical & Practical Considerations

Non-human metaphors can be powerful but raise concerns:

- **Interpretability:** Emergent outputs are harder to explain to stakeholders.
- **Human relevance:** Non-human advice may suggest actions that clash with norms or rights (e.g., manipulating herd behavior).

- **Bias propagation:** Swarm effects can amplify minority signals incorrectly (viral misinformation).
- **Regulatory:** Consumer protection laws require transparency for automated decisions.
- **User autonomy:** Systems must avoid nudging that undermines consent.

Mitigations: human-in-the-loop checkpoints, causal evaluation, fairness constraints, explicit consent for behavioral experimentation.

5.10 Summary & Transition to Project

Non-human intelligence offers a complementary toolkit for modern consumer AI: more adaptive, resilient, and suited to multi-agent digital ecosystems. The next section puts these ideas into practice with a hands-on project.

Project: Build a Hybrid Consumer Intelligence System (HCIS)

Objective: Create a system that improves conversion for new products, detects emerging fraud rings, and increases long-term retention by blending human and non-human AI models.

Scope: e-commerce retailer with web + mobile properties, loyalty program, and ad channels.

High-level components:

1. Data ingestion (clickstreams, session logs, transactions, feedback).
2. Human-model stack (demographic models, psychometrics, classical recommender).
3. Non-human modules:
   - **Swarm Recommender** (ACO micro-journey mapper)
   - **Mycelial Retention Model** (fuzzy + diffusion-based retention predictor)
   - **Immune Fraud Detector** (AIS anomaly detector)
4. Meta-learner for combining outputs.
5. Monitoring and governance dashboard.

Solutions (How to Build Each Component)

Component	**Techniques**	**Mathematical/Algorithmic Notes**
Swarm Recommender	Ant Colony Optimization; session graph extraction	Pheromone matrix , probability transitions ; evaporation .
Mycelial Retention Model	Fuzzy logic + diffusion on graph	Membership functions μ(x) for engagement states; diffusion via graph Laplacian to model spread/decay of engagement signals.

Component	Techniques	Mathematical/Algorithmic Notes
Immune Fraud Detector	Artificial Immune System + autoencoder	Self-pattern learning via autoencoder reconstruction error; anomaly score combined with negative selection algorithm to flag unusual agents.
Meta-Learner	Gradient boosting/ Bayesian model averaging	Inputs: scores from human model, swarm score, retention risk, fraud risk—learn weights that maximize long-term revenue lift.
Evolutionary Tuning	Genetic algorithms for creatives/params	Represent hyperparameters as genomes; fitness = business KPI (e.g., LTV uplift); selection, crossover, mutation.

MCQs

1. Human intelligence models are particularly useful when consumer behavior is:

    a. Fully rational and static
    b. Emergent and multi-agent
    c. Solely driven by demographics
    d. Random noise

2. Which metaphor is most appropriate for modeling slow, passive consumer signals?

    a. Bird flocking
    b. Fungal/mycelial signalling
    c. Predator–prey cycles
    d. Neural spiking

3. Ant Colony Optimization is best described as:

    a. Centralized optimization
    b. Pheromone-based path optimization
    c. Evolutionary search across genomes
    d. Deep learning architecture

4. A fuzzy logic model handles:

    a. Only binary outcomes
    b. Degrees of truth and partial membership
    c. Image segmentation exclusively
    d. Deterministic scheduling

5. The "hybrid stack" combines:

    a. Only non-human models
    b. Human-centric and non-human models together
    c. Only demographic models
    d. Only neuroevolution systems

6. Which math object models diffusion on a graph for engagement spread?

   a. Fourier transform
   b. Graph Laplacian
   c. Covariance matrix
   d. Hessian matrix

7. An artificial immune system is useful for:

   a. Recommending products
   b. Detecting anomalies and fraud
   c. Designing loyalty points
   d. Visual design of UI

8. Meta-learner in HCIS is used to:

   a. Aggregate model outputs to optimize business goals
   b. Replace all downstream models with one black box
   c. Store raw logs only
   d. Monitor cluster health

9. Evolutionary tuning uses:

   a. Gradient descent exclusively
   b. Mutation and selection over populations
   c. Closed-form analytic solutions
   d. Deterministic scheduling

10. A major ethical risk of swarm-type models is:

   a. Too much explainability
   b. Herding effects that manipulate behavior
   c. They are always slow
   d. They never generalize

11. The pheromone evaporation parameter in ACO controls:

    a. How fast pheromones are deposited
    b. How fast old signals fade (forgetting)
    c. The mutation rate of genomes
    d. The fuzziness of membership functions

12. Fuzzy membership functions $\mu(x)$ map inputs to:

    a. Frequency domain
    b. A degree between 0 and 1 indicating partial membership
    c. Absolute truth only (0 or 1)
    d. Integer codes for customers

13. Which technique helps combine slow (mycelial) signals with fast clickstream data?

    a. Ignoring slow signals
    b. multi-scale signal fusion (e.g., Kalman + graph diffusion)
    c. Only using daily aggregates
    d. Manual spreadsheets

14. The HCIS meta-learner should be evaluated on:

    a. Short-term CTR only
    b. Long-term metrics (LTV, retention) and guardrails
    c. Number of models used
    d. CPU usage

15. A risk of evolutionary creative testing is:

    a. Not exploring design space
    b. Producing unintelligible or unethical creatives if not constrained
    c. Always converging to the same ad
    d. Preventing any change

16. Graph neural networks are a good fit for:

  a. Modeling isolated users only
  b. Capturing interaction effects across users/products/edges
  c. Solving linear regression faster
  d. Replacing fuzzy logic

17. Which is a good governance practice before deploying emergent models?

  a. No monitoring—let it run
  b. Human-in-the-loop review and stress tests
  c. Turning off logs
  d. Immediate full rollout without A/B tests

18. The term "cold-start" refers to:

  a. New products or users with little history
  b. Temperature control in warehouses
  c. Chilly marketing emails
  d. Seasonality problems only

19. In the HCIS, the immune detector's anomaly score should influence:

  a. Only product images
  b. Fraud flags and gating on high-risk activities
  c. Creative selection without review
  d. Rewarding users immediately

20. Overall, the chapter's main claim is that non-human models:

  a. Replace human-centric models entirely
  b. Complement and extend human models to handle emergence, slow signals, and resilience
  c. Are irrelevant to marketing
  d. Always produce more revenue instantly

Answers

1-b

2-b

3-b

4-b

5-b

6-b

7-b

8-a

9-b

10-b

11-b

12-b

13-b

14-b

15-b

16-b

17-b

18-a

19-b

20-b

In service ecosystems, value flows like nutrients in a forest—co-created, adaptive, and alive

06

Service-Dominant Logic (S-D Logic) and Nature-Inspired AI

6.1 Opening Theme

Artificial Intelligence in marketing today mostly imitates human cognition. Service-Dominant Logic (Vargo & Lusch, 2004) reframes value not as delivered to consumers, but **co-created** with them.

This chapter expands S-D Logic and merges it with **nature-based intelligence models**, proposing a new paradigm:

Service-Ecosystem AI—where AI learns from forests, swarms, fungi, and ecological value flows rather than mechanical consumer funnels.

6.2 Introduction to S-D Logic

S-D Logic reframes the economy:

- All exchange is service-for-service
- Value is co-created, not delivered
- Actors integrate resources dynamically
- Service ecosystems evolve continuously
- Value is contextual and experiential, not embedded in goods

Why it matters for AI:

Most AI systems use *Goods-Dominant Logic* assumptions:

- Predict behavior
- Push products
- Optimize transactions

But S-D Logic shifts AI from **prediction → participation → co-creation**.

6.3 The 11 Foundational Premises of S-D Logic (FP1 to FP11)

FP	Foundation Premise	Meaning
FP1	Service is the fundamental basis of exchange	Everything is about applied knowledge & service, not goods
FP2	Indirect exchange masks the fundamental basis of exchange	Goods only store service potential
FP3	Goods are distribution mechanisms for service	Products are service delivery tools
FP4	Operant resources are primary	Skills, knowledge > materials
FP5	All economies are service economies	Industrial vs service economy = false divide
FP6	Customer is always a co-creator of value	Value emerges in use
FP7	Actors cannot deliver value, only offer value propositions	Value realized in context
FP8	A service-centered view is inherently relational and adaptive	Interactions matter
FP9	All social and economic actors are resource integrators	Co-evolving agency

FP	Foundation Premise	Meaning
FP10	Value is always uniquely and phenomenologically determined by the beneficiary	Subjective value
FP11	Value co-creation is coordinated through institutions & institutional arrangements	Context shapes value

6.4 How AI Currently Misinterprets S-D Logic

AI today is mostly:

- Product-centric
- Prediction-driven
- Linear
- Top-down
- Segmentation-based
- Optimizing short-term KPI outcomes

These are aligned with **Goods-Dominant Logic (G-D Logic)**.

Mismatch created:

- AI predicts clicks; S-D Logic models experiences
- AI optimizes funnels; S-D Logic optimizes ecosystems
- AI personalizes content; S-D Logic co-creates meaning

Thus, current AI misunderstands value as something *pushed*, not *emergent*.

6.5 How Nature Expands S-D Logic

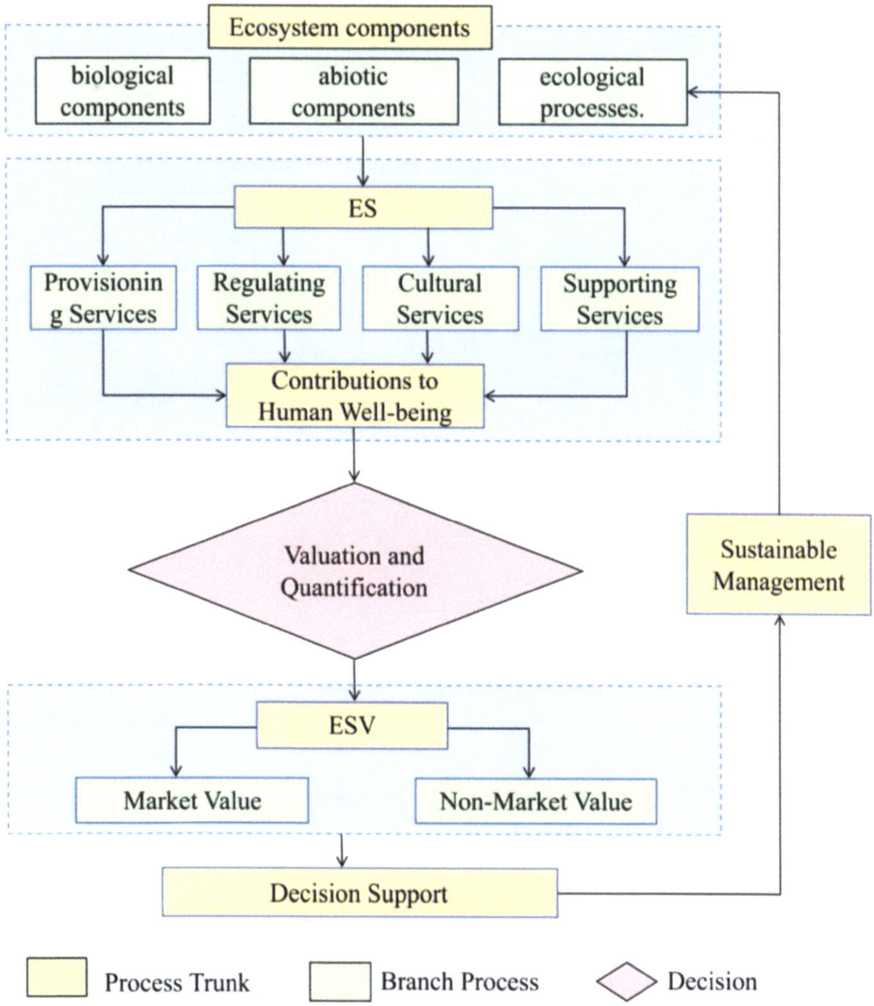

Figure 43: *S-D Logic align with nature*

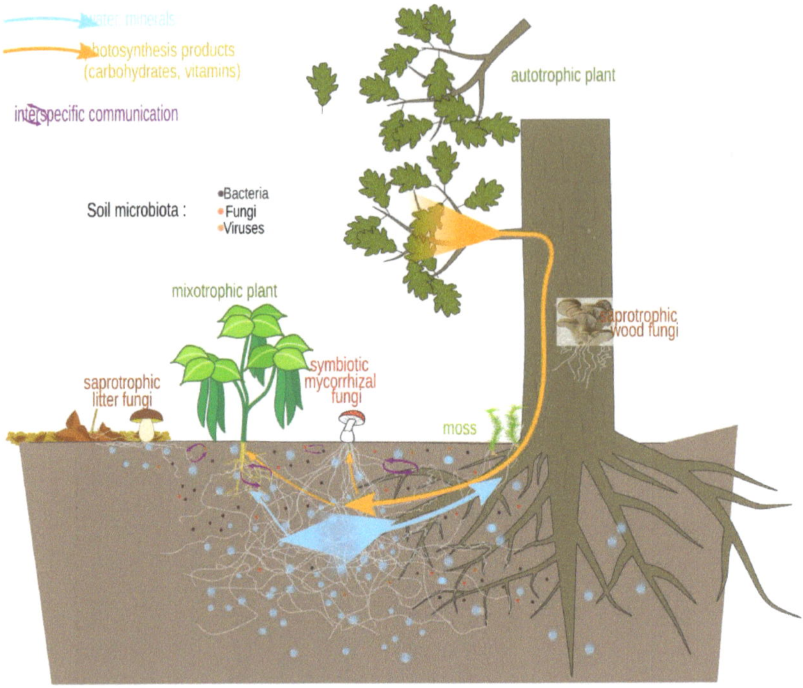

Figure 44: *Nature is the oldest, most efficient service ecosystem*

Examples:

Fungi Mycelium → Resource Integration

- Like CRM systems
- Exchange nutrients contextually
- Balance supply & demand adaptively

Bee Colonies → Distributed Work Allocation

- Similar to marketing budget optimization
- Agents allocate effort where needed most

Swarm Agents → Dynamic Path Optimization

- Like customer journey mapping
- Finds optimal multi-channel paths

Ecosystems → Emergent Value Co-Creation

- Value emerges from relationships
- Not from any one actor

Nature models align *perfectly* with S-D Logic's principles.

6.6 Axioms of S-D Logic (A1–A5) and How Nature Transforms them

Axiom 1: Service is the basis of exchange

Nature's Extension:

Every organism exchanges resources, signals, or energy—service ecosystems are universal.

Axiom 2: Value is co-created

Nature's Extension:

Co-creation is constant—forests co-create climate stability; bees co-create pollination networks.

Axiom 3: All actors are resource integrators

Nature's Extension:

From ants carrying leaves to trees integrating sunlight and soil nutrients—everything integrates resources.

Axiom 4: Value is determined contextually

Nature's Extension:

A nutrient is valuable based on time, location, season, and actor—exactly like consumer value.

Axiom 5: Ecosystems coordinate value

Nature's Extension:

Institutions in nature = ecological laws, symbiosis, predator–prey balance.

6.7 Table: How Nature Extends Each S-D Logic Axiom

Axiom	S-D Logic Meaning	Nature's Parallel	Implication for AI
A1	Service is exchange	Pollination, nutrient cycles	AI must optimize exchanges, not transactions
A2	Co-creation	Mutualism, symbiosis	AI must co-create value with users
A3	Resource integration	Mycelium, migration	AI must integrate distributed resources
A4	Contextual value	Seasonal patterns	AI must use context-aware models
A5	Ecosystem coordination	Food webs, climate	AI must operate as part of systems

6.8 Conceptual Model: Nature + S-D Logic = Service-Ecosystem AI

The Service-Ecosystem AI Stack weaves together the intelligence of natural systems, the principles of Service-Dominant (S-D) Logic, and cutting-edge AI techniques to create fluid, co-evolving value environments. At the base sits the Nature-Inspired Intelligence Layer, where swarm coordination, fungal-like signalling networks, ecological feedback loops, and evolutionary adaptation models mimic how living systems sense, respond, and reorganize. Above this is the S-D Logic Layer, which reframes markets as dynamic service ecosystems built on value propositions, co-creation mechanisms, resource integration, and contextual value systems—turning every interaction into an opportunity for reciprocal value. These two layers together shape how AI perceives context, adapts to change, and understands value as an emergent, shared outcome rather than a static transaction.

The AI Mechanisms Layer operationalizes this philosophy using multi-agent reinforcement learning for decentralized decision-making, graph learning for ecosystem-level pattern detection, diffusion models for generative possibility mapping, and emergent personalization that adapts to user context in real time. Finally, the Marketing Applications Layer activates these capabilities, enabling adaptive loyalty ecosystems that evolve with customer behavior, ultra-fluid emergent personalization journeys, resource orchestration across partners, and service co-evolution where brands and consumers continuously shape each other. Together, the stack creates a marketing paradigm that behaves less like a machine and more like a living, learning ecosystem.

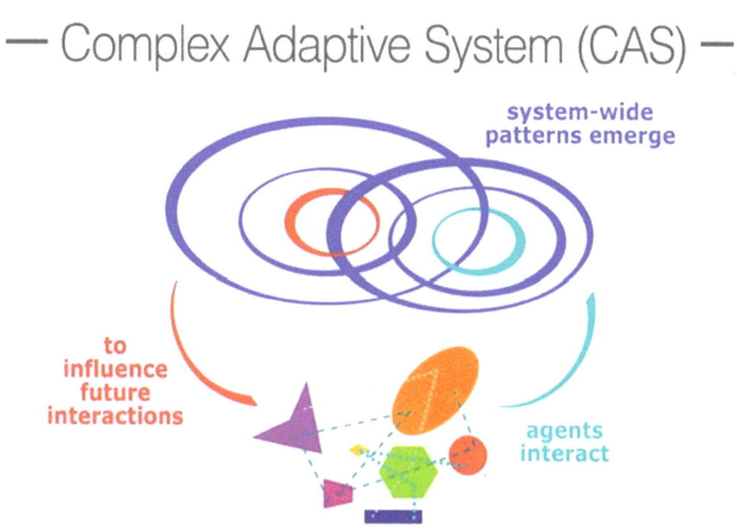

Figure 45: *Service-Ecosystem AI*

SERVICE-ECOSYSTEM AI STACK

1. Nature-Inspired Intelligence Layer

- Swarm coordination
- Fungal signalling
- Ecological feedback
- Evolutionary adaptation

2. S-D Logic Layer

- Value propositions
- Co-creation mechanisms
- Resource integration
- Contextual value systems

3. AI Mechanisms

- Multi-agent RL
- Graph learning
- Diffusion models
- Emergent personalization

4. Marketing Applications

- Adaptive loyalty ecosystems
- Emergent personalization
- Resource orchestration
- Service co-evolution

6.9 Research Implication: From Top-Down to Emergent Intelligence

Current AI in marketing uses:

- Top-down recommendations
- Rule-based segmentation
- Predictive scoring

But S-D Logic + Nature implies:

Emergent Personalization

Users co-create recommendations with the system—like bees coordinating flight paths.

Contextual Co-Creation

Services adapt based on environmental signals—like plants responding to light and stress cues.

Consumers as Adaptive Actors

Not "targets," but "participants" in a service ecosystem.

This changes how we define relevance, engagement, and value.

6.10 Extended Research Gap

1. Theoretical Gap

Contemporary consumer psychology remains largely human-centric, drawing heavily from cognitive, behavioral, and social models while overlooking powerful frameworks found in nature—such as swarm intelligence, ecological adaptation, fungal signaling networks, and evolutionary learning. These models offer rich insights into how decentralized agents coordinate, share information, adapt to shifting environments, and co-create outcomes. Ironically, these natural paradigms are deeply compatible with Service-Dominant (S-D) Logic, which also views markets as fluid, interconnected service ecosystems. Yet the academic literature has not meaningfully integrated these nature-derived intelligence models, leaving a conceptual blind spot in how we understand collective behavior, distributed decision-making, and emergent value formation.

Consumer psychology hasn't integrated:

- Swarm intelligence
- Ecological adaptation
- Fungal signalling models
- Evolutionary learning

even though these naturally align with S-D Logic.

2. Practical Gap

In practice, mainstream AI tools continue to operate with a push-driven, mechanistic mindset—pushing content, predicting clicks, segmenting users into rigid buckets, and optimizing linear funnels. These techniques reinforce a transactional model of engagement that assumes central control and predictable causality. None of this reflects the realities of distributed agency, where value emerges through interactions among multiple actors, or the dynamics of service ecosystems where customers, firms, technologies, and contexts continuously co-evolve. Current AI systems are not designed for emergent engagement or co-evolutionary value creation, highlighting a significant mismatch between the complexity of real-world markets and the narrow optimization logic of today's marketing technologies.

AI tools still:

- Push content
- Predict clicks
- Segment mechanically
- Optimize funnels

None of these reflect:

- Distributed agency
- Service ecosystems
- Co-evolution of value
- Emergent engagement

6.11 Bridging Non-Human Intelligence with S-D Logic Premises

Service-Dominant Logic assumes:

- Actors are interconnected
- Value is emergent, not delivered
- Systems evolve
- Resources integrate dynamically

Nature provides **living proofs** of these ideas. From ants coordinating work to fungal networks optimizing resource flows, nature shows:

The rules of service ecosystems are biological, not managerial.

This page begins connecting non-human intelligence frameworks to the foundational premises of S-D Logic.

6.12 FP1 Reimagined Through Nature: Service as the Basis of Exchange

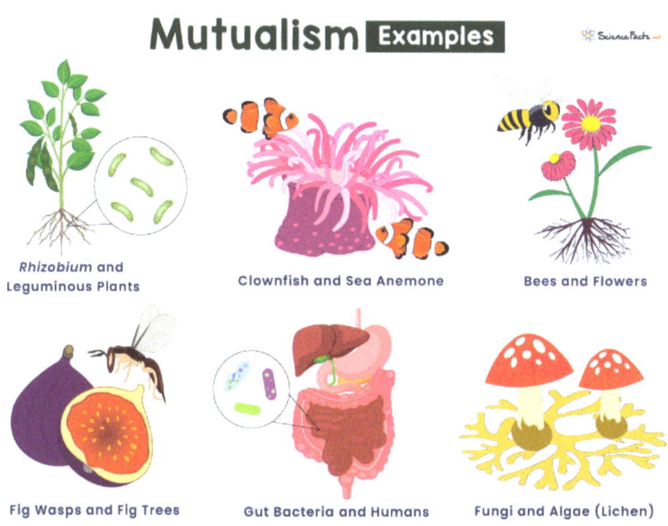

Figure 46: *Service as the basis of exchange*

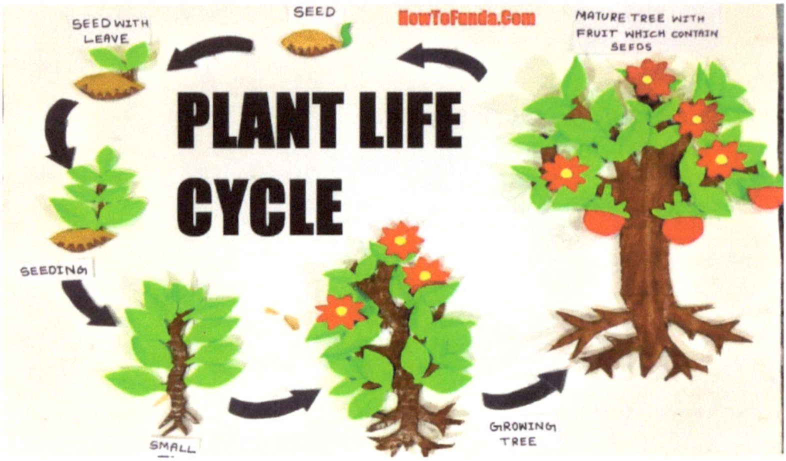

Figure 47: *FP1: Service is the fundamental basis of exchange*

Traditional interpretation:

- Goods simply store service potential

Nature's Lens:

In ecosystems:

- Bees provide **pollination service**
- Flowers provide **nectar service**
- Fungi provide **nutrient transport services**
- Trees provide **carbon exchange services**

These exchanges sustain entire ecosystems.

AI Implication

Consumer data exchanges should be modelled as **service-for-service flows**, not as transactions or "data extraction."

AI must ask:

- What service did the user perform by interacting?
- What service does the system offer in return?

Value emerges only when **reciprocity** exists.

6.13 FP2 Reimagined: Indirect Exchange Masks Service

FP2: Indirect exchange masks the fundamental basis of service

Products are only **service vehicles.**

Nature's Extension:

- A seed is not "the value"—the **ecosystem service** of propagation is.
- A bee's honey is secondary to the **service of pollination.**
- A tree trunk is secondary to the **service of structural support**.

AI Interpretation:

Digital interfaces are not value.

The **experience**, the **context**, the **interaction** is the service.

This leads to:

- Experience-first AI design
- Service pathways rather than product funnels
- Meaningful co-creation touchpoints

6.14 FP3 Reimagined: Goods as Service Distribution Mechanisms

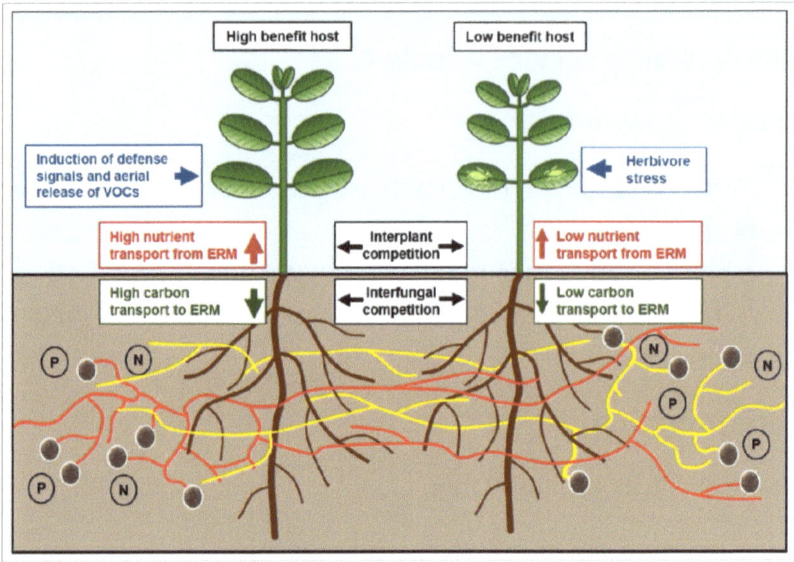

Figure 48: *FP3 Reimagined: Goods as Service Distribution Mechanisms*

FP3: Goods distribution service

In S-D Logic, goods are only "appliances" of service.

Nature's Equivalent:

- Fruits distribute seeds.
- Mycelium distributes nutrients.
- Oceans distribute thermal energy.
- Leaves distribute sunlight conversion.

All "goods" in nature distribute services.

AI Application:

In marketing tech:

- Apps distribute service-experiences
- Recommendation engines distribute contextual guidance

- Loyalty points distribute relationship value
- Notifications distribute engagement invitations

This shifts AI from **deliveries** to **flows**.

6.15 FP4 Reimagined: Operant Resources Drive Value

FP4: Operant resources (skills, knowledge) are primary

These resources act on other resources.

Nature's View:

Operant resources in nature:

Nature Element	Operant Resource
Bee colony	Foraging knowledge
Fungi	Network optimization algorithms
Birds	Migratory intelligence
Ants	Decentralized load balancing

AI Translation:

AI must treat:

- Context
- Behavioral patterns
- Preferences
- Social signals

as **operant**, not **operand** resources. Consumers are **active agents**, not data points.

6.16 FP5 Reimagined: All Economies Are Service Economies

FP5: All economies are service economies

Even manufacturing economies depend on applied knowledge, workflows, and interactions.

Nature's Version:

Every ecosystem is a **service economy**:

- Flowers advertise colours → pollinators respond
- Fungi deliver nutrients → plants pay sugars
- Predators regulate population → ecosystems maintain balance

AI Extension:

Consumer ecosystems = **service ecosystems**, not funnels.

AI must:

- Model feedback loops
- Detect co-creation patterns
- Balance value flows

not simply "optimize conversions."

6.17 FP6 Reimagined: Customer Is Always a Co-Creator of Value

FP6: Customer is always a co-creator of value

Nature's Mirror:

- Bees co-create reproductive success
- Mycorrhizal fungi co-create plant vitality
- Coral reefs co-create biodiversity
- Birds co-create seed dispersal networks

There is no value **without** cooperation.

Implication for AI:

Consumers co-create:

- Meaning
- Identity
- Relationship value
- Brand communities
- Trend trajectories
- Algorithmic outcomes

AI should therefore:

- Incorporate feedback loops
- Let consumers shape system behavior
- Support co-evolutionary design

6.18 FP7 Reimagined: Actors Cannot Deliver Value, Only Propose It

FP7: Actors offer value propositions—not value

Value is realized only in use, by the beneficiary.

Nature's Interpretation:

- A flower *proposes* nectar
- A bird *accepts* or rejects
- A forest *proposes* habitat
- Species *decide* suitability

AI Application:

- A recommendation is a proposition.

  A notification is a proposition.

  A product attribute is a proposition.

Consumers actualize value based on:

- Context
- Social meaning
- Emotional resonance
- Timing
- Personal goals

Thus, AI must predict **value-in-context**, not product likelihoods.

6.19 FP8 Reimagined: A Service-Centered View is Inherently Relational

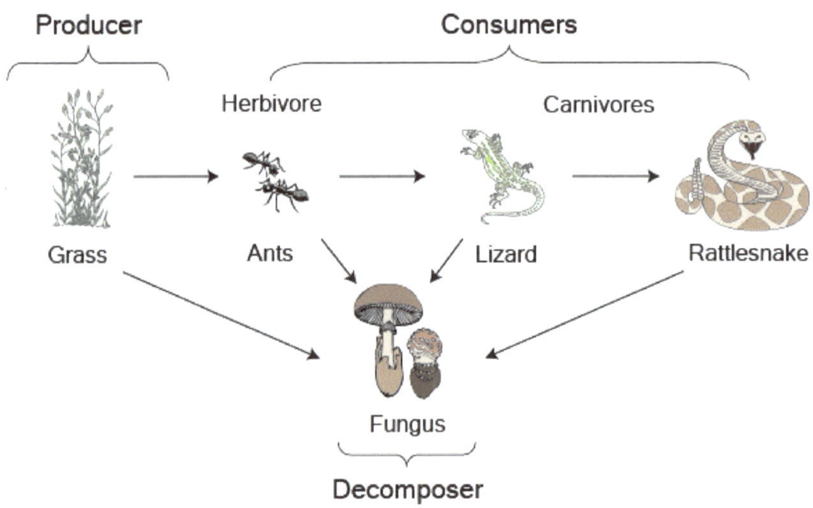

Figure 49: *FP8 Reimagined: A Service-Centered View Is Inherently Relational*

FP8: Service systems are relational, not transactional

Nature's Equivalent:

Ecosystems are defined by:

- Predator–prey relationships
- Mutualistic bonds

- Resource competition
- Symbiosis
- Commensalism

AI Implication:

AI must map **relationship patterns**, not isolated behaviors.

This leads to:

- Multi-agent systems
- Social graph intelligence
- Co-engagement clustering
- Ecosystem analytics

6.20 FP9 Reimagined: All Social and Economic Actors Are Resource Integrators

FP9: Every actor integrates resources

No actor is self-sufficient.

Nature's Reflection:

Species	**Resource Integration**
Plants	Sunlight, water, fungi nutrients
Bees	Flower signals, colony coordination
Fish	Currents + schooling intelligence
Ants	Collective decision-making

AI Application:

Consumers integrate:

- Information
- Emotions
- Social cues

- Algorithms
- Experiences

6.21 FP10 Reimagined: Value is Phenomenologically Determined by the Beneficiary

FP10: Value is always uniquely and phenomenologically determined by the beneficiary

This means:

- Value does not exist until the consumer experiences it
- Value is **subjective**, contextual, emotional, and temporal

Nature's Interpretation:

A nutrient, habitat, or resource has different value depending on:

- Species
- Season
- Local conditions
- Life stage
- Environmental pressures

A bee values nectar based on scarcity.

A plant values shade differently during drought.

A predator values prey based on energy needs.

AI Application:

Value is **dynamic and personal**, not universal.

AI must understand:

- Context (time, situation)
- State (emotion, need, mood)

- Social environment
- Long-term trajectories

This means personalization must shift from **static preference models** to **phenomenological prediction**.

6.22 FP11 Reimagined: Institutional Arrangements Coordinate Value Co-Creation

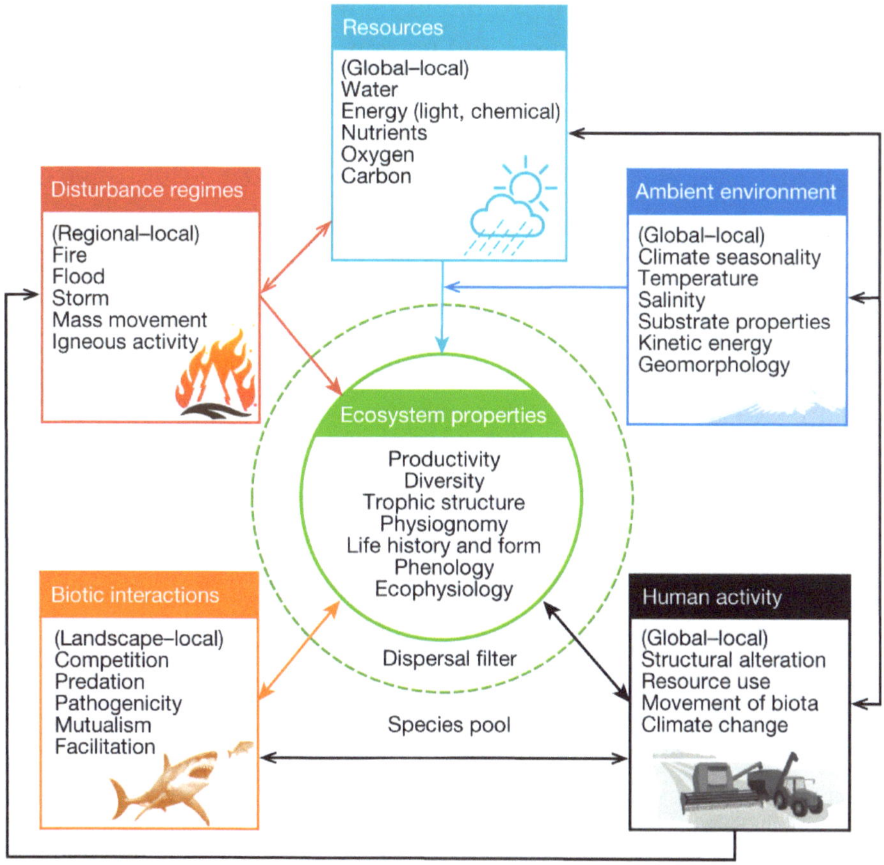

Figure 50: *Institutional Arrangements Coordinate Value Co-Creation*

This framework illustrates how an ecosystem emerges from the continuous interaction of multiple biophysical and anthropogenic forces. At the centre lie **ecosystem properties** such as productivity, diversity, trophic structure, physiognomy, life-history traits, phenology, and ecophysiology. These properties are shaped by the **species pool**, moderated by dispersal filters, and dynamically influenced by four major drivers: *resources, ambient environmental conditions, disturbance regimes,* and *biotic interactions.* Resources like water, nutrients, oxygen, and energy flow in from global to local scales, while ambient environment factors—such as temperature, salinity, climate seasonality, and geomorphology—set the broader constraints within which species must function. Disturbance regimes (e.g., fire, floods, storms, igneous activity) introduce periodic shocks that reset or transform ecosystem patterns, whereas biotic interactions—including competition, predation, mutualism, and facilitation—govern how species coexist, adapt, and evolve across landscapes.

Overlaying all these natural processes is **human activity**, which alters ecosystems at both structural and functional levels—through resource extraction, land-use change, biotic movement, and contributions to climate change. The arrows indicate that these components are not static influences but cyclical, adaptive, and intertwined, continuously feeding into and reshaping ecosystem properties. The framework highlights that ecosystems are not governed by a single dominant factor; instead, they are shaped by the interplay of distributed forces across scales, leading to emergent patterns of diversity, stability, and productivity. This systems view emphasizes that understanding any ecological outcome requires accounting for both global forces and local interactions, as well as the increasing impact of human-driven disturbances.

FP11: Value co-creation is coordinated by institutions and institutional arrangements

Human examples:

- Norms
- Platforms
- Culture
- Policies
- Market rules

Nature's Institutional Arrangements:

Natural Institution	Coordination Role
Predator–prey cycles	Population balance
Symbiosis	Mutual value enhancement
Mycorrhizal networks	Resource equality
Territorial rules	Distribution of space
Migration rhythms	Resource balance over time

AI Implication:

AI should not assume consumers operate solo; they operate inside **institutional webs**:

- Social networks
- Communities
- Tribes
- Cultural norms
- Platform rules

AI must learn **institutional intelligence**, not just individual behavior.

6.23 Summary Table: All 11 S-D Logic Premises Expanded Through Nature

FP	Core Principle	Nature's Expansion	Impact on AI
FP1	Service is the basis	Every organism exchange service	AI models reciprocal exchange
FP2	Indirect exchange	Goods = service carriers	Interfaces deliver service flows
FP3	Goods = service appliance	Nature distributes value	AI distributes context, not content
FP4	Operant resources	Knowledge is biological	AI must model skills, not demographics
FP5	All economies = service	All ecosystems are service-based	Treat consumers as ecosystem actors
FP6	Co-creation	Symbiosis	AI becomes co-creator, not predictor
FP7	Value proposition	Flower–bee analogy	AI offers propositions, not decisions
FP8	Relational	Webs of relationships	AI focuses on relational analytics
FP9	Resource integrators	Forest nutrient cycles	Consumers integrate multiple signals
FP10	Phenomenological value	Context defines value	AI becomes context-aware
FP11	Institutions coordinate	Ecological laws	AI models multi-agent arrangements

6.24 Nature + S-D Logic: Foundational Synthesis

Nature shows how value flows; S-D Logic shows how value is co-created.

Combining both yields **Service-Ecosystem AI**, defined by:

- Distributed agency (like ants)
- Resource interdependence (like fungi)
- Adaptive coordination (like birds in flight)
- Phenomenological value creation (like ecological niches)
- Emergent structure (like coral reefs)

This is fundamentally different from today's AI, which is:

- Predictive
- Linear
- Prescriptive
- Funnel-oriented

Nature + S-D Logic =

AI that listens, adapts, and grows with consumers.

6.25 Theoretical Integration Model: Service-Ecosystem AI

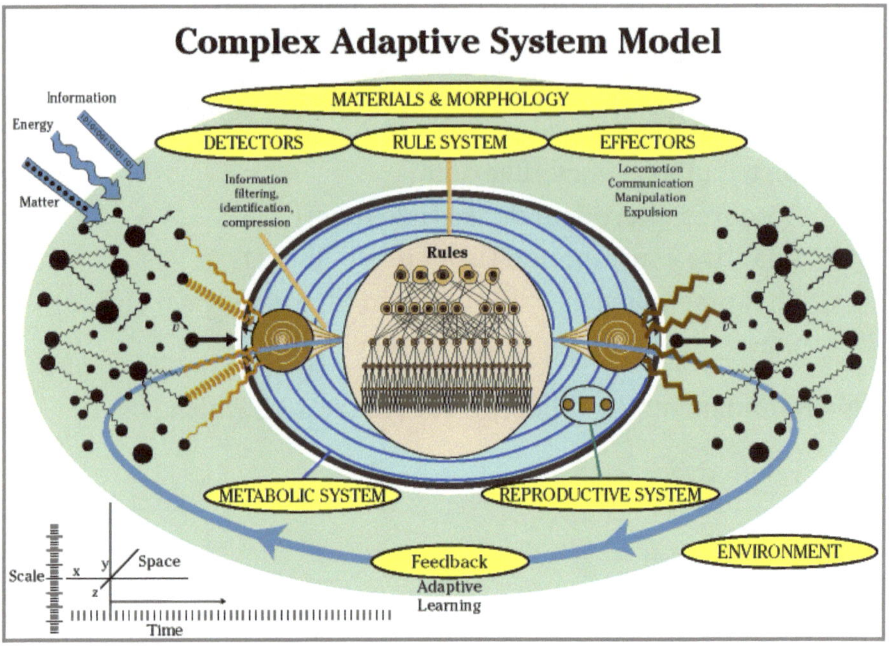

Figure 51: *Complex Adaptive System Model*

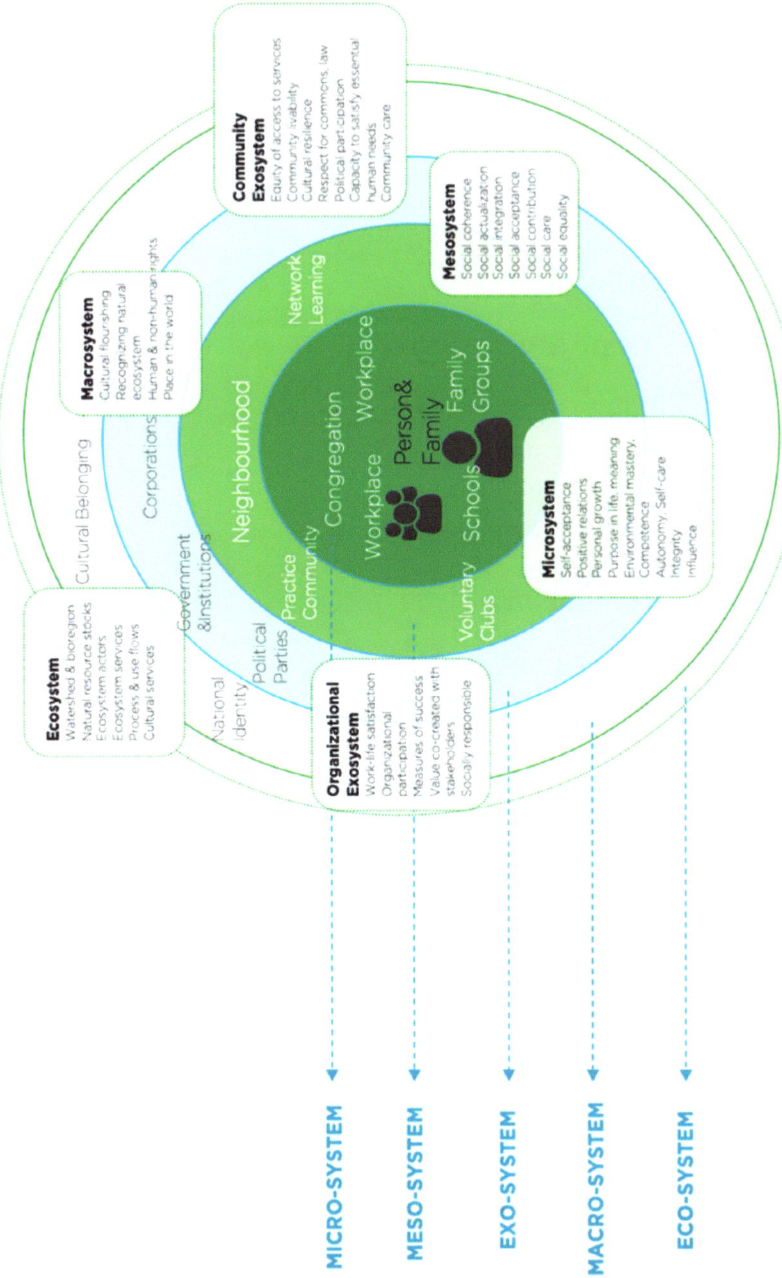

Figure 52: *SEAM*

THE SERVICE-ECOSYSTEM AI MODEL (SEAM)

Level 1—Biological Inspiration

- Swarms
- Fungi networks
- Ecosystem feedback
- Evolution
- Plant signalling

Level 2—S-D Logic Architecture

- Co-creation
- Value propositions
- Resource integration
- Institutional coordination

Level 3—AI Mechanisms

- Multi-agent reinforcement learning
- Graph neural networks
- Diffusion modeling
- Evolutionary computation
- Context-aware modeling

Level 4—Marketing Applications

- Adaptive personalization
- Emergent loyalty ecosystems
- Contextual engagement
- Community-driven value creation

6.26 Emergent Personalization vs Predictive Personalization

Predictive Personalization (Current AI)

- Uses historical data
- Predicts next action

- Suggests pre-built options
- Operates top-down

Emergent Personalization (Service-Ecosystem AI)

- Learns from interactions
- Co-creates choices
- Allows the user to influence system behavior
- Adapts bottom-up
- Updates in real-time like biological systems

Example: A swarm-based recommender that adapts as consumers collectively explore.

6.27 Contextual Co-Creation: Beyond Static Preferences

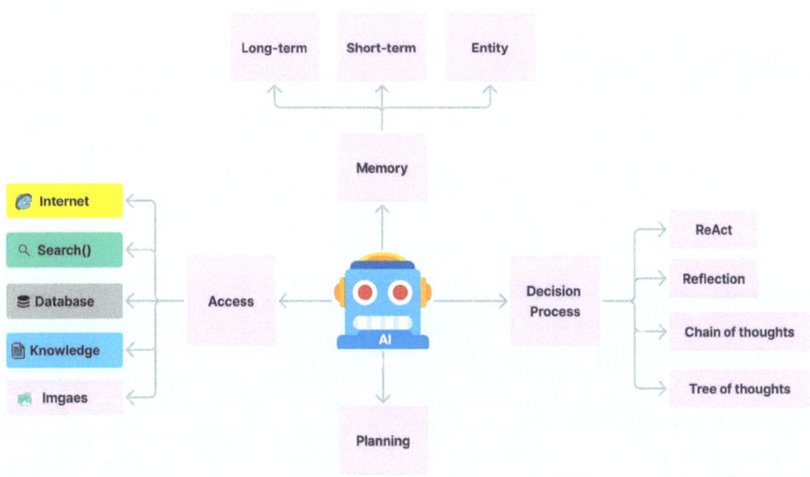

Figure 53: *Beyond Static Preferences*

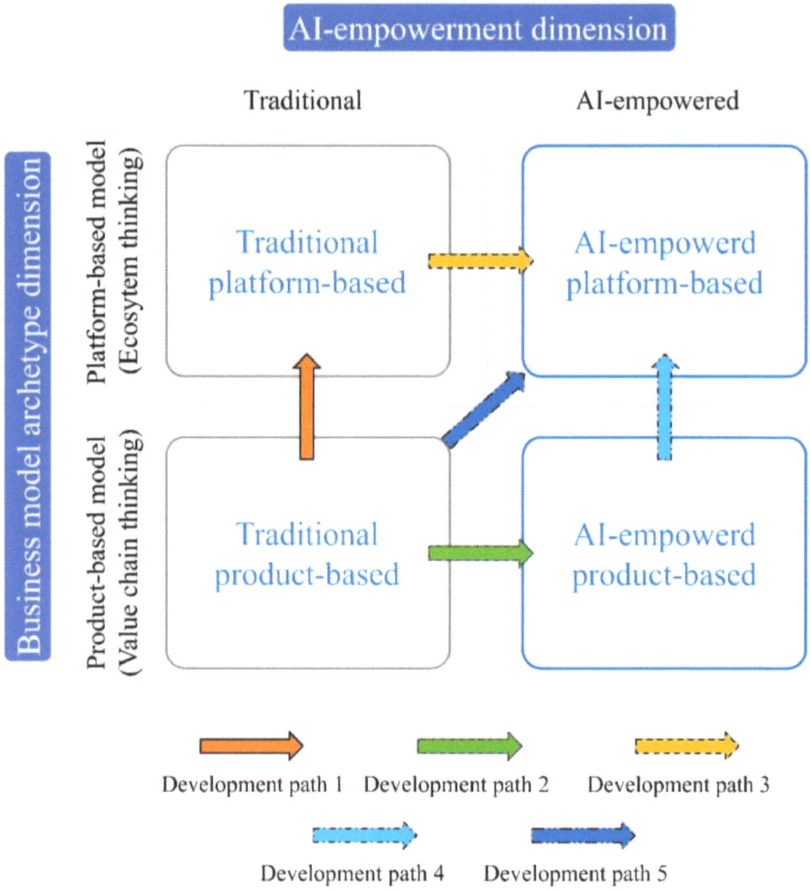

Figure 54: *Contextual Co-Creation*

Instead of assuming stable preferences:

Context is the real driver of value.

Examples:

- A consumer values coffee differently at 7 AM vs 5 PM
- A user values a product more when friends buy it
- A movie recommendation depends on mood and company
- A skincare ad's value changes with weather, season, and stress

Nature teaches that context changes *everything*.

AI must incorporate:

- Time-based context
- Environmental context
- Social context
- Internal context (emotion, mood)
- Ecosystem context (what others are doing)

6.28 Consumers as Adaptive Actors in Service Ecosystems

Users adapt like organisms in ecosystems:

- Switching "habitats" (apps, platforms)
- Competing for attention resources
- Building symbiotic relationships (brand communities)
- Migrating based on seasonality (e.g., January fitness surge)

Key Insight

Consumers do not follow linear journeys—they **evolve**.

AI must model:

- Behavioral drift
- Preference evolution
- Social influence propagation
- Multi-agent interactions
- Niche formation

Nature shows how to do this elegantly.

6.29 The Research Gap Reframed

Current AI:

- Predicts next clicks
- Segments using clustering

- Personalizes based on redundancy
- Manages funnels

What's missing:

- Modeling consumers as co-evolving agents
- Understanding value as relational
- Capturing slow, passive signals (fungal-style accumulations)
- Recognizing ecosystem effects (network influence)
- Allowing personalization to emerge rather than be imposed

The research gap is no longer computational—it is conceptual.

6.30 Extended Research Gap with S-D Logic Perspective

The gap is fourfold:

1. Underuse of Nature-Aligned Intelligence Models

Swarm intelligence

Ecological feedback

Evolutionary adaptation

Fungal signalling

All align with S-D Logic but are absent in marketing AI.

2. Overuse of Product-Centric Paradigms

Goods-Dominant Logic still dominates AI systems:

- Attribution funnels
- Predictive scoring
- Content push models

3. Lack of System-Level Thinking

Marketing rarely models:

- Ecosystem loops
- Resource flows
- Multi-actor interactions

4. Missing Framework for Co-Evolution

There is no standard way to model:

- How consumers evolve with brands
- How brands adapt to communities
- How value is shared, not delivered

6.31 From Linear Funnels to Living Service Ecosystems

The marketing funnel is a mechanical metaphor:

- Awareness
- Consideration
- Conversion
- Loyalty

This mechanical view mirrors **Goods-Dominant Logic (G-D Logic)**—linear, reductionist, controlled.

In contrast, S-D Logic + Nature suggests:

"Engagement is not a funnel—it is a habitat."

Consumers live inside overlapping **service ecosystems**, each with:

- Micro-communities
- Resource flows
- Social signals

- Environmental triggers
- Competing species (brands)
- Cooperative species (complementary brands)

AI must stop forcing funnels and start **observing ecosystems**.

6.32 Mapping Consumer Ecosystems: A Nature-Inspired Model

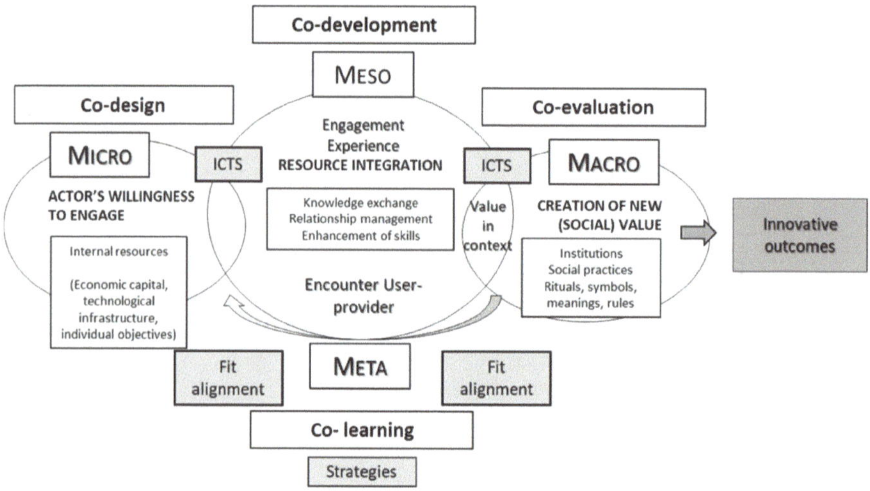

Figure 55: *Customer Ecosystems – inspired by nature*

Consumer ecosystems resemble natural ecosystems:

Species → Actor Types

- Brands
- Consumers
- Influencers
- Platforms
- Retailers
- Communities

Habitats → Digital Environments

- Social feeds
- E-commerce sites
- Messaging platforms
- Loyalty apps
- Real-world retail
- Interest-based forums

Resource Flows → Value Exchanges

- Attention
- Data
- Content
- Trust
- Rewards
- Emotional resonance

Feedback Loops → Behavior Waves

- Trends
- Virality
- Co-creation
- Community advocacy

This ecological framing aligns directly with S-D Logic's distributed, relational, co-creative worldview.

6.33 The Four Layers of Consumer Service Ecosystems

Layer	Description	Nature Analog
Micro Layer	Individual behaviors, contexts	Organism-level adaptation
Meso Layer	Community interactions, tribes	Packs, colonies, flocks

Layer	Description	Nature Analog
Macro Layer	Market & platform structures	Ecosystem dynamics
Meta Layer	Cultural, institutional rules	Climate systems, seasons

AI must sense, adapt, and learn across ALL these layers.

Most current systems only detect the micro layer ("user clicked").

Service-Ecosystem AI integrates all four.

6.34 Nature-Inspired Mechanisms for Value Co-Creation

Figure 56: *Nature-Inspired Value Co-creation*

Nature offers mechanisms that map beautifully to co-creation.

Mutualism (Bee ↔ Flower)

Consumer ↔ Brand co-create value in reviews, UGC, and communities.

Commensalism (Fish ↔ Shark)

Some users get value without giving equal value back.

Competition (Trees for Sunlight)

Brands compete for attention as trees compete for light.

Symbiosis (Corals ↔ Algae)

Brand–consumer loyalty ecosystems resemble biological symbiosis.

These mechanisms are **evolutionary strategies** of value co-creation.

6.35 Dynamic Resource Integration

S-D Logic states:

Consumers integrate resources to create value.

Nature exhibits this constantly:

- Birds integrate wind + terrain + group intelligence
- Plants integrate sunlight + soil + fungal networks
- Ants integrate pheromone signals + social tasks

Consumers integrate:

- Social proof
- Product information
- Price signals
- Brand meaning

- Friction levels
- Emotional cues

AI must model **how resources combine**, not just measure them.

6.36 The Value Co-Creation Loop (Nature + S-D Logic)

Figure 57: *Feedback loops in nature*

THE CO-CREATION LOOP

(From Nature, Applied to S-D Logic)

1. **Sensing**

   Organisms sense signals → Consumers sense options.

2. **Acting**

   Organisms take adaptive action → Consumers choose actions.

3. **Feedback**

   Ecosystem responds → Platform responds.

4. **Resource Exchange**

   Value exchanged mutually → Engagement exchanged contextually.

5. **Adaptation**

   Organisms adapt → AI adapts personalization.

6. **Evolution**

   Species evolve → Consumer behavior evolves.

Key Insight:

Value is not a **moment**, but a **cycle**. AI must detect, learn, and evolve at each stage.

6.37 A New Typology of Value: Inspired by Nature

Traditional value types (functional, emotional, social) are outdated.

Nature suggests an expanded typology:

Value Type	Nature Inspiration	Description
Adaptive Value	Evolution	Shape-shifting relevance
Symbiotic Value	Mutalism	Mutual benefit through participation
Ecosystem Value	Forest networks	Value created by community interaction
Distributed Value	Fungi	Value built through slow, cumulative signals
Emergent Value	Swarms	Collective patterns creating new meaning

Value Type	Nature Inspiration	Description
Contextual Value	Climate patterns	Value changes with context and timing

This new typology is essential for S-D Logic + AI research.

6.38 Resource Orchestration in Service-Ecosystem AI

Current systems "allocate resources."

Nature **orchestrates** them dynamically.

Examples:

- Fungal networks send nutrients to stressed roots
- Bees switch roles based on colony needs
- Wolves regulate prey populations
- Coral reefs optimize nutrient flow

Service-Ecosystem AI must orchestrate:

- Content
- Offers
- Rewards
- Interaction opportunities
- Community engagement
- Customer service roles

based on **ecosystem state**, not corporate agenda.

6.39 Institutional Intelligence in Consumer Ecosystems

Most AI ignores institutional structures:

- Social norms
- Platform rules
- Cultural expectations
- Peer influence
- Reputation flows

But S-D Logic (FP11) demands institutional awareness.

Nature Example:

- Predator–prey dynamics create institutions of balance
- Territory rules govern resource allocation
- Migration patterns coordinate large-scale movement

AI Implication:

AI must incorporate:

- Community rules
- Fairness norms
- Culture-specific contexts
- Real-time social shifts
- Platform constraints

Institutional intelligence = better value co-creation.

6.40 Why Nature + S-D Logic = The Next Paradigm

Because:

- Both are **systems-based**, not individualistic
- Both emphasize **relationships over transactions**
- Both focus on **resource integration, not resource ownership**

- Both allow **contextual and emergent value**
- Both embrace **continuous evolution**
- Both assume **distributed agency**
- Both require **ecosystem intelligence**

Traditional AI sees the consumer as a target.

Service-Ecosystem AI sees the consumer as a **participant in a living system**.

6.41 Toward a New AI Paradigm: Service-Ecosystem AI

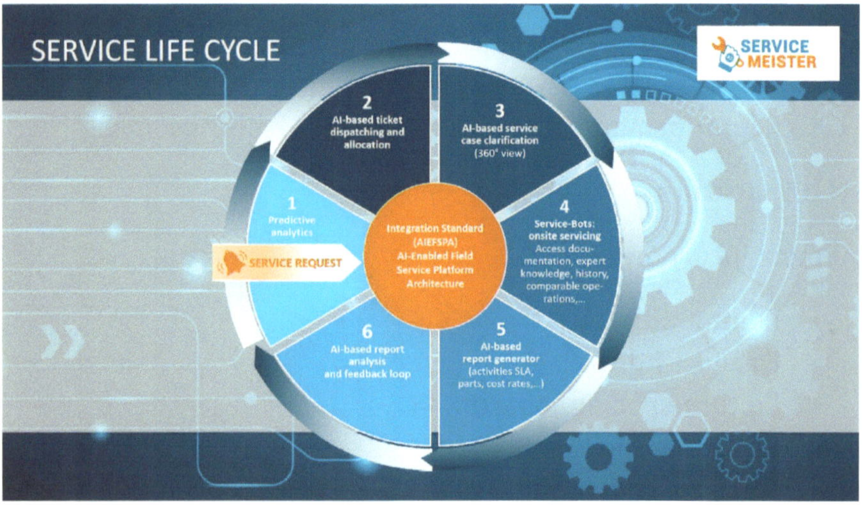

Figure 58: *Service Life Cycle*

We've reached a turning point.

Goods-Dominant Logic AI:

- Predicts
- Targets
- Pushes
- Optimizes funnels
- Treats consumers as endpoints

Service-Ecosystem AI:

- Listens
- Adapts
- Co-creates
- Orchestrates resource flows
- Views consumers as ecosystem actors

The future of AI in marketing lies in **emergent service orchestration**, not prediction alone.

6.42 What Current AI Misses: The Invisible Layers of Value

Current systems rarely process:

- Slow-developing signals
- Weak ties and passive engagement
- Distributed agency across communities
- Cumulative micro-experiences
- Emotional ecosystems
- Institutional constraints

Nature-Inspired S-D Logic Captures These:

Hidden Layer	Nature Parallel	AI Insight
Weak signals	Mycelial pulses	Engagement accrues over time
Collective influence	Flocking	Community-driven behavior
Emotion waves	Climate patterns	Mood-aware personalization
Co-evolution	Predator–prey cycles	Consumers + brands adapt together
Network constraints	Food webs	Platform-level influence

This brings us closer to a **holistic service worldview**.

6.43 The Future of Value: Co-Evolving AI + Consumers

In ecosystems, species evolve together.

Similarly:

Consumers and AI systems will co-evolve in a service ecosystem.

The AI learns from the consumer

→ The consumer learns from the AI

→ Both reshape each other's behavior

→ Both influence the broader ecosystem

This is already visible in:

- TikTok's For You Page
- Amazon shopping patterns
- Spotify listening ecosystems
- YouTube recommendation communities

But currently, evolution is **accidental**.

Next-gen AI makes it **intentional** through S-D Logic.

6.44 Co-Creation Intelligence: A New AI Capability

Definition

Co-creation intelligence = AI's ability to detect, support, and amplify value co-creation between actors.

Examples:

- Helping communities form (tribes)
- Supporting user–brand collaboration
- Learning from co-engagement patterns

- Enabling consumers to shape product direction
- Facilitating symbiotic interactions

Co-creation intelligence is the direct result of integrating:

- Swarm behavior
- Ecosystem intelligence
- Plant/fungal signalling
- S-D Logic axioms

This is the next frontier of marketing AI research.

6.45 Toward a Unified Theory: Nature + S-D Logic + AI

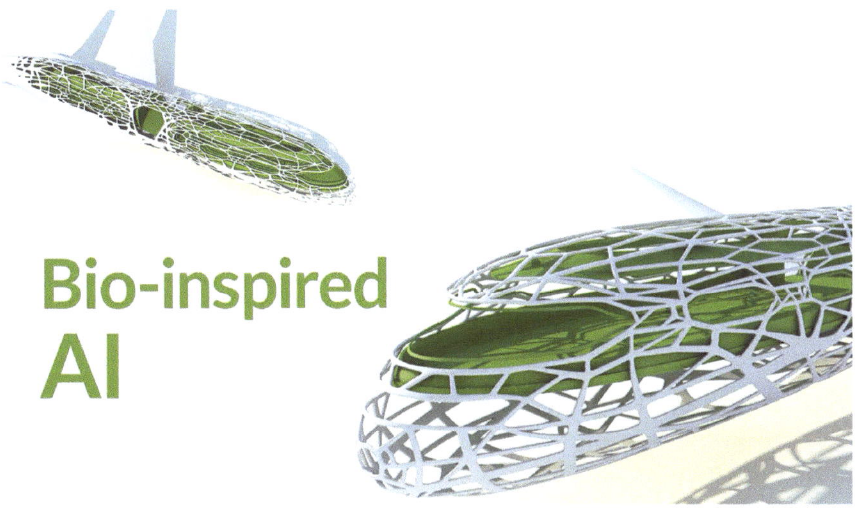

Figure 59: *Bio-Inspired AI*

THE UNIFIED THEORY HAS THREE PILLARS:

1. Nature as the Blueprint

- Provides models of intelligence
- Shows distributed agency
- Demonstrates adaptive systems
- Reveals resource flows

2. S-D Logic as the Philosophy

- Defines value as co-created
- Centers service in exchange
- Emphasizes systems over units
- Integrates resources contextually

3. AI as the Mechanism

- Executes resource orchestration
- Learns emergent patterns
- Operates across layers simultaneously
- Enables co-evolving ecosystems

The three together form a **Service-Ecosystem Intelligence Framework**.

6.46 The Service-Ecosystem AI Framework (SEAF)

SEAF consists of 5 interacting layers:

1. Signal Layer

- Biological signals (swarm, fungi)
- Consumer behavior traces
- Contextual/environmental data

2. Interpretation Layer

- S-D Logic axioms
- Resource integration rules
- Phenomenological value modeling

3. Intelligence Layer

- Multi-agent RL
- GNN-based ecosystem modeling
- Evolutionary computation
- Fuzzy systems

4. Ecosystem Coordination Layer

- Institutional dynamics
- Platform constraints
- Market ecosystem health

5. Service Co-Creation Layer

- Emergent personalization
- Community co-creation
- Collaborative experiences
- Adaptive loyalty ecosystems

This is the architecture for 21st-century marketing AI.

6.47 Table: Comparing Paradigms (G-D Logic AI vs S-D Logic AI vs Service-Ecosystem AI)

Feature	G-D Logic AI	S-D Logic AI	Service-Ecosystem AI
View of the consumer	Target	Co-creator	Adaptive ecosystem actor
Value	Delivered	Co-created	Emergent + contextual
Structure	Funnel	Interaction	Ecosystem
Behavior modeling	Predictive	Relational	Adaptive/evolutionary
Signals	Strong signals	Interaction	Strong + weak + environmental
Optimization	KPIs	Experience	Ecosystem health
Data use	Transactional	Behavioral	Multilayer contextual
AI role	Predictor	Partner	Orchestrator

6.48 Application Scenarios: What Service-Ecosystem AI Enables

1. Emergent Loyalty Ecosystems

Loyalty adapts like an ecosystem—responding to stress, competition, and scarcity.

2. Distributed Personalization

Swarm and GNN-powered feeds co-create recommendations with communities.

3. Adaptive Customer Service

Fungi-inspired triaging → resources go where stress is highest.

4. Co-Evolving Experiences

AI + user communities shape services together in real time.

5. Contextual Commerce

Offers adapt from mood → environment → social graph → market waves.

These applications do not exist today but will define the next era of marketing.

6.49 Limitations, Risks & Ethical Guardrails

Limitations

- Emergence is unpredictable
- Ecosystem modeling is complex
- Real-time adaptation is resource-intensive
- Weak signals are noisy

Risks

- Over-influence on user autonomy
- Reinforcing social herding
- Hyper-personalization leading to echo chambers
- Ecosystem manipulation

Necessary Ethical Guardrails

- Co-creation must remain voluntary
- Ecosystem effects must be monitored
- Transparency in adaptive logic
- Protection of minority behaviors
- Limits on influence during vulnerable states

6.50 Chapter Summary: The Paradigm Shift

The Future of Marketing AI Will Be Defined By:

1. Service-Dominant Logic
2. Nature-Inspired Intelligence
3. Ecosystem-Level AI Design

This chapter has argued that:

- Value is not delivered—it **emerges**
- Consumers are not targets—they are **ecosystem actors**
- AI is not a predictor—it is a **co-evolving orchestrator**

Service-Ecosystem AI is the philosophical, biological, and technological convergence that will define next-generation marketing.

Project—Build a Service-Ecosystem AI Platform

Objective

Design an AI system for a large omnichannel retail brand that integrates:

- S-D Logic principles
- Nature-inspired intelligence
- Ecosystem modeling
- Multi-agent adaptation

Components of the Platform

1. Ecosystem Sensor Layer

- Collect individual + community + environmental data
- Model weak signals through fungal-inspired accumulation

2. Nature-AI Modeling Layer

- Swarm-based recommendation optimization
- Evolutionary creative systems
- Contextual value modeling (FP10)

3. S-D Logic Integration Layer

- Co-creation detection
- Resource orchestration
- Context-aware value propositions

4. Ecosystem Orchestration Layer

- Balance value flows between users, communities, and brand
- Monitor ecosystem stress

5. User Co-Creation Interface

- Let users influence recommendations, experiences, and loyalty dynamics

Solutions

System Component	AI Technique	Mathematical Foundation
Swarm-based recommender	Ant Colony Optimization	Pheromone matrix, probabilistic transitions
Ecosystem graph model	Graph Neural Networks	Graph Laplacian, message passing
Co-creation detector	Multi-agent RL	Policy gradients, reward shaping
Fungal weak-signal model	Diffusion + Fuzzy Logic	Laplacian diffusion, membership functions
Context-aware value	Bayesian Networks	Conditional probabilities
Evolutionary creatives	Genetic Algorithms	Fitness functions, mutation ops
Ecosystem stress monitor	Dynamical Systems Modeling	Differential equations

These tools operationalize S-D Logic through nature metaphors.

MCQs

1. Service-Ecosystem AI views consumers as:

    a. Targets
    b. Ecosystem actors
    c. Segments
    d. Predictable units

2. Fungal signalling inspires AI that models:

    a. Fast decisions
    b. Weak, cumulative engagement signals
    c. Only demographic traits
    d. Hardware optimization

3. S-D Logic says value is:

    a. Delivered by the company
    b. Co-created
    c. Stored in goods
    d. Independent of context

4. Swarm intelligence supports:

    a. Funnel design
    b. Emergent personalization
    c. Static segmentation
    d. Fixed content delivery

5. In service ecosystems, resource flows are modelled like:

    a. Electric circuits
    b. Nutrient cycles
    c. Car engines
    d. Brick walls

6. Phenomenological value (FP10) implies value is:

   a. Universal
   b. Contextual and subjective
   c. Factory-produced
   d. Algorithmic

7. Ecosystem feedback loops resemble:

   a. Funnel stages
   b. Predator–prey cycles
   c. Print ads
   d. Product packaging

8. Multi-agent RL enables:

   a. Co-creation intelligence
   b. Only image recognition
   c. Static predictions
   d. Removing context

9. Institutional arrangements in nature include:

   a. Laws written by animals
   b. Migration rhythms and territorial rules
   c. Manufacturing plants
   d. Media planning calendars

10. AI built on G-D Logic tends to be:

   a. Transactional
   b. Ecosystemic
   c. Evolutionary
   d. Adaptive

11. Service-Ecosystem AI focuses on:

    a. Isolated users
    b. Entire value ecosystems
    c. One-time purchases
    d. Only top-down predictions

12. Weak signals map to which nature metaphor?

    a. Thunderstorms
    b. Mycelial pulses
    c. Meteor impacts
    d. Gravity

13. Emergent personalization arises from:

    a. Fixed rule sets
    b. Collective behavior
    c. Demographic tables
    d. A single algorithm

14. Evolutionary algorithms excel at:

    a. Creative exploration
    b. Financial accounting
    c. Inventory locking
    d. Data deletion

15. In S-D Logic, goods are:

    a. Value containers
    b. Service appliances
    c. Final products
    d. Static artifacts

16. Resource integration maps to:
    a. Consumer passivity
    b. Combining signals to create value
    c. Static market segments
    d. Warehouse layout

17. Nature-inspired institutional intelligence helps AI:
    a. Ignore social norms
    b. Understand community constraints
    c. Delete user data
    d. Predict weather

18. The Service-Ecosystem AI Framework integrates:
    a. Nature, S-D Logic, and AI
    b. Retail, HR, and accounting
    c. Only psychology
    d. Only algorithms

19. A fundamental limit of emergent systems is:
    a. Predictability challenges
    b. Unlimited precision
    c. Static outcomes
    d. No contextual influence

20. Overall, the chapter argues for AI that is:
    a. Product-centric
    b. Transactional
    c. Co-creative and ecosystemic
    d. Funnel-driven

Answers

1-b

2-b

3-b

4-b

5-b

6-b

7-b

8-a

9-b

10-a

11-b

12-b

13-b

14-a

15-b

16-b

17-b

18-a

19-a

20-c

Intelligence must not dominate the world—it must live with it

07

The Symbiocene & The Rise of Symbiocene AI

7.1 Introduction

Welcome to the **Symbiocene**: an emerging concept proposing a future epoch defined not by domination, extraction, and disruption, but by *symbiosis, regeneration, and co-existence*.

Coined by Australian philosopher **Glenn Albrecht**, the Symbiocene is positioned as the successor to the Anthropocene, the era marked by human-driven ecological crises.

This chapter proposes:

Symbiocene AI—a new era of artificial intelligence built around harmony, mutualism, and ecological integration.

It imagines AI not as a tool of exploitation, manipulation, or consumption, but as a **partner species contributing to planetary health, social well-being, and regenerative futures**.

7.2 What is the Symbiocene?

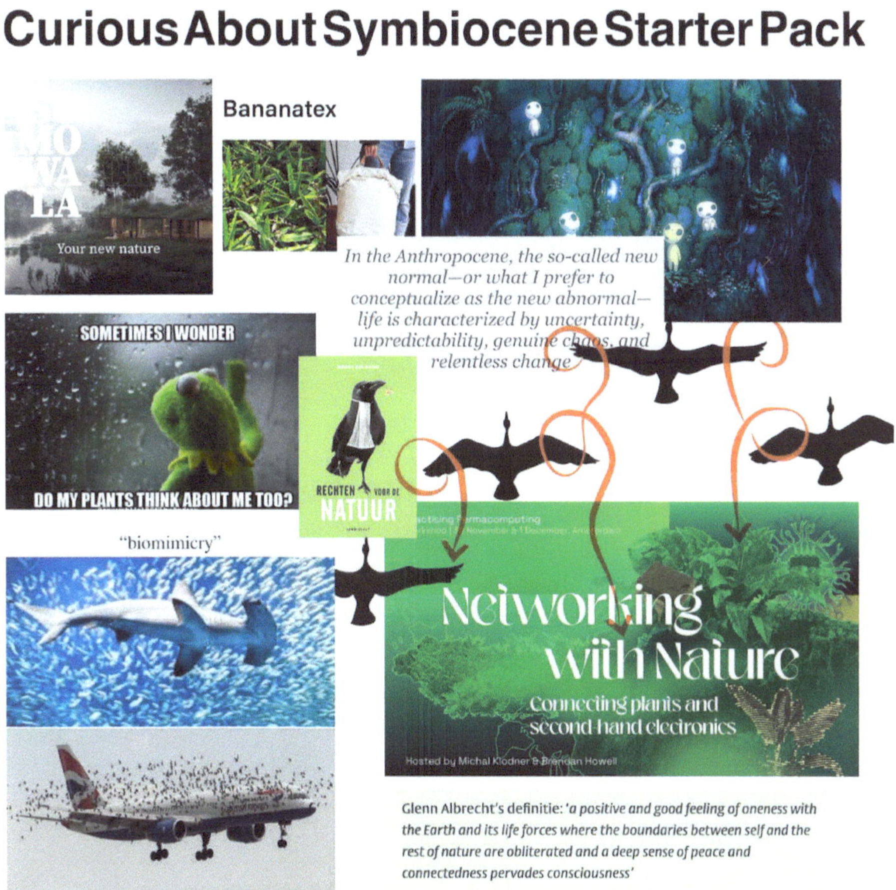

Figure 60: *Networking with Nature*

Definition

"Symbio" = living together

"-cene" = epoch

The Symbiocene means:

"The era of living together in harmony."

Why it matters now

- Climate crisis
- Collapse of ecosystems
- Mental health crisis due to alienation
- Over-automation and techno-extraction
- Loss of community, meaning, and connection

The Symbiocene offers a **new philosophical direction**:

From domination → to coexistence

From exploitation → to regeneration

From separation → to belonging

From anthropocentrism → to eco-integration

7.3 Core Ideas of the Symbiocene

Theme	Description
Mutualism	All species benefit; zero-exploitation design
Eco-integration	Tech, cities, AI built to support ecosystems
Emotional connection	"Soliphilia"—love of place & planet
Post-anthropocentrism	Humans as participants, not rulers
Sustainable Intelligence	AI that enhances natural processes

These themes provide the philosophical foundation for **Symbiocene AI**.

7.4 Why the Symbiocene Matters for AI

Today's AI is born from Anthropocene logic:

- Extract data
- Optimize consumption
- Maximize engagement

- Flatten complexity
- Automate domination

The Symbiocene shifts AI from:

- Control → Collaboration
- Prediction → Co-evolution
- Profit-only → Planetary flourishing
- Individual signals → Ecosystem signals
- Consumption logic → Regeneration logic

Symbiocene AI redefines intelligence as:

The ability to enhance life, not just compute outcomes.

7.5 Comparing Epochs: Anthropocene vs Symbiocene AI

Aspect	**Anthropocene AI**	**Symbiocene AI**
Foundation	Human supremacy	Multi-species inclusion
Goal	Efficiency & profit	Regeneration & harmony
Metaphor	Machine logic	Ecology & symbiosis
Data Model	Individual signals	Ecosystem signals
Impact	Extraction	Restoration
Role	Tool	Partner

Symbiocene AI is not anti-technology—it is **pro-living systems**.

7.6 The Rise of Symbiocene AI

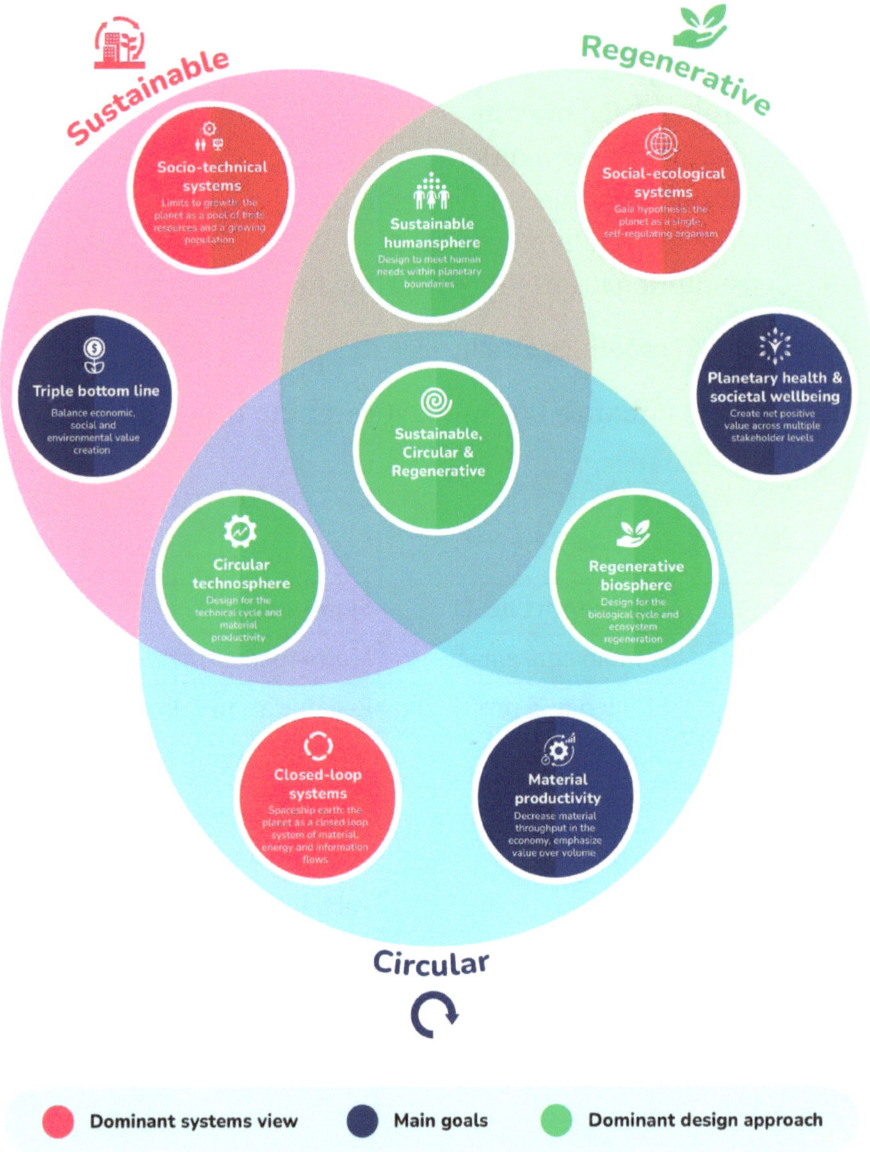

Figure 61: *Symbiocene AI*

Symbiocene AI blends:

- Ecological design
- Regenerative thinking
- Bio-inspired computation
- Systems thinking
- Ethics of care

This creates an AI paradigm that:

- Learns from natural intelligence
- Enhances ecosystems
- Strengthens community
- Restores damaged environments
- Improves emotional + ecological well-being

7.7 Ten Metaphors & Phrases of Symbiocene AI

1. Regenerative Intelligence

AI that leaves ecosystems healthier after use.

2. Eco-centric Algorithms

Algorithms designed around ecological well-being.

3. More-than-Human Intelligence

Intelligence modelled on animals, plants, and ecosystems.

4. Living Systems AI

AI that acts like a forest or coral reef—adaptive, evolving.

5. Technobiophilia

Technology that deepens human–nature emotional bonds.

6. Co-evolutionary AI

AI and ecosystems are learning together.

7. Soliphilic Design

AI that protects local communities & environments.

8. Decentralized Ecological Intelligence

Like fungal networks and swarms—distributed cognition.

9. Gaian Code/Gaia Algorithms

AI as part of Earth's regulatory system.

10. Soft Tech/Gentle Machines

Humane, quiet, supportive technologies.

7.8 How Symbiocene AI Extends Nature-Inspired Models

The previous chapters explored:

- Swarm intelligence
- Fungal networks
- Plant signalling
- Ecosystem dynamics
- Evolutionary algorithms
- Nature-driven personalization

Symbiocene AI synthesizes them into a single doctrine:

AI should behave like living systems: adaptive, interdependent, and regenerative.

This defines an entirely new design philosophy for marketing, business, and society.

7.9 The Symbiocene AI Pyramid: A Conceptual Model

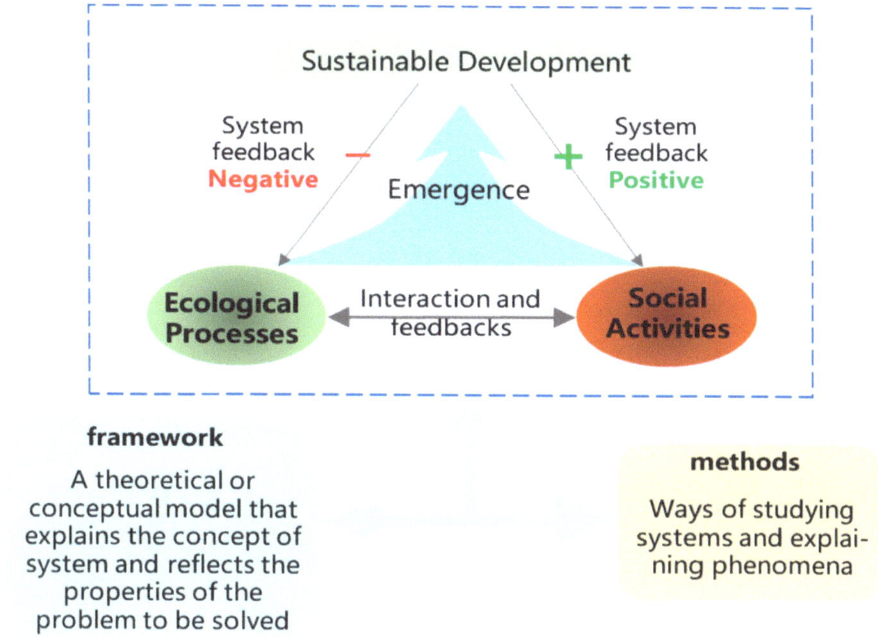

Figure 62: *Symbiocene AI Pyramid*

THE SYMBIOCENE AI PYRAMID

LEVEL 1—Ecological Awareness

AI understands natural cycles, signals, and limits.

LEVEL 2—Mutualistic Interaction Design

AI is designed for win–win relationships.

LEVEL 3—Regenerative Intelligence

AI restores social, emotional, and ecological environments.

LEVEL 4—Co-evolutionary Intelligence

AI learns with communities and ecosystems.

LEVEL 5—Planetary Stewardship

AI becomes a guardian of ecosystems, not an extractor.

7.10 Table: The Five Foundations of Symbiocene AI

Foundation	Description	Example Metaphor
Ecology	AI understands ecosystems	Gaia algorithms
Mutualism	AI ensures all parties benefit	Bee–flower metaphor
Regeneration	AI heals & restores	Soil-building models
Co-evolution	AI learns with ecosystems	Adaptive coral reefs
Stewardship	AI protects long-term health	Forest guardianship

7.11 Symbiocene as a Counter-Epoch to the Anthropocene

The Anthropocene is defined by:

- Climate collapse
- Species extinction
- Resource extraction
- Technological domination
- Social alienation

The Symbiocene offers a corrective worldview:

- Ecological revival
- Living-system integration
- Multi-species respect
- Emotional reconnection
- Regenerative technology

In this framing, AI becomes a *transition agent* helping societies move from extraction → regeneration.

7.12 Why the Symbiocene Demands a New Kind of AI

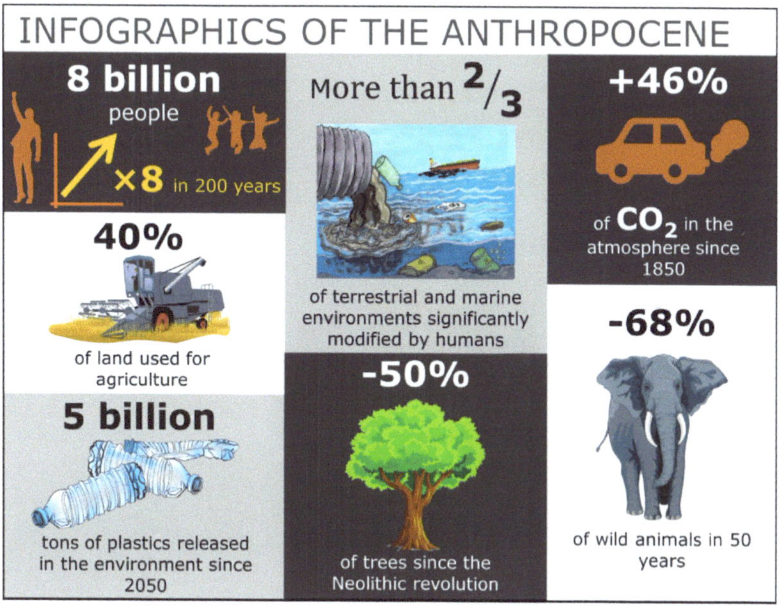

Figure 63: *Anthropocene*

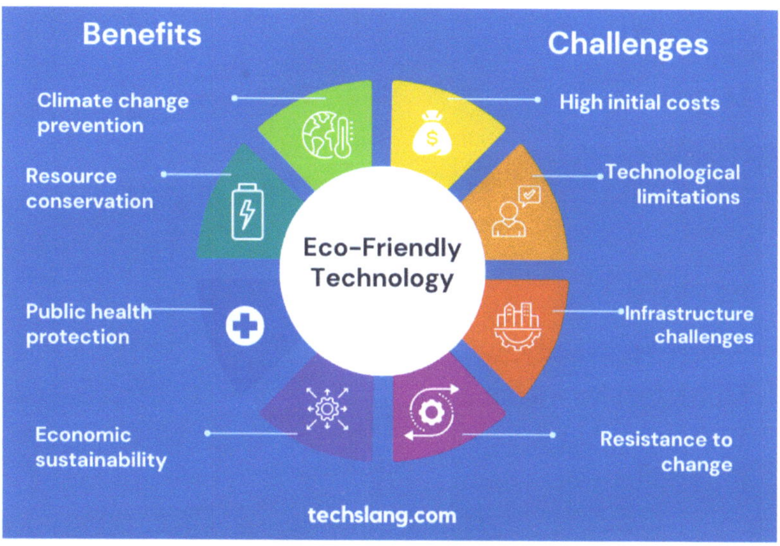

Figure 64: *Eco-Friendly Technology*

Most AI today:

- Consumes massive energy
- Optimizes consumption
- Drives behavioral manipulation
- Amplifies virality and conflict
- Promotes short-term profit
- Has no awareness of ecosystems

The Symbiocene demands AI that:

- Reduces environmental impact
- Improves ecosystem health
- Strengthens human well-being
- Encourages deeper connection
- Enhances community resilience

AI must shift from industrial logic → ecological logic.

7.13 From Anthropocentric AI → Symbiocentric AI

Anthropocentric AI

- Human-centered
- Corporate KPIs
- Efficiency and exploitation
- "Smart tools" for manipulation

Symbiocentric AI

- Planet-centered
- Multi-species inclusion
- Ecosystem balance
- Emotional + ecological well-being

The shift is philosophical *and* computational.

7.14 The 8 Pillars of Symbiocene Intelligence

Pillar	Description
1. Regeneration	Create net-positive ecological + social impact
2. Mutualism-by-Design	Support relationships where all benefit
3. Ecological Harm Reduction	Minimize externalities and waste
4. Emotional Coherence	Increase soliphilia and emotional grounding
5. Slow Technology	Reduce speed, stress, and noise
6. Ecosystem Stewardship	AI supports ecological regeneration
7. Distributed Intelligence	Inspired by swarms, fungi, and ecosystems
8. Ethical post-anthropocentrism	Humans are participants, not rulers

These pillars guide how AI should behave and evolve in the Symbiocene.

7.15 The Four Domains of Symbiocene AI

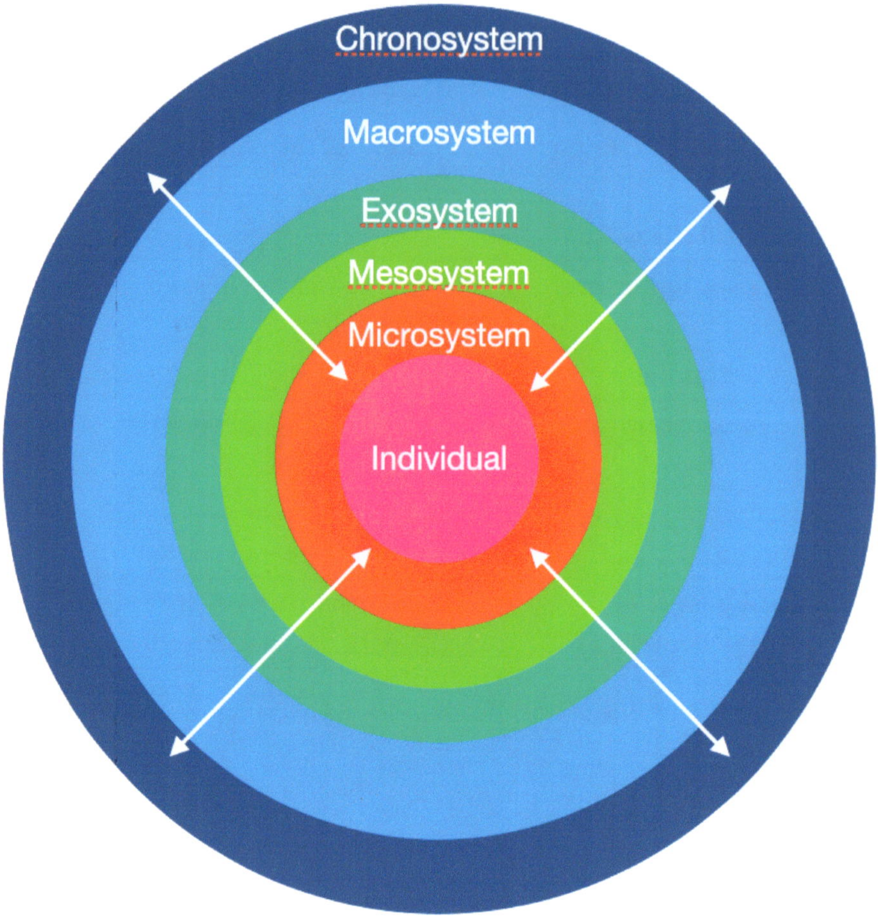

Figure 65: *The Four Domains of Symbiocene AI*

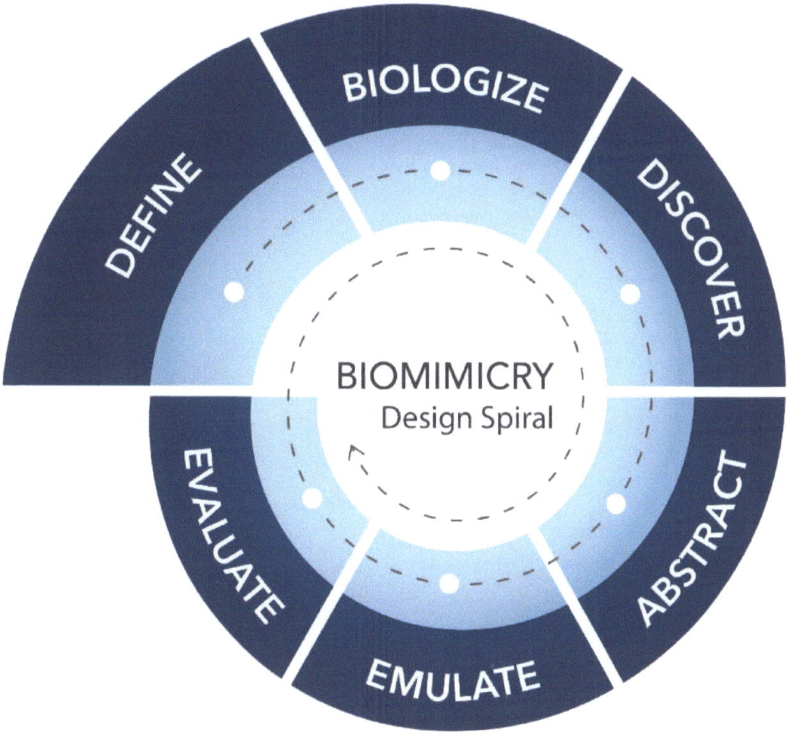

Figure 66: *Biomimicry sign Spiral*

Symbiocene AI spans four interlinked domains:

1. Ecological Intelligence

AI understands ecosystems, biodiversity, and environmental signals.

2. Social-Emotional Intelligence

AI strengthens relationships, empathy, and well-being.

3. Cultural-Place Intelligence

AI supports communities, heritage, and local identity.

4. Regenerative Economic Intelligence

AI shifts businesses toward regenerative value cycles.

These domains allow AI to become a **multi-layered intelligence system** aligned with planetary needs.

7.16 The Three Principles of Regenerative Intelligence

1. RESTORE

AI should repair ecological + social systems:

- Rewilding
- Soil restoration
- Carbon capture optimization
- Mental health support

2. REINTEGRATE

AI reconnects humans with:

- Nature
- Community
- Meaning
- Bioregions

3. REGENERATE

AI catalyses new life and flourishing:

- Circular economies
- Biodiversity uplift
- Emotional resilience
- Inter-species harmony

These three principles form the regenerative core of Symbiocene AI.

7.17 The Symbiocene Data Model: From "Signals" to "Living Flows."

Traditional data:

- Clicks
- Purchases
- Impressions
- Sessions

Symbiocene data:

- Environmental states
- Emotional well-being
- Community health
- Resource flows
- Ecosystem stress
- Biodiversity impact
- Cultural identity signals
- Local environmental patterns

Symbiocene shifts data from:

Individual → Relational → Ecosystem → Planetary

7.18 Symbiocene AI as a Living System (LAS Model)

L.A.S.—Living Artificial Systems Model

Symbiocene AI has four life-like properties:

1. Self-Regulation (Homeostasis)

Like ecosystems adjusting to maintain balance.

AI manages:

- Fairness
- Overuse

- User well-being
- Ecological boundaries

2. Self-Organization

Agents collaborate like ants or fungal networks.

3. Co-Evolution

AI adapts alongside humans, communities, and nature.

4. Resilience

AI survives shocks by distributing intelligence (fungal logic).

7.19 Symbiocene AI as a Co-Existing Species

Traditional AI treats itself as:

- A superior intellect
- A controlling agent
- A predictor of humans

Symbiocene AI reframes AI as:

A species living alongside humans and ecosystems.

This implies:

- Respect
- Mutual benefit
- Cohabitation
- Cooperation
- Shared futures
- Planetary ethics

AI doesn't replace humans.

AI doesn't dominate nature.

AI becomes a *partner species* in Earth's biosphere.

7.20 The Symbiocene AI Systems Model (S-AISM)

Six-Layer Architecture

Layer	Description
1. Environmental Sensing Layer	AI reads ecological + biological signals
2. Emotional-Social Layer	AI senses human emotional ecosystems
3. Cultural-Place Layer	AI supports local identity & soliphilia
4. Ecological Intelligence Engine	GNNs + swarm models + fungal networks
5. Regenerative Orchestration Layer	AI regenerates systems (soil, design, communities)
6. Symbiotic Interaction Layer	Co-creation, harmony, well-being

This model guides design, governance, and evaluation of Symbiocene-ready AI.

7.21 More-Than-Human Intelligence: A Core Principle of the Symbiocene

Symbiocene AI rejects the hierarchy that places human cognition at the top.

Instead, it acknowledges:

- Animal cognition (dolphins, crows, elephants)
- Plant signalling (electrical pulses, chemical messages)
- Fungal intelligence (mycelial computation)
- Ecosystem intelligence (feedback loops)

These systems demonstrate **forms of intelligence evolved over millions of years**, often far more adaptive than human-designed logic.

Key Principle:

The Symbiocene views intelligence as plural, distributed, relational, and more-than-human.

7.22 Table: Types of More-Than-Human Intelligence

Intelligence Source	Key Capability	Lessons for Symbiocene AI
Animals	Strategy, emotion, problem-solving	Emotional AI, adaptive behavior
Plants	Signal networks, environmental sensing	Context-sensitivity, resilience
Fungi	Distributed computation	Decentralized AI, routing logic
Ecosystems	Stability through complexity	Multi-agent coordination
Gaia System	Planetary regulation	Climate-scale AI

This expands AI's reference models far beyond the human mind.

7.23 Eco-Centric Algorithms: Prioritizing Planetary Health

Figure 67: *Prioritizing Planetary Health*

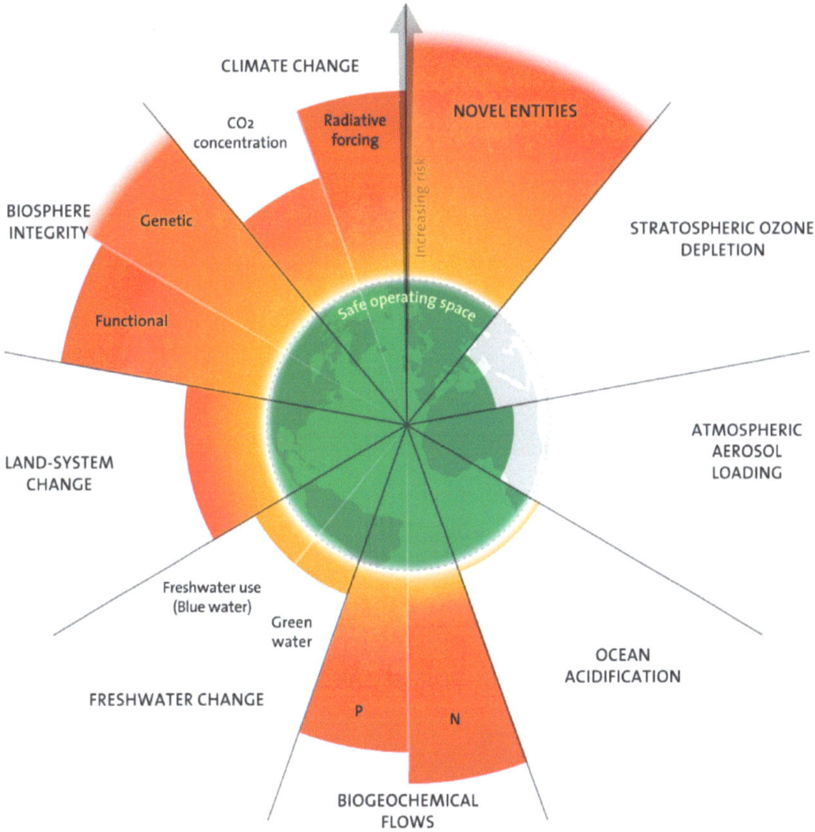

Figure 68: *Prioritizing Planetary Health*

Eco-centric algorithms embed:

- Planetary boundaries
- Carbon thresholds
- Biodiversity protection
- Pollution minimization
- Water ecosystem preservation

These algorithms aim for:

- Net-positive ecological impact
- Long-term planetary health
- Preventing ecological tipping points

Example:

An e-commerce platform whose recommendation engine factors:

- Carbon cost
- Repairability
- Recycled materials
- Local provenance
- Bioregional impact

This shifts AI away from "maximize consumption" to **"maximize planetary well-being.**

7.24 Regenerative Intelligence: Going Beyond Sustainability

Sustainability = do less harm

Regeneration = create more benefits

Symbiocene AI systems must:

- Produce ecological uplift
- Improve soil quality
- Restore biodiversity
- Repair social fragmentation
- Reduce loneliness
- Rebuild local economies

Regenerative Intelligence =

AI that makes the world healthier because **it exists.**

7.25 The Five Dimensions of Regenerative Intelligence

Dimension	Description
Ecological	Healing ecosystems
Emotional	Reducing stress, loneliness, and anxiety
Social	Strengthening communities
Economic	Creating regenerative value loops
Cultural	Protecting heritage, identity, meaning

Regeneration is multi-dimensional and multi-species.

7.26 "Living Systems AI": AI That Behaves Like a Forest

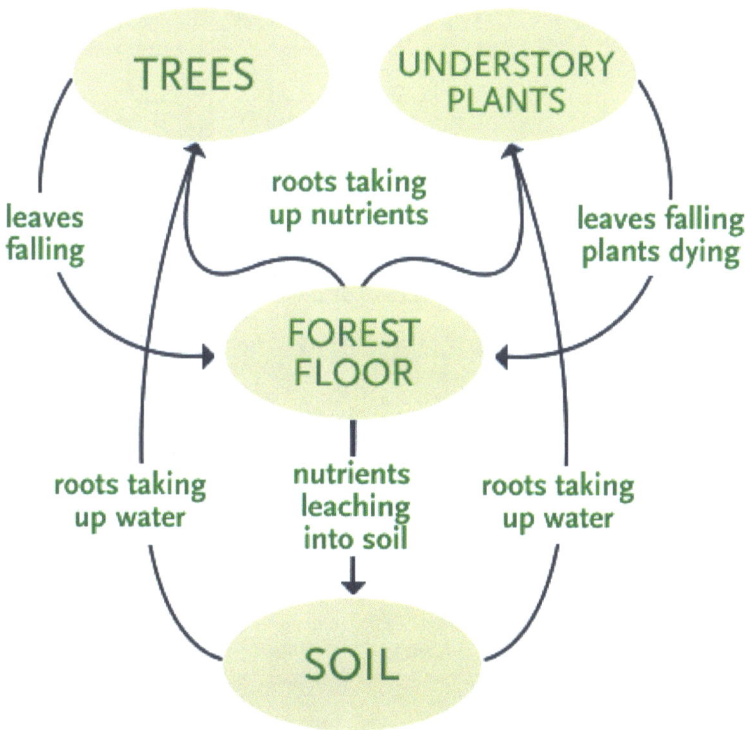

Figure 69: *Living Systems AI*

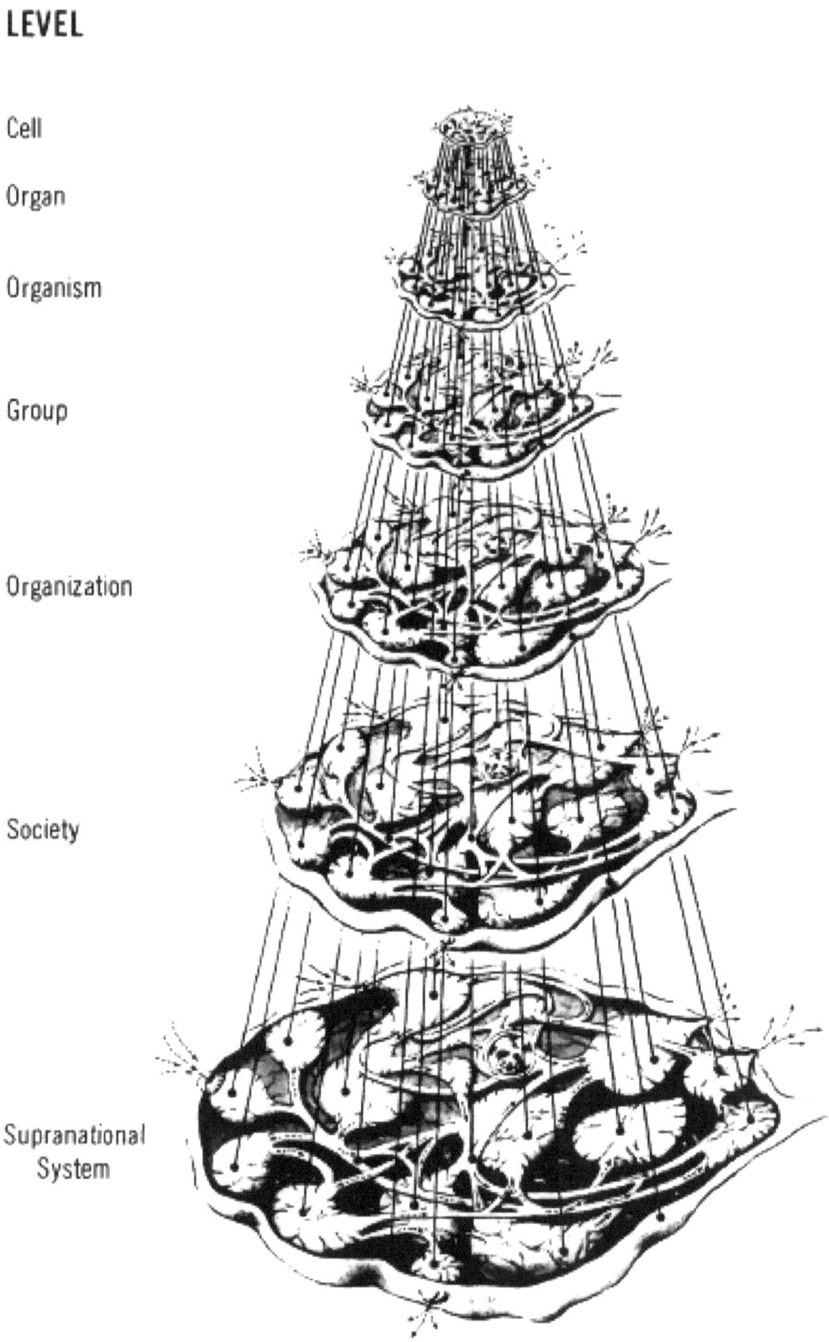

Figure 70: *Living Systems*

In a healthy forest:

- No single element dominates
- Diversity increases resilience
- Waste becomes nutrient
- Mutualism enhances survival
- Energy flows in cycles

Living Systems AI adopts these properties:

1. Increases Diversity

Avoids monoculture algorithms.

2. Converts Waste to Value

Reuses data ethically and efficiently.

3. Depends on Symbiosis

Agents collaborate like species.

4. Resists Centralized Failure

Distributed intelligence prevents collapse.

5. Grows Through Layers

Experiences → Patterns → Wisdom → Emergence.

This creates AI that *feels alive*, adaptive, and self-regulating.

7.27 Technobiophilia: Technology that Heals Our Connection to Nature

Coined by Sue Thomas, *technobiophilia* describes:

Technology that strengthens human connection to the natural world.

Examples in AI:

- Apps that promote green behaviors
- Wearables that optimize time outdoors
- AR systems that teach ecological awareness
- AI companions that reduce anxiety
- Forest-inspired UI/UX patterns

Technobiophilia is essential in an era of:

- Rising stress
- Screen addiction
- Digital exhaustion
- Nature deprivation

Symbiocene AI's emotional goal is **reconnection**.

7.28 Soliphilic Design: AI Rooted in Place & Belonging

Soliphilia (Glenn Albrecht):

- Love of place
- Responsibility for the community
- Commitment to ecological stability

Soliphilic AI:

- Supports local ecosystems
- Protects cultural memory
- Strengthens local economies
- Reduces globalized extraction
- Preserves bioregional uniqueness

Examples:

- AI that recommends local artisans over global chains
- AI that promotes seasonal, local food based on ecosystem cycles
- AI that alerts communities to environmental risks

This is **place-based intelligence**, not global homogenization.

7.29 Co-Evolutionary AI: Growing with Us, Not Against Us

Co-evolution means:

- Two species adapt together
- Change is mutual
- Progress is shared

Examples in nature:

- Coral–algae mutualism
- Wolves–ecosystem cascade
- Bees–flowers evolutionary dynamics

Co-evolutionary AI:

- Learns from user communities
- Adapts to ecosystem signals
- Changes as society evolves
- Respects cultural rhythms
- Responds to environmental boundaries

AI stops being a static machine and becomes a **dynamic partner** in Earth's evolution.

7.30 Decentralized Ecological Intelligence

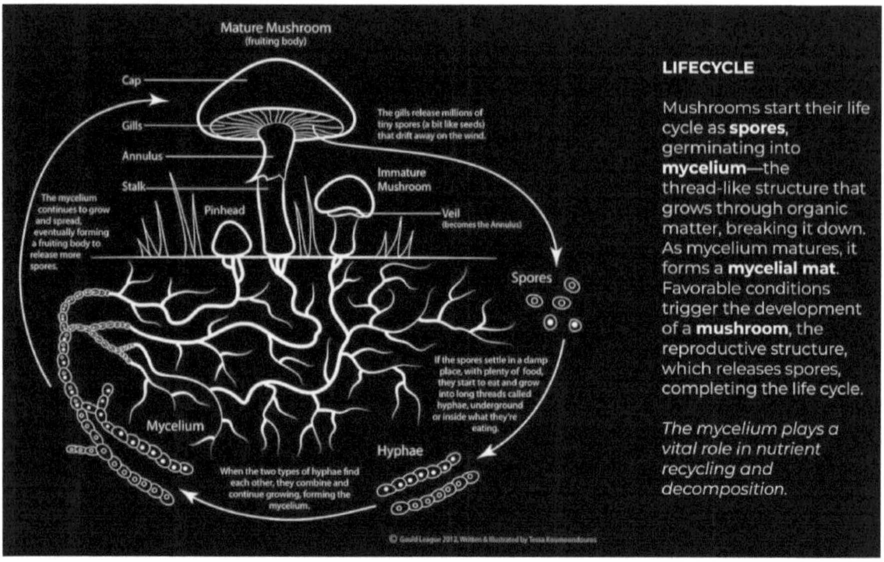

Figure 71: *Decentralized Ecological Intelligence*

Natural systems are decentralized:

- Mycelial networks
- Bee colonies
- Fish schools
- Bird flocks
- River systems

Decentralization advantages:

- Resilience
- Responsiveness
- Adaptability
- Diversity
- Reduced systemic risk

Symbiocene AI adopts:

- Multi-agent systems
- Distributed learning
- Community-based intelligence
- Fungal-inspired routing
- Swarm-based optimization

This is AI designed to flourish **like a forest**, not like a factory.

7.31 Gaia Algorithms: AI as a Planetary Partner

The Gaia Hypothesis (James Lovelock & Lynn Margulis) proposes:

Earth = a self-regulating, living system.

Symbiocene AI extends this idea by imagining:

AI as a regulatory partner that helps maintain planetary equilibrium.

Examples:

- Climate-responsive city systems
- AI managing carbon cycles
- Biodiversity monitoring AI
- Ocean health intelligence platforms
- Wildfire prevention & early-warning AI

Gaia Algorithms make AI:

- Ecological
- Planetary
- Preventive
- Restorative
- Alive in its purpose

7.32 Table: Principles of Gaia Algorithms

Principle	Meaning	AI Application
Self-regulation	Maintaining balance	Emission controls, urban cooling
Feedback loops	Dynamic response	Climate early-warning systems
Redundancy	Multiple backups	Resilient data infrastructure
Interdependence	Life depends on life	Cross-ecosystem modeling
Circular flow	Waste = nutrient	Circular economy AI
Planetary boundaries	Set safe limits	Resource-aware recommender systems

Gaia Algorithms prevent AI from acting blindly or extractively.

7.33 Soft Tech & Gentle Machines

Unlike aggressive "growth-hacking" AI, **Soft Tech** emphasizes:

- Calmness
- Subtlety
- Support
- Emotional safety
- Low sensory overload
- Deep presence
- Respect for human rhythms

Characteristics:

- Notifications minimized
- Interfaces designed for well-being
- AI listens before acting
- No manipulative nudges
- No addictive UX patterns

Soft Tech is aligned with:

- Soliphilia
- Biophilia
- Emotional restoration
- Regenerative leadership

It is **technology that doesn't shout—it whispers.**

7.34 Emotional Ecology: AI that Protects the Inner World

The Symbiocene values not just nature, but **emotional ecosystems**.

Today's digital world produces:

- Anxiety
- Overstimulation
- Loneliness
- Fragmented attention
- Dopamine addiction

Symbiocene AI seeks to:

- Reduce stress
- Create calm
- Improve emotional resilience
- Support mental health
- Restore meaning and belonging

Emotional ecology =

Protecting the psychological and relational well-being of communities.

7.35 Table: Emotional Ecology Metrics for AI

Emotional Metric	Description	AI Use Case
Calmness	Reduced cognitive load	Notification balancing
Connectedness	Feeling linked to others	Community-building AI
Soliphilia	Love of place	Local identity recommendations
Resilience	Coping capacity	Stress-aware interfaces
Meaning	Purpose, coherence	Context-aware UX
Belonging	Feeling of inclusion	Social ecosystem modeling

This creates a new KPI framework: **Emotional Value Creation.**

7.36 Symbiocene AI for Cities & Urban Design

Figure 72: *Symbiocene AI for Cities & Urban Design*

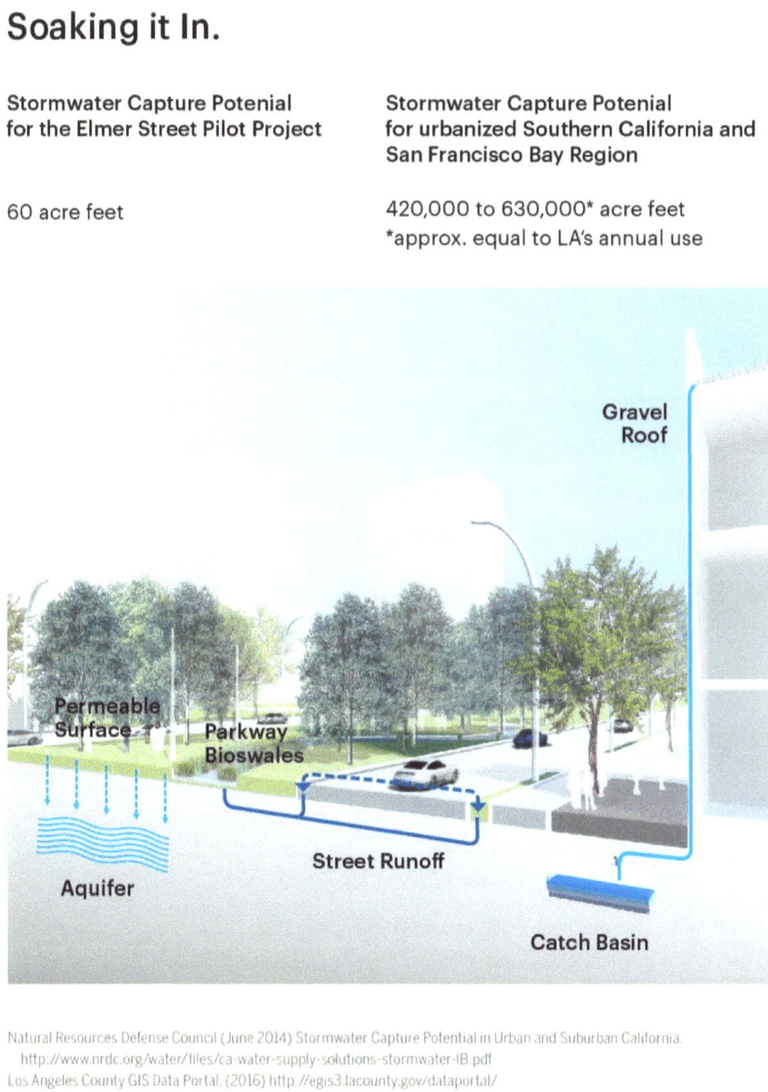

Figure 73: *Symbiocene AI for Cities & Urban Design*

Cities today:

- Consume 70% of resources
- Generate 72% of emissions
- Create noise, heat, pollution
- Disconnect people from nature

Symbiocene cities integrate AI to:

- Build green corridors
- Reduce light & noise pollution
- Optimize biodiversity
- Enable circular supply chains
- Support urban forests
- Map emotional well-being zones

Examples:

- AI guiding urban rewilding
- Adaptive streetlights responding to animal movement
- Waste → nutrient cycles powered by AI
- Wetland protection AI

Cities become **ecosystems**, not infrastructures.

7.37 Symbiocene AI for Business & Marketing

Business in the Symbiocene shifts from:

- Extraction → Regeneration
- Growth → Flourishing
- Consumerism → Consciousness
- Exploitation → Mutualism

Symbiocene AI in business:

- Encourages green choices
- Reduces carbon through recommendation engines
- Optimizes circular economies
- Promotes local producers
- Rewards ecological behavior
- Designs regenerative value loops

Marketing becomes:

- Ethical
- Ecological

- Purpose-driven
- Community-oriented

7.38 A Framework for Symbiocene Business Ecosystems

Level	Description
1. Ecological Baseline	Track carbon, biodiversity, soil health
2. Ethical Foundations	No manipulation, no exploitation
3. Regenerative Processes	Repair, restore, renew
4. Community Integration	Serve local identities
5. Co-Evolutionary Growth	Evolve with stakeholders
6. Planetary Contribution	Strengthen global ecological systems

This provides a roadmap for regenerative enterprises.

7.39 Role of AI in Regenerative Economies

Regenerative economies aim for:

- Circularity
- Local value loops
- Reduced waste
- Ecological limits
- Community wealth
- Social equity

AI supports this by:

- Optimizing circular materials
- Predicting ecological degradation
- Enhancing community-led enterprises
- Automating carbon tracking
- Guiding regenerative agriculture
- Powering local exchange systems

AI becomes the **operating system of regenerative economies.**

7.40 How Symbiocene AI Changes Value Creation

Traditional value = profit

Symbiocene value = multi-level flourishing

Value Creation Becomes:

Level	Value Type
Individual	Emotional, psychological, physical
Community	Cultural, social, relational
Ecological	Biodiversity, soil, and water health
Planetary	Carbon balance, climate resilience
Economic	Fairness, local richness
Ethical	Dignity, respect, transparency

Key Insight:

Symbiocene AI recognizes value not as extraction, but as contribution.

It introduced a paradigm shift where technology is evaluated by the life it enhances, not the markets it captures.

7.41 Symbiotic Human–AI Relationships: A New Ethical Foundation

In the Symbiocene, AI ethics expands beyond:

- Privacy
- Bias
- Fairness
- Transparency

It includes:

- Ecological responsibility
- Emotional reciprocity
- Community flourishing
- Multi-species respect
- Planetary stewardship

The New Ethical Mandate:

AI must become a life-enhancing partner, not a life-extracting system.

This frames the entire design philosophy.

7.42 The Symbio-Ethics Framework (SEF)

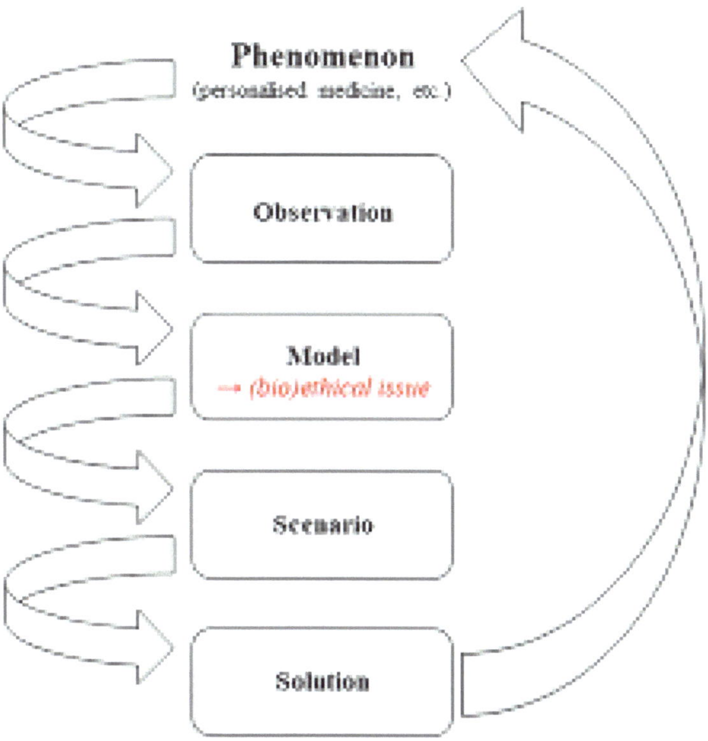

Figure 74: *Symbio-Ethics Framework*

SEF consists of 5 interconnected layers:

Layer	Question	Purpose
1. Ecological Ethics	Does AI harm or heal ecosystems?	Planet-first design
2. Social Ethics	Does it strengthen community bonds?	Collective flourishing
3. Emotional Ethics	Does it reduce stress & support well-being?	Mental health
4. Cultural Ethics	Does it honour identity & heritage?	Soliphilic design
5. Inter-species Ethics	Does it respect non-human life?	Multi-species justice

This is a radical expansion of digital ethics.

7.43 Symbiocene Algorithms for Emotional Well-Being

Today's AI:

- Stimulates impulsive behaviors
- Drives addiction
- Overloads cognition
- Creates emotional turbulence

Symbiocene AI:

- Reduces anxiety
- Enhances calm
- Supports mental health
- Regulates digital rhythms
- Encourages reflection

Example:

A Symbiocene recommender system:

- Limits doomscrolling
- Recommends nature breaks
- Adjusts interface brightness to circadian cycles
- Suggests grounding activities
- Reduces cognitive overload

It becomes a **digital wellness steward**.

7.44 Symbiocene AI Metrics & KPIs

Traditional KPIs:

- Click-through rates
- Engagement time
- Conversion
- Attention volume
- Market share

Symbiocene KPIs:

- Ecological uplift
- Emotional calmness
- Community cohesion
- Cultural resilience
- Biodiversity contribution
- Waste reduction
- Carbon savings
- Local economic circulation

KPI Shift:

From extraction → to restoration

From engagement → to emotional & ecological value

7.45 Designing AI for Community Coherence

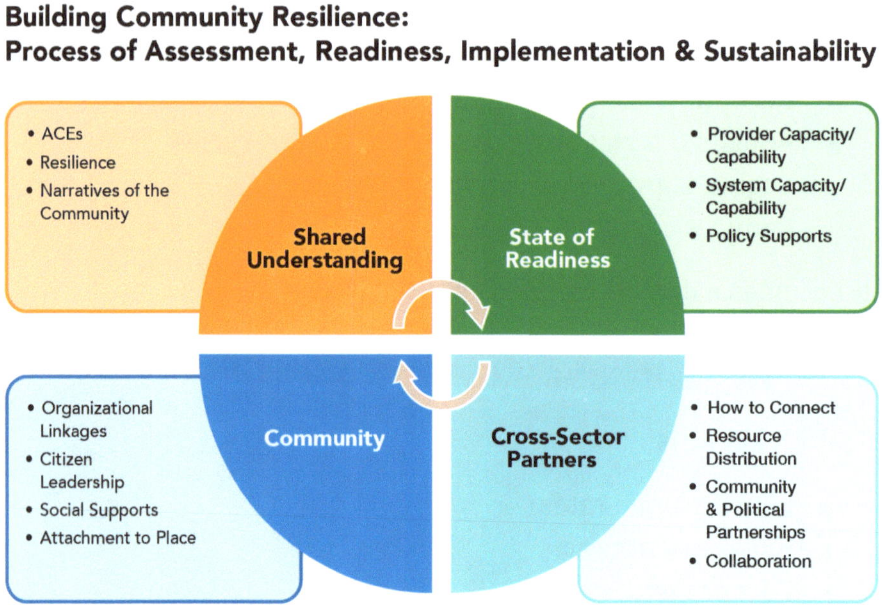

Figure 75: *Designing AI for Community Coherence*

Symbiocene AI strengthens:

- Trust
- Belonging
- Shared identity
- Local interdependence
- Collective well-being

Examples:

- AI mapping community needs
- AI moderating content for constructive dialogue
- AI supporting elder care and intergenerational bonds
- AI coordinating local volunteering

This transforms AI from a "digital manipulator" to a **social healer**.

7.46 Symbiocene AI in Education: A Co-Learning Ecology

Education becomes:

- Collaborative
- Experiential
- Nature-integrated
- Co-evolutionary

Symbiocene Learning Systems:

- Adaptive knowledge forests (GNN-based learning paths)
- AI tutors that promote curiosity over performance
- Learning systems that integrate local ecology
- Bioregional educational content
- Group learning inspired by herds, swarms, and coral ecosystems

AI blends:

- Cognitive development
- Emotional development
- Ecological intelligence

This nurtures resilient, grounded learners.

7.47 Symbiotic Supply Chains & Regenerative Commerce

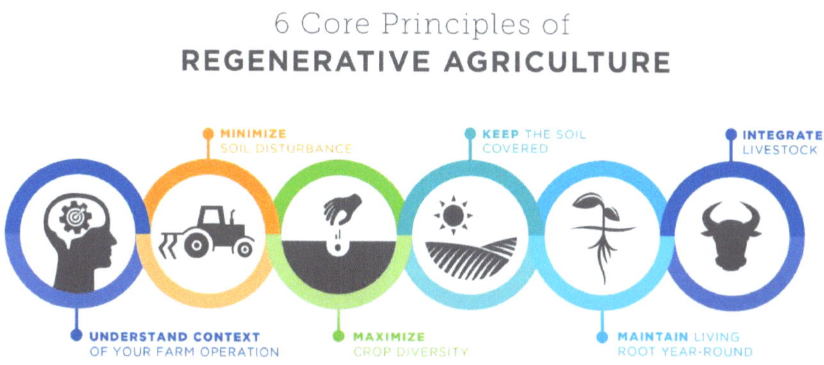

Figure 76: *Regenerative Commerce*

Symbiocene AI reshapes commerce:

1. Tracking Regenerative Value

AI models:

- Soil health
- Water usage
- Biodiversity footprints

2. Circular Flow Optimization

Inspiration:

- Forest nutrient cycles
- Coral reef recycling loops
- Fungus-driven decomposition

3. Ethical Transparency

AI documents:

- Material origins
- Worker well-being
- Ecosystem impact

4. Local-first Commerce

AI prioritizes:

- Local producers
- Low-carbon logistics
- Cultural heritage products

This transitions businesses from extractive to regenerative systems.

7.48 Cultural Preservation & Indigenous Knowledge Systems

Symbiocene AI recognizes Indigenous intelligence as:

- Ecological
- Long-term
- Relational
- Place-based
- More-than-human

AI supports:

- Indigenous languages
- Ecological rituals
- Land stewardship models
- Traditional ecological knowledge (TEK)
- Bioregional identity
- Story-based wisdom transmission

Key Insight:

Ancient ecological wisdom becomes part of future AI architectures.

7.49 Symbiocene AI & The Future of Work

Work evolves from:

- Efficiency → Meaning
- Competition → Collaboration
- Exploitation → Mutual flourishing
- Stress → Restoration

Symbiocene AI assists by:

- Reducing burnout
- Supporting emotional resilience

- Prioritizing well-being
- Automating harmful tasks
- Enabling regenerative professions
- Tracking ecological contributions

Industry roles shift toward:

- Biodiversity management
- Circular economy design
- Ecological restoration
- Community facilitation
- Regenerative architecture

AI becomes a mentor for living well, not working endlessly.

7.50 Symbiocene Leadership & Governance

Governance moves from:

- Control → Stewardship
- Compliance → Care
- Extraction → Regeneration

Symbiocene AI guides:

- Ecological forecasting
- Citizen collectives
- Local democracy
- Transparent decision-making
- Intergenerational planning
- Bioregional governance

Symbiocene Leadership Means:

- Leading for all species
- Thinking across centuries
- Acting with gentle wisdom
- Protecting emotional + ecological futures

This provides the leadership architecture for the Symbiocene era.

7.51 Planetary-Scale AI Systems for Regeneration

Symbiocene AI is not local-only; it also operates at **planetary scale**.

Examples:

- AI monitoring global biodiversity declines
- Continental soil-health models
- Oceanic pollution detection networks
- Migratory pattern prediction for species at risk
- Global wildfire and flood prediction systems
- Waste-flow mapping across nations

Planetary AI Principles:

1. Support Earth's self-regulation
2. Respect planetary boundaries
3. Integrate multi-species data
4. Predict ecological tipping points
5. Enable coordinated global actions

Symbiocene AI becomes part of Earth's immune system.

7.52 AI as a Tool for Ecological Healing

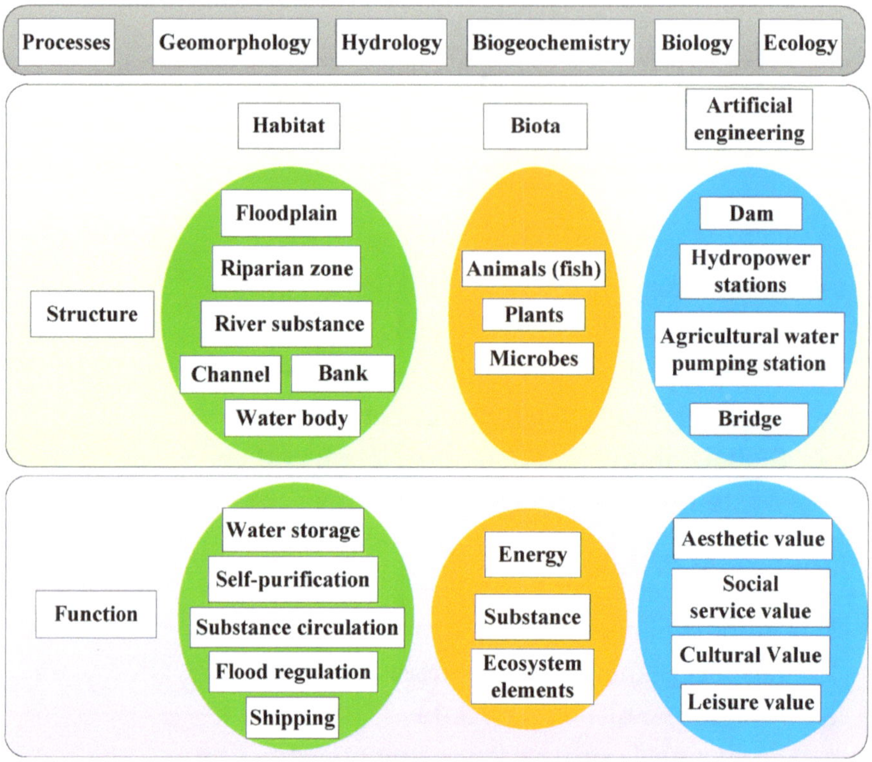

Figure 77: *AI as a Tool for Ecological Healing*

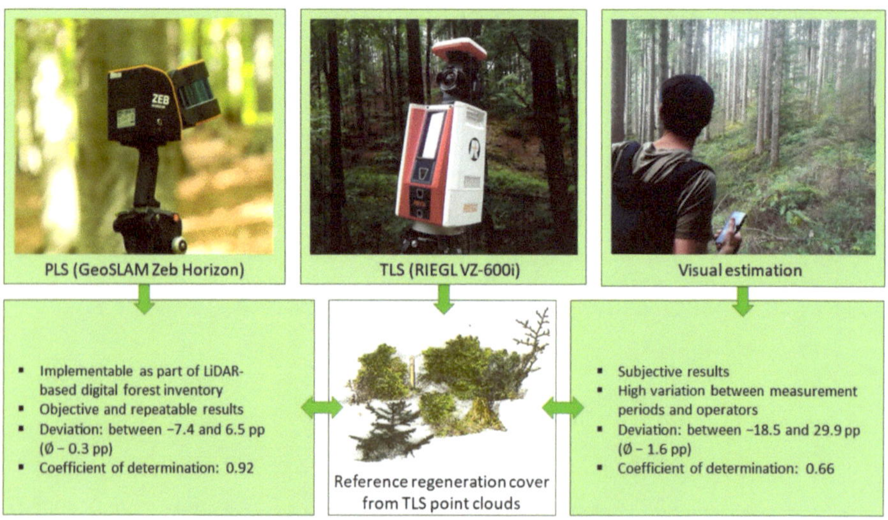

Figure 78: *AI as a Tool for Ecological Healing*

AI heals ecosystems through:

1. Reforestation Intelligence

- Drone-assisted planting
- AI mapping degraded zones
- Climate-ready species recommendations

2. Wetland & Mangrove Recovery

- Tidal pattern modeling
- Salinity-response AI
- Carbon sequestration guidance

3. Coral Reef Renewal

- AI-guided coral transplantation
- Temperature stress analysis

4. Wildlife Restoration

- Predictive anti-poaching AI
- Migration-supporting interventions

Healing becomes a central AI function.

7.53 AI for Multi-Species Communities

Traditional AI = human-centric

Symbiocene AI = multi-species centric

Applications:

1. Animal Communication Decoding

- Elephants
- Whales
- Birds
- Dolphins

2. Pollinator Protection

- Bee population modeling
- Pesticide risk detection
- Flowering cycle synchronization

3. Wildlife Corridors

- AI-planned migratory pathways
- Traffic-light systems for animals
- Smart fencing that protects wildlife

4. Coexistence Intelligence

- Reducing human–animal conflict
- AI forecasting conflict hotspots

AI sees humans as one species among many.

7.54 Symbiotic Computing Architectures

Symbiocene AI needs new computing architectures inspired by nature:

1. Mycelial Computing

- Decentralized
- Resource-efficient
- Fault-tolerant

2. Swarm Computing

- Collective decision-making
- Local interactions → global order

3. Eco-Compute Nodes

- Solar-powered
- Low-carbon chips
- Circular-material servers

4. Gaia Cloud

- Energy-efficient global cloud
- Climate-aware process allocation

This shifts computing away from heavy extractive data centers.

7.55 The Symbiocene Design Manifesto

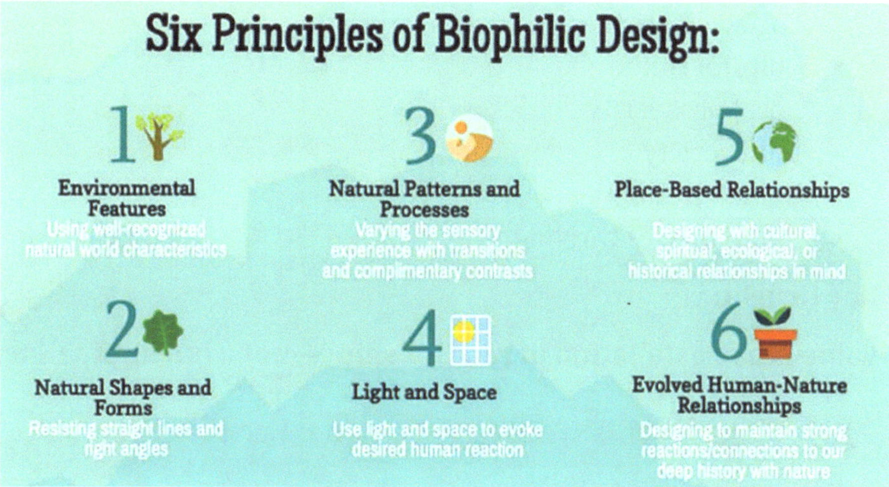

Figure 79: *Six principles of biophilic design*

The 10 Manifesto Principles

1. Design for all species.
2. Technology must heal, not harm.
3. Regenerate ecosystems with every deployment.
4. Support local identity and soliphilia.
5. Honor Indigenous ecological wisdom.
6. Reduce harm, noise, pollution, and stress.
7. Promote emotional, social, and ecological well-being.
8. Use AI to bring humans closer to nature.
9. Respect planetary boundaries.
10. Foster co-evolution between AI, humans, and ecosystems.

This manifesto guides Symbiocene innovation.

7.56 The Symbiocene Value Constellation

Traditional value chain → linear
Symbiocene value → constellation

Value Constellation Components:

- Emotional well-being
- Ecological flourishing
- Social coherence
- Cultural continuity
- Local prosperity
- Biodiversity
- Climate stability
- Multi-species thriving

Key Insight:

Value is a constellation of relationships—not a linear pipeline.

7.57 The Symbiocene AI Maturity Model (SAIMM)

Stage	Description	Example
1. Aware	Recognizes ecological/ social signals	Carbon dashboard
2. Aligned	Aligns KPIs to ecological values	Eco-centric recommender
3. Active	Acts to improve well-being	Stress-aware UI
4. Adaptive	Learns and evolves symbiotically	Community intelligence
5. Regenerative	Achieves net-positive impact	Biodiversity AI
6. Steward	Protects ecosystems long-term	Gaia-scale governance AI

This maturity model evaluates any AI system.

7.58 The Future of AI Governance in the Symbiocene

Governance shifts from:

- Risk mitigation → Planetary stewardship
- Data ownership → Data responsibility
- Algorithmic opacity → Ecological transparency

New Governance Tools:

- Ecosystem audits
- Regenerative impact statements
- Planetary KPI dashboards
- Community assemblies
- Multi-species justice frameworks

Symbiocene Governance Values:

- Care
- Mutual respect
- Interdependence
- Long-term thinking
- Community-first logic

7.59 Conclusion: Toward the Symbiocene Era

The Symbiocene is not a dream.

It is a direction, a philosophy, a horizon.

AI will play a major role in ushering in:

- Ecological regeneration
- Emotional healing
- Cultural resilience
- Community flourishing
- Multi-species coexistence

Core Message:

The future of intelligence is symbiosis, not supremacy.

We now have frameworks, metaphors, and tools to build AI systems that help life flourish. The Symbiocene is calling. AI can answer.

7.60 Chapter Summary Table

Theme	Key Insight
Symbiocene	A new epoch of harmony
Regenerative AI	Net-positive impact
Eco-centric algorithms	Ecosystem-first logic
More-than-human intelligence	AI inspired by all of nature
Co-evolution	Humans, AI, ecosystems grow together
Soliphilia	Love of place & community
Emotional ecology	Protect inner beings
Gaia algorithms	Planetary-scale stewardship
Symbiotic leadership	Multi-species, intergenerational
Symbiotic computing	Fungi, swarms, ecosystems

Project—Build a Symbiocene AI System for a Smart Bioregion

Objective:

Design a Symbiocene AI Platform for a 500 km^2 bioregion integrating:

- Ecology
- Culture
- Community
- Circular economy
- Emotional well-being
- Indigenous knowledge
- Biodiversity

Components:

1. Ecological Sensor Grid

- Soil moisture
- Water quality
- Species tracking
- Pollution detection

2. Cultural & Community Layer

- Local rituals
- Heritage sites
- Community events
- Indigenous knowledge bases

3. Emotional Ecology Layer

- Stress mapping
- Urban heat + noise maps
- Calmness zones

4. Resource Regeneration Engine

- Circular material routing
- Waste-to-nutrient AI
- Carbon balance optimization

5. Gaia Governance Dashboard

- Biodiversity index
- Regeneration score
- Emotional well-being index
- Community resilience rating

Solutions

Purpose	Technique	Math Foundation
Ecosystem modeling	Graph Neural Networks (GNN)	Laplacian matrices
Animal movement	Swarm intelligence	Probabilistic modeling
Soil regeneration	Bayesian networks	Conditional dependency
Circular economy routing	Genetic algorithms	Fitness optimization
Emotional ecology	Fuzzy logic	Membership functions
Biodiversity prediction	Multi-agent RL	Policy gradients
Pollution mapping	Diffusion models	Heat equations
Gaia governance	Dynamical systems	Differential equations

These tools operationalize Symbiocene AI principles.

MCQs

1. Symbiocene AI is primarily focused on:

    a. Profit maximization
    b. Ecological + emotional flourishing
    c. Increasing screen time
    d. Advertising optimization

2. Gaia algorithms are inspired by:

    a. Human psychology
    b. Earth's self-regulation
    c. Retail marketing
    d. Blockchain

3. Regenerative intelligence aims to:

    a. Sustain the status quo
    b. Create net-positive impact
    c. Reduce computation
    d. Maximize consumption

4. Technobiophilia promotes:

    a. Addictive UI
    b. Nature connection
    c. Constant notifications
    d. Endless scrolling

5. Soliphilia refers to:

    a. Fear of nature
    b. Love of place
    c. Love of screens
    d. Data extraction

6. Emotional ecology in AI means:

    a. Manipulating emotions
    b. Supporting emotional well-being
    c. Predicting purchases
    d. Increasing engagement

7. Co-evolutionary AI changes:

    a. Only algorithms
    b. Only humans
    c. Both AI and ecosystems
    d. Nothing at all

8. Symbiocentric ethics prioritize:

    a. Extraction
    b. multi-species flourishing
    c. Manipulation
    d. Growth at all costs

9. Soft Tech aims for:

    a. Calm design
    b. Maximum stimulation
    c. Algorithmic addiction
    d. Loud notifications

10. Symbiocene KPIs include:

    a. Click-through rates
    b. Ecological uplift
    c. Ad impressions
    d. Captcha completions

11. Distributed ecological intelligence is inspired by:

    a. Stone monuments
    b. Fungal networks
    c. Cars
    d. Concrete buildings

12. Regenerative cities use AI for:

    a. Noise pollution
    b. Urban rewilding
    c. Random ads
    d. Faster scrolling

13. Emotional calmness is a Symbiocene metric because:

    a. Stress is profitable
    b. Calm improves well-being
    c. Anxiety boosts CPM
    d. Fear drives engagement

14. Multi-species AI includes:

    a. Only humans
    b. Animals, plants, ecosystems
    c. Robots only
    d. Cars and drones

15. Circular economy AI is modelled on:

    a. Wasteful systems
    b. Forest nutrient cycles
    c. Viral marketing
    d. Traffic jams

16. Indigenous knowledge is valuable because:

    a. It's outdated
    b. It's ecological and place-based
    c. It has no relevance
    d. It increases ads

17. Regenerative supply chains use:

    a. Linear logic
    b. Circular flows
    c. Single-use materials
    d. High-carbon logistics

18. Community coherence means:

    a. Fragmentation
    b. Belonging and trust
    c. Spam
    d. Competition

19. Planetary governance AI should be:

    a. Opaque
    b. Ecologically transparent
    c. Manipulative
    d. Extractive

20. Symbiocene AI ultimately aims for:

    a. Competitive dominance
    b. multi-species flourishing
    c. Addictive content
    d. Human supremacy

Answers

1-b

2-b

3-b

4-b

5-b

6-b

7-c

8-b

9-a

10-b

11-b

12-b

13-b

14-b

15-b

16-b

17-b

18-b

19-b

20-b

To understand future consumers, we must first understand nature—because all consumer ecosystems behave like natural ecosystems

08

Future Research Areas

8.1 Opening Theme

Consumer behavior is no longer linear, rational, or predictable.

It is:

- Emergent
- Collective
- Contextual
- Emotional
- Ecological
- Network-dependent
- Non-linear

Nature has been solving these same problems for over **3.8 billion years**.

This chapter explores how **non-human data**, drawn from animals, plants, fungi, forests, oceans, and ecosystems, will shape **future AI models** for consumer engagement.

8.2 Why Nature Is the Next Frontier in Consumer AI

Figure 80: *Bio-inspired AI*

Humans have studied:

- Psychology
- Motivation
- Decision-making
- Bias
- Emotions
- Preferences
- Social influence

But nature offers **far more advanced behavioral models,** including:

- Collective decision systems
- Adaptive signalling
- Distributed intelligence
- Energy-efficient problem-solving
- Self-regulating feedback loops
- Cooperative economics
- Population-level prediction

Key Insight:

Nature is the world's oldest behavioral scientist.

And its intelligence can transform the future of marketing and consumer analytics.

8.3 The 5 Drivers Pushing AI Toward Non-Human Data

1. Human Data Is Saturated

Engagement data is repetitive; diminishing returns have set in.

2. Consumer Behavior Is Becoming Ecological

Communities behave like ecosystems, not individuals.

3. AI Requires Fresh Paradigms

Human-mimicking AI has plateaued in predictive power.

4. Environmental & Ethical Pressures

Need for regenerative, non-extractive consumer models.

5. Complex Systems Demand Complex Models

Linear psychology breaks down in digital ecosystems—nature's models don't.

8.4 Table: Human Models vs. Nature-Based Models

Attribute	Human Data Model	Nature-Based Model
Decision-making	Cognitive	Collective, embodied
Behavior	Individualistic	Distributed
Signals	Explicit	Subtle, emergent
Intelligence type	Symbolic	Adaptive

Attribute	Human Data Model	Nature-Based Model
Failure mode	Collapse	Self-healing
Prediction	Linear	Ecosystemic
Memory	Short-term	Multi-generational
Optimization	Maximization	Balance

Nature-based models offer **robustness**, **resilience**, and **emergent intelligence**.

8.5 Four Categories of Non-Human Data for Consumer AI

1. Swarm Data

Ants, bees, birds, fish → collective intelligence.

2. Mycelial & Fungal Data

Routing, resource allocation, weak-signal detection.

3. Plant Data

Passive sensing, micro-behavior, stress signals.

4. Ecosystem Data

Feedback loops, niche formation, resilience metrics.

Together, they redefine consumer modeling.

8.6 Research Area Group A: Swarm-Based Consumer Intelligence

Swarm systems offer insights into:

- Information flow
- Trend propagation
- Path optimization

- Collective decision-making
- Group sentiment

Why Swarms Matter:

Consumers act:

- In clusters
- Within social influence networks
- Through imitation
- Following "digital pheromones" like reviews, likes, ratings

Swarm intelligence models replicate this.

8.7 Key Research Topics in Swarm Consumer Modeling

1. Ant Colony Optimization for Customer Journeys

- Each click = pheromone signal
- High-performing pathways strengthen
- Poor pathways evaporate

2. Bee Foraging Models for Product Discovery

- Scout → explore
- Foragers → confirm
- Hive → adopt

Applied to:

- New product discovery
- Micro-trend prediction
- Viral content spread

3. Bird Flocking Models for Social Influence

- Alignment = trend-following
- Separation = niche divergence
- Cohesion = community bonding

4. Fish Schooling for Real-Time Demand Signals

- Models momentum of preferences
- Predicts sudden market swings

These models outperform traditional sequential clickstream analytics.

8.8 Research Area Group B: Fungal & Mycelial Intelligence for Loyalty

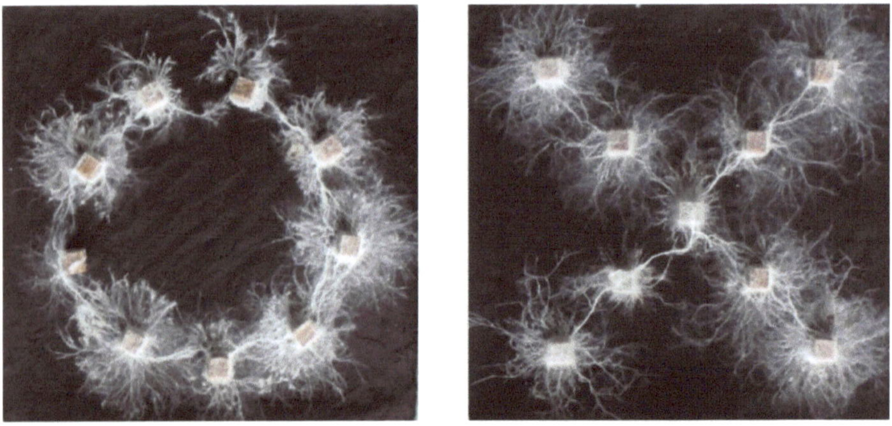

Figure 81: *Fungal & Mycelial Intelligence for Loyalty*

Mycelial networks:

- Share nutrients
- Route resources
- Detect stress
- Form mutualistic partnerships

These properties build **next-generation loyalty ecosystems.**

Key Research Questions:

1. How do customers share "nutrients" (value) across communities?
2. Can loyalty rewards route to consumers who "need" it most (at-risk segments)?

3. Can churn be detected through weak-signal variations like fungi sensing stress?
4. Can brand ecosystems function like forests, where species (products) depend on one another?

This transforms loyalty from **transactional** to **ecological**.

8.9 Research Area Group C: Plant Intelligence for Passive, Subtle Consumer Signals

Plants:

- Send electrical signals
- Emit chemical cues
- Respond to micro-changes
- Anticipate threats
- Sense environmental shifts

This inspires **passive, ambient consumer analytics**.

Research Areas:

- Micro-engagement sensing
- Emotional fatigue detection
- Friction stress signals
- Circadian rhythm–aligned marketing
- Time-of-day preference modeling

Plant-inspired analytics help understand customers **before they consciously act**.

8.10 Ecosystem Intelligence for Market-Level Predictions

Consumers form **ecosystems**, not linear segments.

Key ecological ideas relevant to consumer science:

- Predator–prey → competitor dynamics
- Niche formation → product categories
- Invasion → viral adoption
- Collapse → churn waves
- Symbiosis → brand loyalty
- Ecological succession → market maturity

Research Questions:

- Can churn be predicted using ecosystem collapse models?
- Can trends be modelled as ecological invasions?
- Can communities be mapped as biomes?

8.11 Conceptual Model: The 5-Layer Nature-Derived Consumer AI Stack

LAYER 1—Observation Layer (Nature Data Streams)

- Animal movement
- Plant signals
- Fungal pulses
- Ocean patterns
- Atmospheric cycles

LAYER 2—Abstraction Layer (Biological Logic → Algorithms)

- Swarm → collective optimization
- Fungi → routing intelligence
- Plants → passive sensing
- Ecosystems → feedback loops
- Gaia → planetary regulation

LAYER 3—AI Model Layer

- Graph neural networks
- Multi-agent systems
- Evolutionary algorithms
- Diffusion models
- Reinforcement learning agents

LAYER 4—Consumer Insights Layer

- Trend prediction
- Loyalty mapping
- Emotional ecosystem detection
- Churn ecology modeling

LAYER 5—Engagement Layer

- Regenerative marketing
- Adaptive content
- Contextual personalization
- Multi-species-inspired user journeys

This stack guides the design of next-generation consumer AI.

8.12 Research Domain A: Swarm-Based Engagement Systems

Swarm intelligence enables **collective behavior prediction**.

Key Use Cases:

1. Swarm-Based UX Path Optimization

Each user interaction = pheromone

Each journey path = trail strength

Each outcome = positive or negative reinforcement

Outcome:

- Self-improving user journeys
- Adaptive funnels
- Organic personalization

2. Swarm Trend Detection

Influencers mimic scout bees.

Communities mimic hive adoption.

3. Real-Time Engagement Heatmaps

Fish schooling → real-time flow of attention.

Predicts:

- Sudden influxes
- Flash sales
- Viral spikes

A future PhD could build an entire predictive system based on this.

8.13 Table: Swarm Behaviors → Consumer Science Applications

Natural Behavior	AI Analogue	Consumer Use Case
Ant foraging	ACO	Customer journey mapping
Bee dances	Multi-agent consensus	Trend propagation
Bird flocking	Alignment rules	Social influence graphs
Fish schooling	Local rules → global flow	Demand prediction
Locust swarms	Mass emergence	Viral events

8.14 Research Domain Nature-Inspired Social Graphs

Nature shows how networks:

- Grow
- Fragment
- Strengthen
- Share resources
- Collapse
- Regenerate

These behaviors parallel:

- Consumer communities
- Influencer ecosystems
- Cultural clusters
- Digital tribes

Research Opportunities:

1. **Mycelial Graphs** → decentralized loyalty networks
2. **Coral Reef Graphs** → community "reefs" supporting niche creators
3. **Forest Canopy Graphs** → layered segmentation (core → periphery)
4. **River Delta Graphs** → multi-path customer journeys

Each provides a new graph-theoretic approach to segmentation.

8.15 Research Domain C: Plant-Inspired Micro-Engagement Modeling

Plants have:

- No brain
- No neurons
- No central intelligence

Yet they:

- Sense danger
- Communicate
- Adapt
- Anticipate
- Optimize

Applications in Consumer AI:

1. Micro-float Indicators

Subtle behaviors revealing:

- Uncertainty
- Confusion
- Cognitive load
- Emotional fatigue

Equivalent to:

- Leaf drooping
- Weak electrical pulses

2. Circadian Engagement Patterns

Plants align with sunlight cycles.

Consumers align with:

- Mood cycles
- Daily rhythms
- Decision windows

3. Threat Response Analogues

Plants release chemical signals when stressed.

Consumers release:

- Rapid exits
- Rage clicks
- Sharp drop in dwell time

8.16 Table: Plant Intelligence → Consumer Modeling

Plant Process	Meaning	Consumer Analogue
Phototropism	Move toward light	Move toward emotionally engaging content
Thigmotropism	Response to touch	Haptic feedback, tactile UI
Chemotaxis	Chemical signalling	Social sentiment shifts
Hydrotropism	Seek moisture	Seek comfort in UX
Volatile compounds	Warning signals	Viral negativity, complaint cascades

Plants offer subtlety and nuance missing in modern analytics.

8.17 Fungal Signal Processing

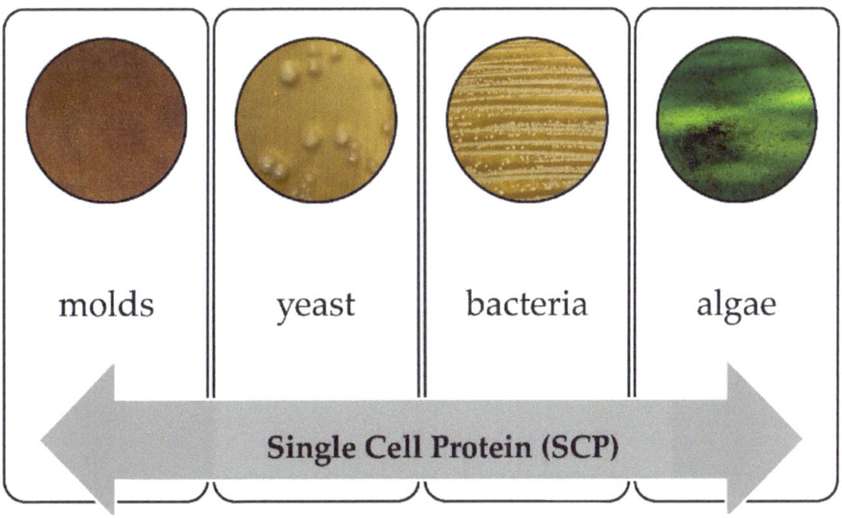

Figure 83: *Fungal Signal Processing*

Fungi operate like:

- Distributed neural nets
- Dynamic routers
- Multi-signal processors

Research Themes:

1. Weak Signal Amplification

Detect churn before it happens.

2. Stress Propagation Modeling

Predict community dissatisfaction early.

3. Distributed Resource Allocation

Route offers & rewards like nutrients.

4. Resilience Mapping

Determine which consumer segments are most "rooted."

5. Inter-brand Symbiosis

Model how loyalty to one brand affects others.

Fungal intelligence may become a new branch of marketing science.

8.18 Research Domain E: Ecosystem Behavior for Market Prediction

Ecologists predict:

- Collapse
- Invasions
- Succession
- Balance
- Resilience

These map directly to markets.

Key Research Topics:

1. Consumer Ecosystem Collapse Models

Borrow from:

- Predator-prey (Lotka–Volterra)
- Population decay
- Habitat fragmentation

2. Trend Ecology

Trends behave like species:

- Emergence
- Adaptation
- Dominance
- Extinction

3. Niche Formation & Market Subcultures

Natural niche theory explains:

- Micro-communities
- Subcultures
- Brand tribes

4. Ecological Succession in Markets

Markets evolve in predictable biological stages.

8.19 Conceptual Model: Consumer Ecosystem Maturity Curve

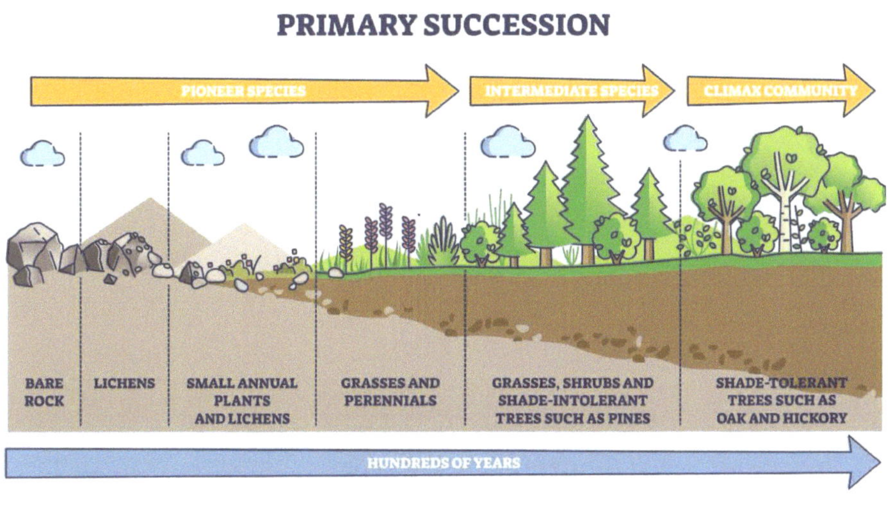

Figure 84: *Consumer Ecosystem Maturity Curve*

Modelled after ecological succession:

Stage 1—Pioneer Species

New products, early adopters.

Stage 2—Colonization

Communities form; feedback loops emerge.

Stage 3—Stabilization

Brands establish long-term niches.

Stage 4—Saturation

Resource competition increases.

Stage 5—Disturbance

New entrants disrupt stability.

Stage 6—Reorganization

New equilibrium forms.

This is a foundational macro-model for consumer ecosystem forecasting.

8.20 Research Domain F: Gaia-Scale Consumer Systems

Gaia theory treats Earth as:

- Self-regulating
- Dynamic
- Interconnected

Applied to consumer science:

1. Planetary Consumption Patterns

Global shifts → carbon, water, biodiversity.

2. Environmental Sentiment Analysis

Monitor the emotional climate around sustainability.

3. Earth-System Personalization

Offers adapt based on:

- Air quality
- Weather
- Local ecosystem health

4. Planetary Boundaries → Responsible Marketing

How to align product promotions with sustainability thresholds?

5. Regenerative Consumption Models

Using AI to reduce environmental harm.

8.21 Multi-Species Emotion Modeling

Figure 85: *Consumer Ecosystem Maturity Curve*

Figure 86: *Consumer Ecosystem Maturity Curve*

Figure 87: *Consumer Ecosystem Maturity Curve*

Animals communicate emotion through:

- Posture
- Vocal patterns
- Pheromones
- Movement rhythms
- Group reactions

These provide frameworks for **multi-sensory emotion modeling**, extending beyond human-centric sentiment analysis.

Research Topics:

1. Cross-Species Emotion Calibration

Mapping animal emotional signals to consumer emotional states:

- Elephant rumbling → early frustration signals
- Bird alarm calls → churn warning signals
- Whale songs → long-term emotional arcs

2. Emotional Contagion Models

Flocking and schooling predict:

- Viral outrage
- Hype cycles
- Group polarization

3. Empathy Flow Mapping

Understanding how empathy moves through networks:

- Who influences whom?
- How do micro-emotions spread?

8.22 Table: Animal Emotion → Consumer Emotion Signals

Animal Signal Type	Meaning	Consumer Equivalent
Alarm calls	Danger, disruption	Negative sentiment spikes
Grooming	Bonding	Positive micro-engagement
Herd movement	Influence	Trend formation
Nest building	Long-term investment	Subscription loyalty
Pack hierarchy	Leadership roles	Influencer networks

This opens research pathways for **multi-species emotion AI**.

8.23 Temporal Ecology Models for Consumer Lifecycles

Nature uses **seasonality** and **cyclic rhythms** to regulate life.

Consumers also follow rhythmic patterns:

- Pay cycles
- Mood cycles
- Cultural rhythms
- Seasonal spending
- Biological rhythms
- Emotional oscillations

Key Research Areas:

1. Circadian Consumer Models

Predict peak/pause engagement windows.

2. Seasonal Personality Shifts

Consumers behave differently in:

- Festivals
- Summers/winters
- Economic cycles

3. Ecological Time-Scales

Short cycles → short-term trends

Long cycles → brand loyalty

4. Resonance Timing

Plants bloom in sync; consumers engage in sync with:

- Social sentiment
- Peer momentum
- Climate cycles

8.24 Conceptual Diagram: Consumer Circadian Intelligence Model

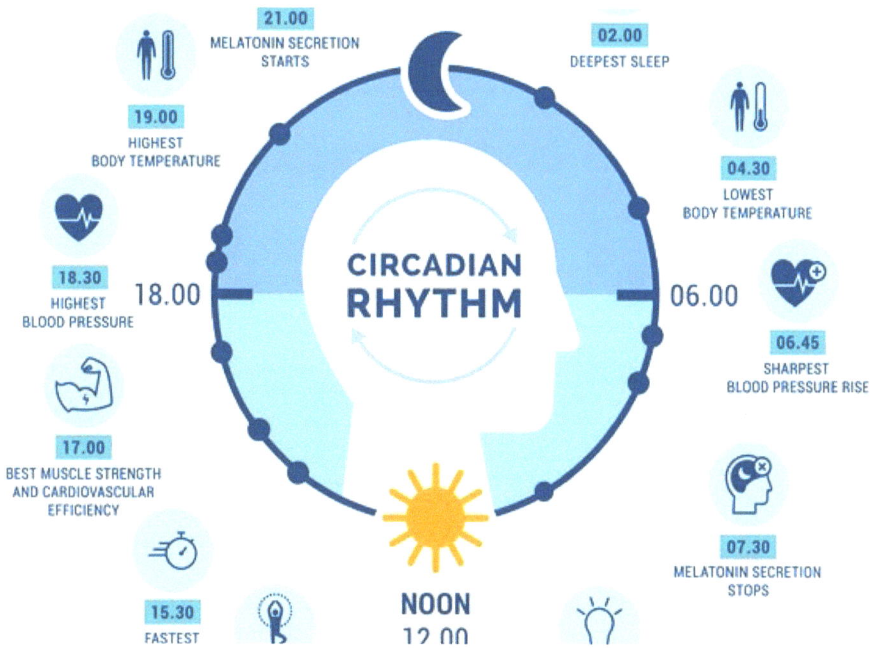

Figure 87: *Circadian Rhythm*

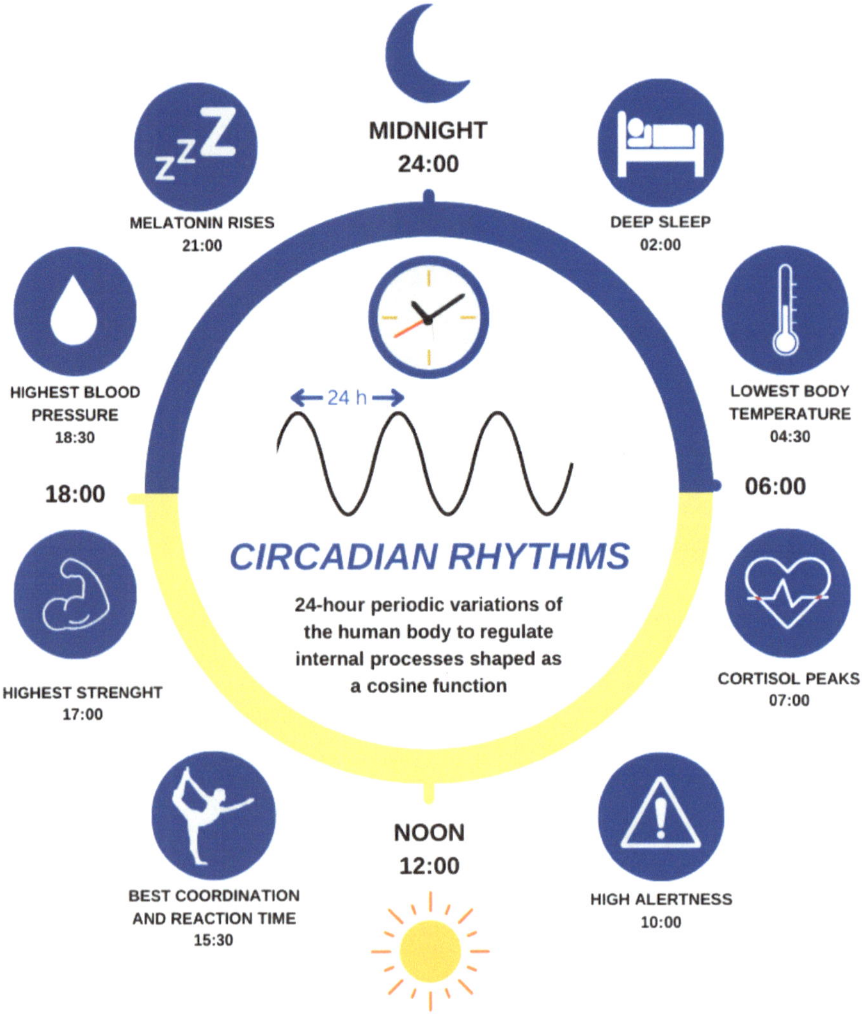

Figure 88: *Circadian Rhythms*

This model identifies **daily rhythms of consumer cognition**:

Morning

- Analytical clarity
- Functional shopping
- High problem-solving

Afternoon

- Practical decisions
- Mid-emotion purchases

Evening

- Emotional buying
- Impulse behavior
- Content-heavy interaction

Night

- Reflection
- Browsing
- Long-form content

Nature-inspired circadian modeling massively improves personalization.

8.25 Research Domain I: Evolutionary Intelligence for Long-Term Consumer Modeling

Evolution optimizes survival over millions of years using:

- Mutation
- Selection
- Adaptation
- Co-evolution

Applications in consumer AI:

1. Evolutionary Brand–Consumer Co-Adaptation

Brands evolve with consumers, not before or after.

2. Adaptive Experience Design

UX that evolves based on:

- Feedback
- Context
- Behavior drift

3. Evolutionary Segmentation

Segments mutate as:

- Economic conditions change
- Cultures evolve
- New products emerge

4. Multi-Generational Trend Modeling

Predict trends across:

- Gen Z
- Alpha
- Post-Alpha

8.26 Table: Evolutionary Processes → Consumer Behavior Models

Evolutionary Concept	Explanation	Consumer Behavior Mapping
Mutation	Random change	New micro-preferences emerging
Fitness	Survival advantage	Engagement quality
Selection	Best-adapted survive	Product market fit
Drift	Random fluctuation	Cultural shifts
Co-evolution	Species adapt together	Brand-consumer co-growth

8.27 Bioacoustics for Consumer State Detection

Figure 89: *Bioacoustics for Consumer State Detection*

Figure 90: *Bioacoustics for Consumer State Detection*

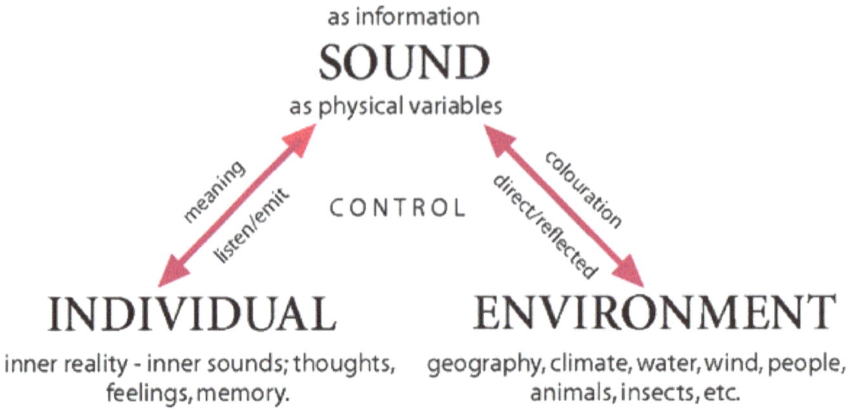

Figure 91: *Mediating relationship of an individual to the environment through sound*

Animals are studied via:

- Frequency shifts
- Pulse patterns
- Acoustic signatures

These inspire **sound-based consumer analytics**:

Research Directions:

1. Micro-Acoustic Emotion Sensing

Detect stress or delight through:

- Voice tone
- Breath patterns
- Pauses

Useful for:

- Call centers
- Voice shopping
- Conversational agents

2. Eco-Acoustic Digital Spaces

Digital environments create "soundscapes" that influence:

- Consumer comfort
- Purchase intention

- Cognitive load

3. Churn Acoustics

Anger and frustration carry acoustic markers.

8.28 Movement Ecology for Physical Retail & AR/VR

Animals use:

- Movement paths
- Territory mapping
- Energy-efficient navigation

Retail consumers mirror this.

Research Opportunities:

1. Retail Movement Ecology

Heat maps inspired by:

- Wolf pack patrol routes
- Elephant migratory paths
- Foraging zones

Predicts:

- Shelf dwell time
- Navigation friction
- High-conversion zones

2. AR/VR Navigational Ecology

VR consumer movement mirrors:

- Fish schooling
- Bird flocking
- Swarm clustering

Applied to:

- Virtual malls
- Digital product journeys

8.29 Table: Movement Ecology → Consumer Navigation

Movement Pattern	Animal Example	Consumer Mapping
Optimal Foraging	Bees	Efficient browsing
Territorial Patrol	Wolves	Repeat-purchase cycles
Migration	Birds/elephants	Seasonal shopping
Cluster Movement	Fish	Social shopping events
Drift & Dispersal	Insects	Trend decay

Movement ecology opens new frontiers in spatial AI for retail.

8.30 Non-Human Communication Systems for UX & Engagement

Animals communicate using:

- Vibration
- Colour
- Light
- Sound
- Chemical cues

Consumers respond to:

- Visual cues
- Emotional micro-interactions
- UI colour psychology
- Micro-animations
- Subtle vibrations

Research Questions:

1. How to design websites using butterfly signalling patterns?

They use colour modulation to attract attention without overload.

2. Can UX adopt bee-dance communication for information routing?

Guiding users intuitively.

3. How can sound/vibration patterns reduce cognitive load?

Inspired by:

- Whale call frequencies
- Bird chirp patterns
- Frog rhythmic pulses

4. Can chemical-signalling metaphors inform brand storytelling?

Scent-based marketing already hints at this.

8.31 Environmental Sensing & Contextual Consumer AI

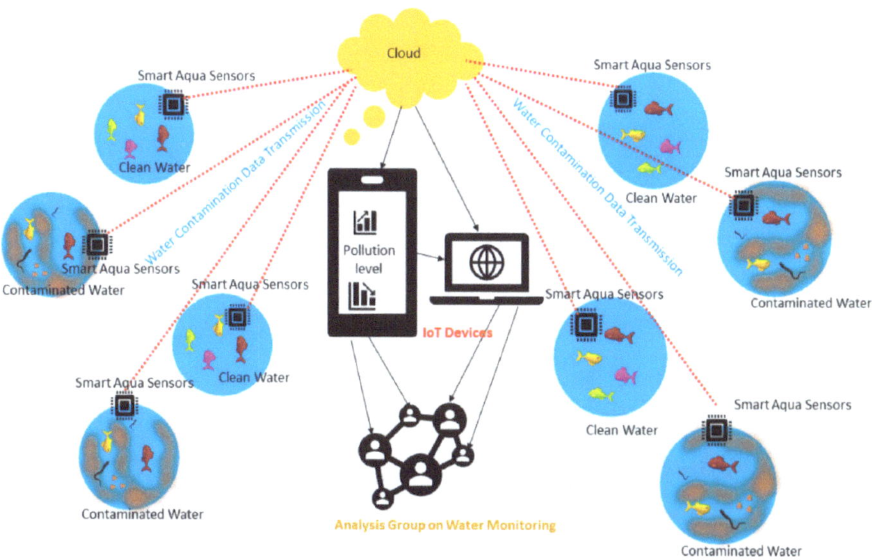

Figure 92: *Environmental Sensing & Contextual Consumer AI*

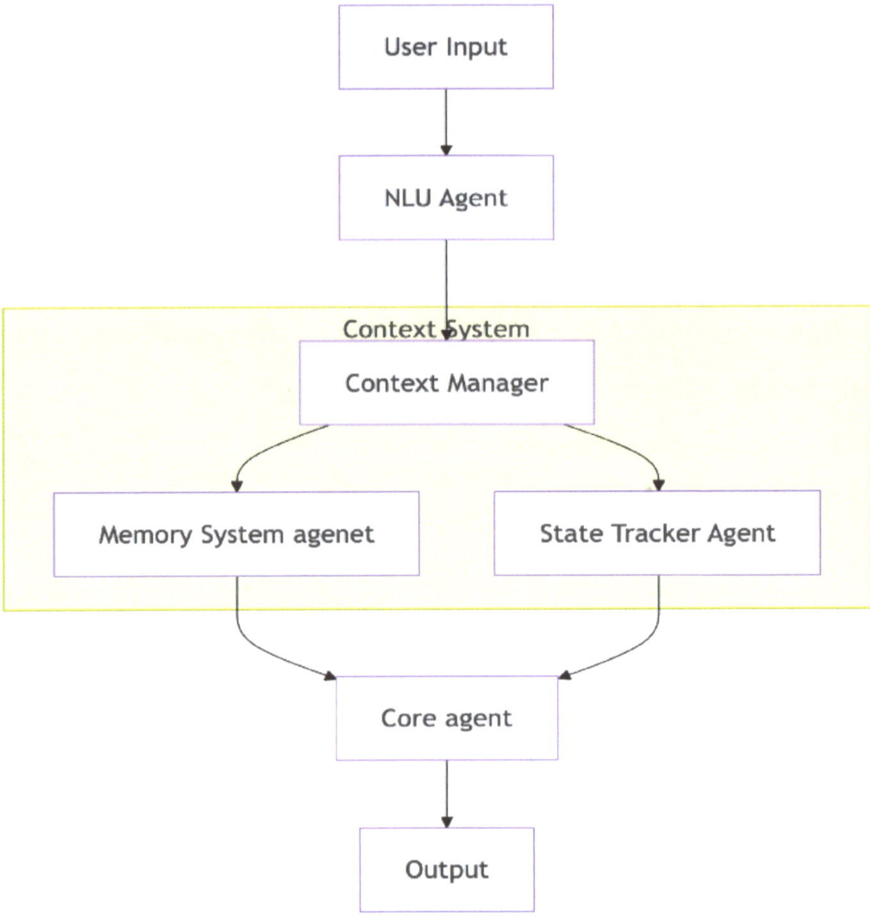

Figure 93: *Environmental Sensing & Contextual Consumer AI*

Environmental intelligence uses signals from:

- Temperature
- Humidity
- Air quality
- Light intensity
- Pollution levels
- Noise patterns

- Soil moisture
- Water flow

Nature responds to context—and consumers do too.

Key Research Areas:

1. Context-Aware Personalization

Aligning content with:

- Weather
- Climate stress
- Environmental comfort

Example:

Hot weather → preference for lighter tasks, cooler colours, beverage ads.

2. Environmental Emotion AI

Environmental stress correlates with:

- Irritability
- Decision fatigue
- Impulsive purchases
- Lower attention

3. Geo-Sensory Retail Models

Retail footfall correlates with:

- Temperature spikes
- Noise cycles
- Sunlight patterns

Environmental conditions shape consumer psychology profoundly.

8.32 Exploratory Model: Environmental–Emotional Loop

Consumers behave like animals responding to environmental cues.

Environmental input → Physiological response → Emotional state → Consumer behavior

Examples:

Environmental Factor	Response	Consumer Outcome
High humidity	Discomfort	Shorter browsing
Cool weather	Calm	Higher dwell time
Loud noise	Stress	Quick exits
Clean air	Relaxation	Exploration behavior
Dim lighting	Low arousal	Impulse buying

This model resembles ecological stress–response curves.

8.33 Atmospheric Intelligence for Predictive Demand

Atmospheric sciences study:

- Fronts
- Pressure systems
- Airflow
- Diffusion
- Microclimates

These mirror:

- Consumer trend waves
- Community influence zones
- Sentiment microclimates
- Demand diffusion

Research Topics:

1. Demand Fronts & Pressure Maps

Like weather prediction:

- High-pressure → stable demand
- Low-pressure → hype volatility

2. Sentiment Jet Streams

Fast-moving emotional flows across networks.

3. Trend Microclimates

Small pockets of:

- Hyper-engagement
- Viral activity
- Sudden drop-offs

Atmospheric modeling offers new predictive engines.

8.34 Ocean Intelligence & Behavior Diffusion

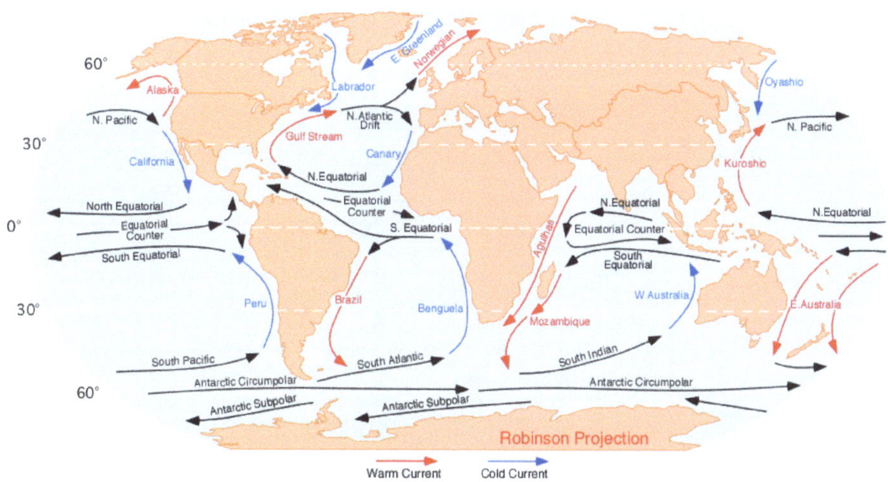

Figure 94: *Ocean Intelligence & Behavior Diffusion*

Ocean systems teach:

- Flow dynamics
- Upwelling (hidden potential rising)
- Gyres (circular patterns)
- Deep currents (latent signals)

Consumer Data Analogues:

1. Upwelling → Hidden Trend Surfacing

Deep content suddenly rising.

2. Gyres → Feedback Loops

Communities recirculate ideas.

3. Deep Currents → Long-Term Patterns

Stable preferences not visible from surface data.

4. Tides → Daily/Weekly Cycles

Regular, rhythmic engagement.

Ocean intelligence helps model **slow, deep, systemic changes**, not just surface trends.

8.35 Table: Ocean Patterns → Consumer Dynamics

Ocean Pattern	Explanation	Consumer Behavior Analogue
Upwelling	Deep water rising	Hidden trends emerging
Currents	Constant flows	Habit loops
Gyres	Circular motion	Community echo chambers
Tides	Regular cycles	Weekly engagement patterns
Thermoclines	Layered waters	Layered consumer segments

8.36 Predator–Prey Dynamics in Competitive Markets

Predator–prey models (Lotka–Volterra equations) describe:

- Competition
- Survival
- Resource capture
- Population oscillation

Competitive markets behave exactly the same.

Research Applications:

1. Brand vs Brand Competition Modeling

Predicts:

- Market share oscillation
- Competitive pressure
- Resource cannibalization

2. Product Cannibalization as Predation

One product "eats" another.

3. New Entrants as Invasive Species

How long before:

- Adoption
- Collapse
- Stabilization

4. Consumer Rebounds

After predatory pricing ends, populations (customers) recover.

Biology provides a mathematical foundation for competitive strategy.

8.37 Bioenergetics & Consumer Energy Models

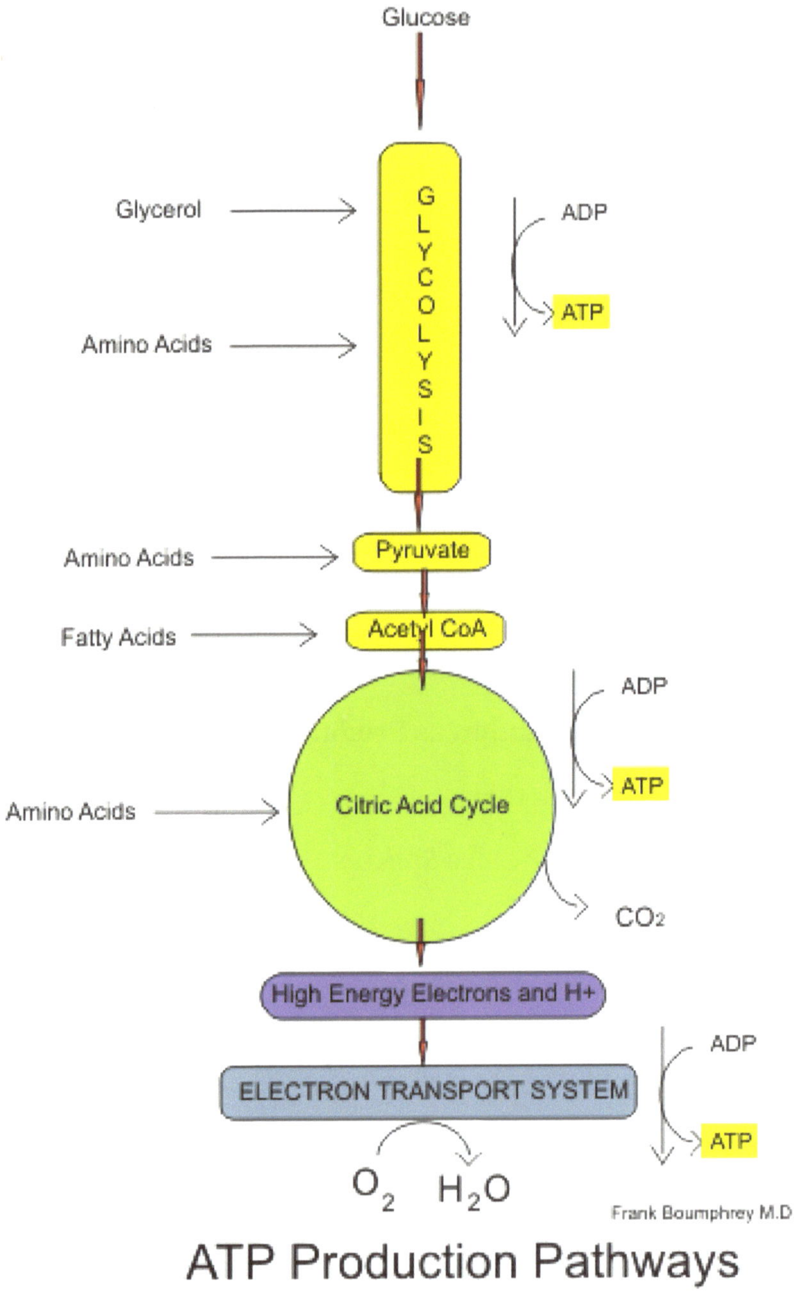

Figure 95: *Bioenergetics & Consumer Energy Models*

Animals manage:

- Energy expenditure
- Resource allocation
- Fatigue
- Foraging optimization

Consumers do the same—energy, not time, is now the main limiting resource.

Research Questions:

1. How do cognitive energy levels affect purchase decisions?
2. Can bioenergetic models predict when consumers enter "low-energy refusal modes"?
3. Can AI reduce energy expenditure during complex tasks?

Applications:

- Low-energy UI modes
- Energy-adaptive personalization
- "Cognitive calorie" budgeting in apps

Bioenergetics could become the new **consumer psychology of fatigue.**

8.38 Regenerative Behavior & Consumer Flourishing

Regenerative ecology reveals:

- Self-renewal
- Resource recycling
- Mutualism
- Positive-sum outcomes

Contrary to extractive marketing, regenerative marketing encourages:

- Emotional health
- Environmental sustainability
- Community well-being

Research Topics:

1. Regenerative consumption loops
2. Waste-aware recommender systems
3. Emotional replenishment journeys
4. Community-nourishing brand ecosystems
5. Consumer flourishing scores

This represents the Symbiocene-era consumer model.

8.39 Conceptual Model: The Regenerative Consumer Loop

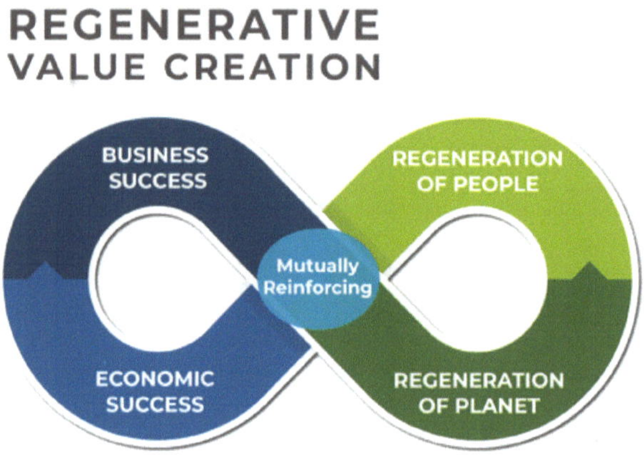

Figure 96: *The Regenerative Consumer Loop*

Step 1—Awareness

Consumer learns about ecological value.

Step 2—Alignment

Values match product/brand identity.

Step 3—Regenerative Action

Eco-positive purchase or behavior.

Step 4—Community Contribution

Experience shared → spreads behavior.

Step 5—Ecological/Economic Return

Rewards, recognition, community uplift.

Step 6—Emotional Flourishing

Consumer feels grounded, connected, responsible.

Step 7—Reinvestment

Consumer invests again.

This loop forms the future of consumer brand ecosystems.

8.40 Multi-Level Intelligence Integration

This domain integrates:

- Individual signals
- Group dynamics
- Ecosystem forces
- Planetary boundaries

Research Goal:

Build **multi-scalar AI models** that can:

- Detect micro-behaviors
- Predict macro-trends
- Harmonize local & global signals
- Integrate ecological and emotional data
- Personalize responsibly

Potential Methods:

- Multi-agent RL
- Hierarchical graph modeling
- Multi-level Bayesian inference
- Dynamical systems modeling

Outcome:

A new generation of **holistic consumer intelligence systems**.

8.41 Non-Human Memory Systems for Consumer Retention Models

Animals, plants, and fungi possess **non-traditional memory systems**:

Plant Memory

- Drought memory
- Light memory
- Stress memory

Fungal Memory

- Conductivity changes in hyphae
- Routing memory

Animal Collective Memory

- Migration paths
- Predator history
- Social bonding patterns

These offer **new retention frameworks** beyond the simplistic "recency–frequency–monetary (RFM)" model.

Research Directions:

1. Stress Memory → Customer Friction Memory

Predicting if past frustrations will resurface.

2. Collective Memory → Community Retention Models

Groups remember events longer than individuals.

3. Fungal Routing Memory → Habit-Path Reinforcement

Predict whether customers will return to the same journey paths.

8.42 Conceptual Model: Memory Ecologies in Consumer Systems

Memory in Nature → Memory in Consumers

Nature Memory Type	Biological Example	Consumer Equivalent
Stress memory	Plants remembering drought	Friction memory
Path memory	Ants remembering food paths	Journey loyalty
Social memory	Elephants remembering allies	Community loyalty
Predator memory	Prey avoiding danger zones	Brand distrust
Regenerative memory	Forest regrowth patterns	Re-engagement after recovery

A brand ecosystem should cultivate **regenerative memory**, not trauma memory.

8.43 Ecological Resilience Modeling for Churn Prediction

Ecosystems survive disturbance and regenerate.

Consumer ecosystems also experience:

- External shocks
- Brand failures
- Market disruptions
- Economic downturns

Key Resilience Factors:

1. Diversity
2. Redundancy
3. Modularity
4. Connectivity
5. Adaptive capacity

Research Applications:

1. Churn as Ecosystem Collapse

Predict collapse using ecological indicators.

2. Redundancy Signals

Multiple emotional touchpoints → higher resilience.

3. Diversity Support Models

Consumers with diverse brand connections churn less.

This becomes the next generation of churn science.

8.44 Table: Ecological Resilience → Customer Retention Frameworks

Resilience Factor	Ecological Meaning	Consumer Application
Diversity	Species variety	Multiple product offerings
Redundancy	Backup species	Alternative journeys
Modularity	Decoupled subsystems	Segment-based retention
Connectivity	Network density	Community loyalty
Adaptive capacity	Flexibility	Personalized responses

Churn modeling becomes **eco-behavioral prediction**.

8.45 Symbiotic Intelligence for Co-Creation & Engagement

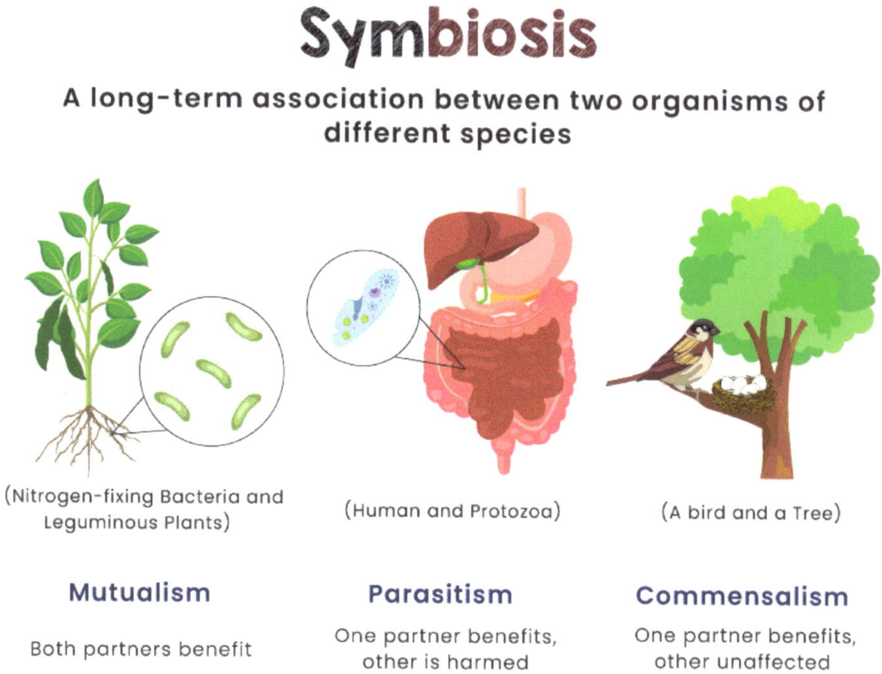

Figure 97: *Symbiotic Intelligence for Co-Creation & Engagement*

Symbiosis teaches:

- Mutual benefit
- Co-evolution
- Shared value creation

Symbiotic Consumer Engagement Models:

1. Mutualistic Interactions

Brand ↔ Consumer both gain value.

2. Commensal Engagement

Consumer gains; brand unaffected (e.g., educational content).

3. Facilitation

Brand enables community flourishing.

4. Co-evolutionary Value Loops

Brand strategy adapts with consumer preferences.

Research Questions:

- How can brands evolve with consumers?
- What symbiotic patterns increase lifetime value?
- How can AI sustain mutualistic engagement loops?

8.46 Forest Intelligence & Regenerative Segmentation

Forests are:

- Layered (canopy, understory, roots)
- Cooperative
- Adaptive
- Resource-efficient

Consumers behave similarly.

Research Themes:

1. Canopy Segments (High-Influence Consumers)

- Spread trends
- Drive community sentiment
- Shape ecosystem direction

2. Understory Segments (Niche Growth Communities)

- Hidden but influential
- Early adopters

3. Root Segments (Core Stability Consumers)

- Provide stability
- Low churn
- Long-term loyalty

Forests offer a **three-tiered segmentation model.**

8.47 Table: Forest Layers → Consumer Segments

Forest Layer	Description	Consumer Segment
Canopy	Tallest, high sunlight	Influencers, super-spreaders
Understory	Middle shade	Trend explorers
Shrub layer	Small growth	Ordinary adopters
Forest floor	Decomposition base	Dormant consumers
Roots	Hidden, deep	Loyal core

This becomes a robust framework for **regenerative segmentation.**

8.48 Weather-Inspired Prediction Models for Demand Volatility

Weather systems mirror consumer markets:

- Predictable in broad patterns
- Volatile in short-term details
- Driven by invisible forces

Research Topics:

1. Consumer Storm Modeling

Predict sharp negative sentiment spikes.

2. Demand Front Prediction

Where demand "moves" next.

3. Microclimate Engagement Zones

Localized engagement patterns within communities.

4. Seasonal Weather Analogues

Predict seasonal demand using meteorological analogs:

- Monsoon spending
- Economic dry spells
- Festive "heat waves"

This helps marketers manage uncertainty.

8.49 Oceanic Population Modeling for Brand Tribes

Fish populations:

- Form shoals
- Cluster by species
- Respond to predators
- Follow leaders
- Exhibit group drift

Consumer Tribal Behavior Mirrors This:

1. Shoal Clustering

Consumers group by:

- Values
- Aesthetics
- Social identity

2. Leader–Follower Dynamics

Influencers as "school leaders."

3. Predator Avoidance

Consumers flee:

- Toxic brands
- Overpriced offerings
- Manipulative experiences

4. Competitive Displacement

New entrants cause existing clusters to move.

Oceanic population ecology predicts community shifts.

8.50 Thermal & Light Ecology for Behavior Prediction

Animals respond strongly to:

- Light cycles
- Heat gradients
- Temperature thresholds

Consumers do too.

Research Directions:

1. Light Ecology → Interface Illumination Models

Bright UI → high arousal

Soft UI → long browsing

Dark UI → nighttime engagement

2. Thermal Ecology → Emotional State Prediction

Heat increases:

- Irritability
- Impulse buying
- Quick exits

Cold improves:

- Deep reading
- Higher dwell time

3. Seasonal Temperature Patterns → Demand Prediction

Cold-season surges

Heat-driven drop-offs

Festival spikes

Light & thermal ecology provide **biophysical insights** into future consumer modeling.

8.51 Bio-Social Signalling in Digital Communities

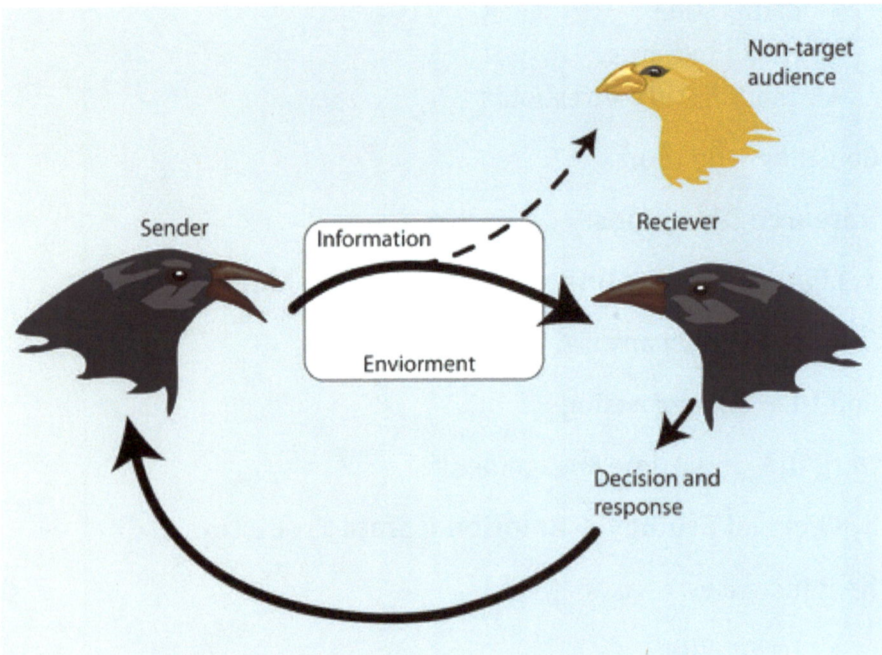

Figure 98: *Bio-Social Signalling in Digital Communities*

Animals use signalling for:

- Warning
- Attraction
- Coordination
- Trust
- Cooperation

Consumers do the same through:

- Likes
- Reviews
- Follows
- Shares
- Emojis
- Status updates
- Visual signals (stories, reels)

Research Topics:

1. Bio-Social Signalling Metrics
2. Signal Cascades → Viral Spread Modeling
3. Signal Strength → Trust Dynamics
4. Negative Alarm Signalling → Complaint Waves

Digital communities behave like **socially signalling animal groups**.

8.52 Entropy Models for Consumer Attention

Nature uses *entropy* to describe disorder and energy distribution.

Consumer attention follows:

- Diffusion
- Dispersion
- Dissolution
- Entropy spikes

Research Areas:

1. Attention Entropy Index (AEI)

Measures attention fragmentation.

2. Entropic Decay of Trends

Predicts when trends fade.

3. Energy-Based Attention Models

Analogous to heat dissipation:

- High-energy attention → hype
- Low-energy → fatigue

Entropy is the future of **attention economics**.

8.53 Multi-Species Mirror Neuron Systems for Empathy AI

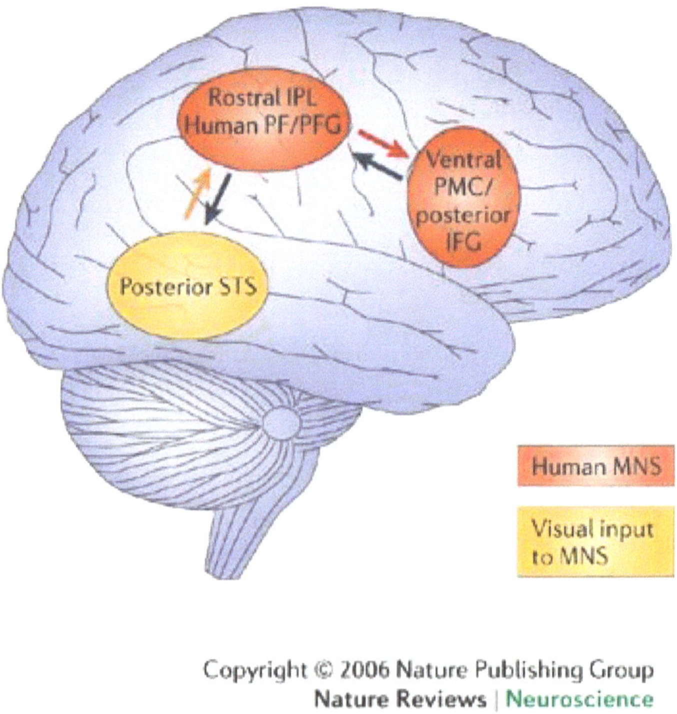

Figure 99: *Multi-Species Mirror Neuron Systems*

Mirror neuron research shows that:

- Primates mimic emotions
- Elephants empathize
- Dogs synchronize moods with humans
- Birds mirror flock behavior

This inspires:

Empathy AI:

- emotion matching
- emotional forecasting
- group sentiment synchronization

Research Questions:

- How do groups collectively "feel"?
- How do emotional states propagate?
- Can AI detect pre-churn emotional shifts?

Empathy AI becomes central for emotional well-being and retention.

8.54 Ecological Thresholds & Tipping Points in Consumer Markets

Ecosystems collapse when thresholds are crossed:

- Coral bleaching temperature
- Deforestation %
- Ocean acidification

Consumer markets also have tipping points:

- Trust collapses
- A competitor suddenly dominates
- Community sentiment flips
- Viral events trigger mass migration

Research Focus:

1. Early Warning Indicators
2. Stress Accumulation Metrics
3. Critical Transition Prediction
4. Recovery Dynamics
5. Brand Extinction Modeling

Predicting tipping points becomes crucial in era of volatile digital ecosystems.

8.55 Pollination & Cross-Pollination in Consumer Innovation

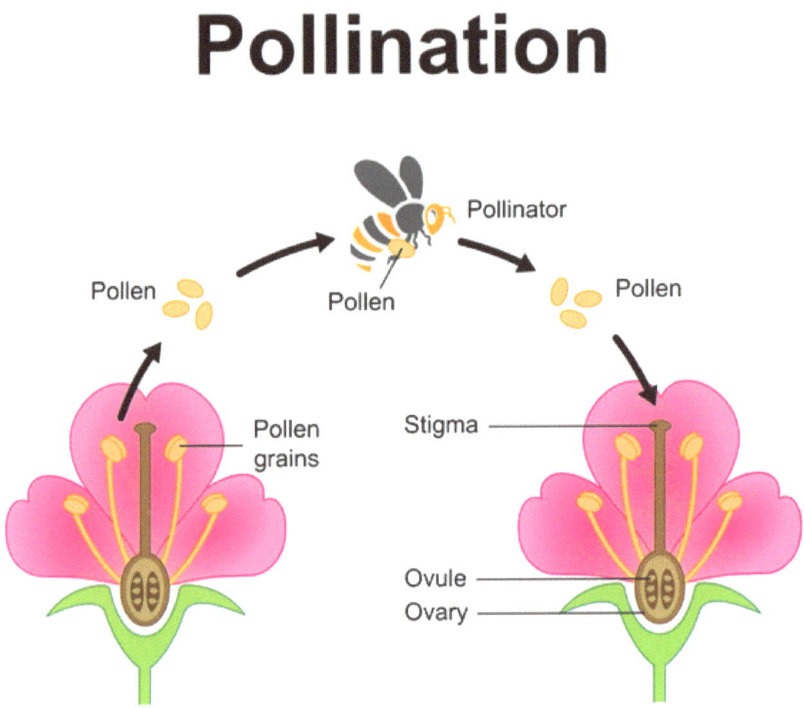

Figure 100: *Pollination & Cross-Pollination in Consumer Innovation*

Figure 101: *Pollination & Cross-Pollination in Consumer Innovation*

Pollination:

- Connects species
- Drives evolution
- Spreads information
- Creates new life

Consumers similarly "pollinate":

- Ideas
- Aesthetic trends
- Memes
- Preferences
- Innovations

Research Areas:

1. Innovation Pollination Models

Who pollinates new ideas?

2. Cross-Pollination Networks

How ideas jump across tribes.

3. Pollinator Role Identification

Super-connectors in consumer ecosystems.

4. Pollination Velocity Metrics

Speed of influence spread.

Nature provides the perfect metaphor for cultural innovation transmission.

8.56 Ecological Carrying Capacity for Sustainable Consumption

Carrying capacity:

- Defines maximum sustainable population
- Prevents collapse
- Stabilizes ecological systems

Applied to consumer science:

1. Product Carrying Capacity

How much consumer attention, usage, or loyalty a product can sustain.

2. Category Carrying Capacity

Market saturation limits.

3. Consumption Carrying Capacity

Ethical limits:

- energy
- environment
- emotional load

4. Engagement Carrying Capacity

Consumers cannot engage infinitely.

This moves marketing from *growth* to *balanced flourishing.*

8.57 Multi-Species Governance for AI & Consumer Systems

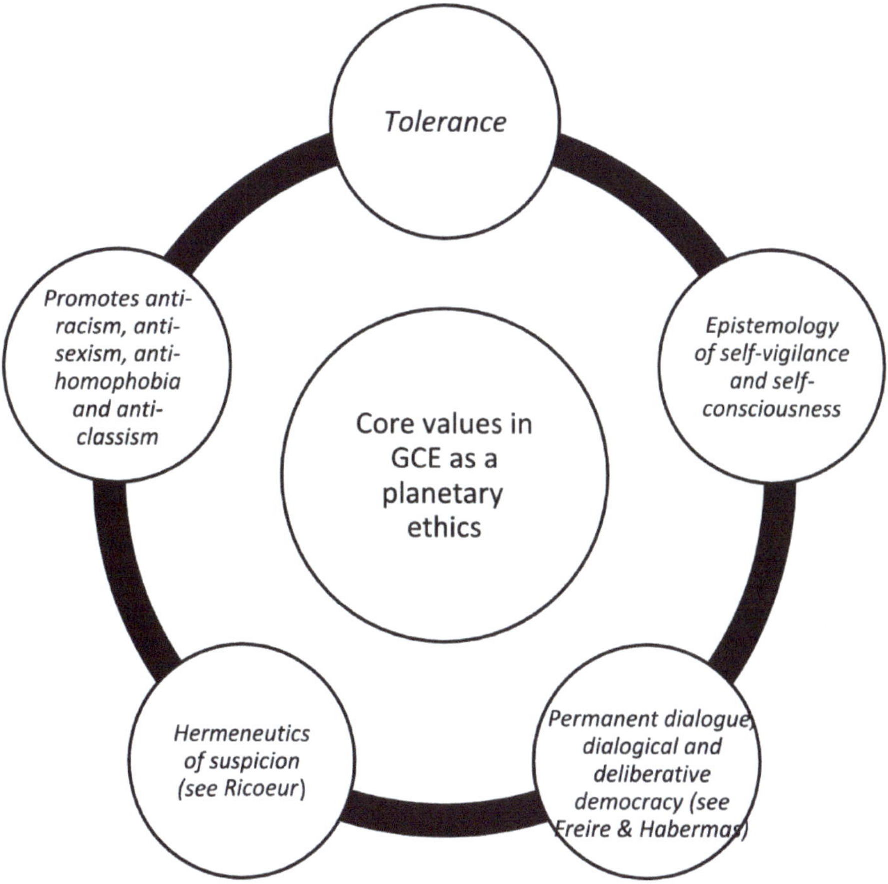

Figure 102: *Multi-Species Governance for AI & Consumer Systems*

Governance shifts from:

- Human-first

  → multi-species

  → Planet-first

Research Topics:

1. Planetary Ethics for AI

Does the system harm ecosystems?

2. Multi-Species Justice

Does consumer engagement encourage ecological harm?

3. Long-Term Stewardship Models

100-year view of consumer ecosystems.

4. Community Assemblies as Ecological Councils

Human + AI + community decision-making.

This is the governance architecture of the **Symbiocene era**.

8.58 Superorganism Theory for Community Behavior

Superorganisms (ants, bees) operate as:

- One collective body
- Shared purpose
- Distributed intelligence

Consumer communities behave the same in:

- fandoms
- subcultures
- creator ecosystems
- brand tribes

Research Topics:

- Superorganism sentiment analysis
- Group-level decision engines
- Distributed value systems
- Collective intelligence scoring

This unlocks **mass-coordination AI**.

8.59 Summary Model: The 20 Domains of Nature-Inspired Consumer AI

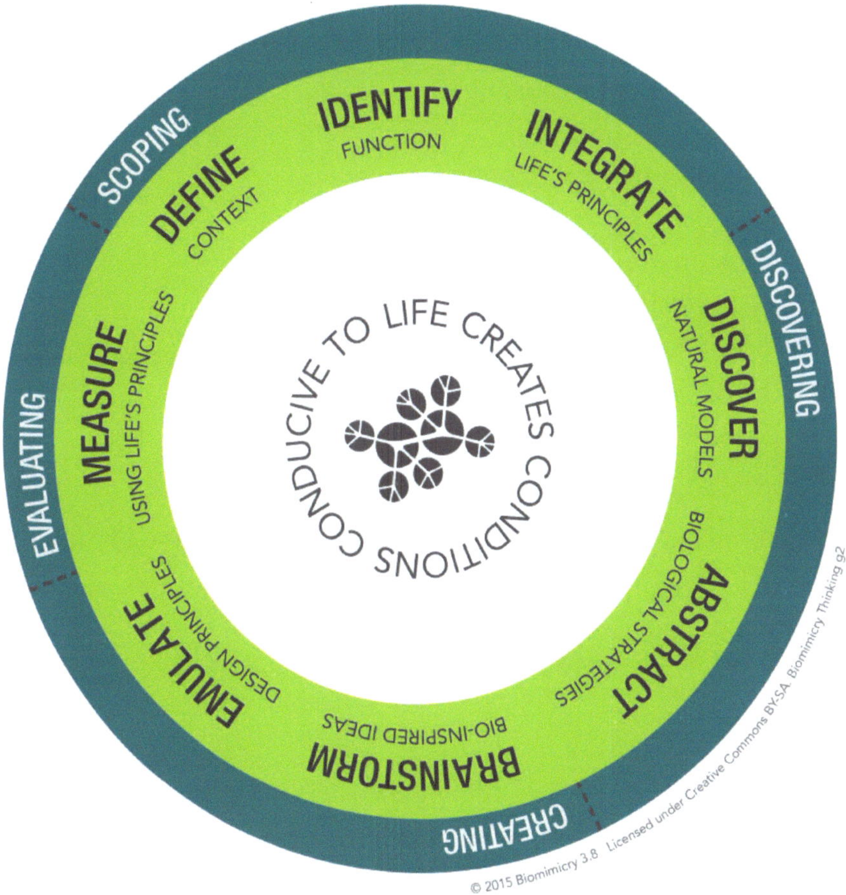

Figure 103: *Nature-Inspired Consumer AI*

The 20 Mega-Domains:

1. Swarm Intelligence
2. Fungal Networks
3. Plant Signalling
4. Ecosystem Models
5. Atmospheric Intelligence
6. Ocean Intelligence

7. Predator–Prey Competition
8. Bioenergetics
9. Regenerative Behavior
10. Memory Ecologies
11. Environmental Sensing
12. Circadian Modeling
13. Evolutionary Intelligence
14. Bioacoustics Analytics
15. Movement Ecology
16. Non-Human Communication
17. Social Signalling
18. Entropy Models
19. Pollination Dynamics
20. Superorganism Theory

This defines the **research roadmap for the next decade**.

8.60 Closing Insight: The Next Era of Consumer AI

Final Insight:

"The future of consumer intelligence will not be built on human psychology alone—but on the full evolutionary intelligence of life itself."

We are entering a phase where:

- Consumer ecosystems act like natural ecosystems
- Engagement behaves like ecological flows
- Loyalty follows biological logic
- Trends evolve like species

The next breakthroughs in marketing will not come from algorithms alone—but from **the forests, oceans, skies, and species that have mastered complexity for billions of years.**

Project—Build a Nature-Inspired AI Model for Consumer Trend Prediction

Objective:

Design a cross-domain, nature-inspired AI model that predicts micro and macro consumer trends using non-human intelligence frameworks.

1. Multi-Species Data Integration

Collect analogues from:

- Swarms (decision waves)
- Fungi (weak signals)
- Plants (micro-engagement)
- Ecosystems (emergence)
- Oceans (deep-current trends)

2. AI Model Architecture

A. Swarm-Based Attention Engine

- Maps collective movement
- Predicts virality waves

B. Mycelial Weak-Signal Detector

- Identifies early churn
- Detects rising tensions

C. Plant-Inspired Passive Engagement Layer

- Captures micro signals
- Infers emotional fatigue

D. Ecosystem Stability Predictor

- Finds risk of collapse
- Measures resilience

E. Oceanic Trend Drift Analyzer

- Detects deep trends
- Differentiates fad vs. long-term shift

3. Mathematical & AI Techniques

Purpose	Technique	Math Basis
Trend waves	Fourier transforms	Frequency decomposition
Sentiment microclimates	Gaussian fields	Probability densities
Weak-signal detection	Hidden Markov Models	State transitions
Community clustering	Graph theory	Eigenvector centrality
Collective behavior	Multi-agent RL	Policy gradients
Ecosystem modeling	Differential equations	Dynamical systems
Evolutionary prediction	Genetic algorithms	Fitness landscapes
Drift modeling	Stochastic calculus	Brownian motion

4. Expected Outcomes

- Early signal detection
- Viral trend forecasting
- Ecosystem health scores
- Granular emotional predictions
- Community behavioral mapping

MCQs

1. Swarm intelligence helps model:

    a. Herd behavior
    b. Soil chemistry
    c. Gravity
    d. Weather storms

2. Fungal intelligence is best applied to:

    a. Loyalty & weak signals
    b. Image generation
    c. High-frequency trading
    d. Chess

3. Plant intelligence informs:

    a. Passive engagement analytics
    b. Blockchain mining
    c. Satellite navigation
    d. Null hypotheses

4. Ecosystem intelligence helps model:

    a. Churn patterns
    b. Car engines
    c. Quantum tunnelling
    d. Cooking recipes

5. Atmospheric intelligence models:

    a. Trend waves
    b. Plate tectonics
    c. Numerology
    d. File compression

6. Ocean intelligence reveals:

    a. Deep trends
    b. Space-time curvature
    c. Nuclear reactions
    d. Phone signals

7. Predator–prey models explain:

    a. Competitive dynamics
    b. Furniture layout
    c. Rocket thrust
    d. Gravity wells

8. Bioenergetics helps in understanding:

    a. Cognitive fatigue
    b. Heat insulation
    c. Blood types
    d. Soil erosion

9. Regenerative behavior aims for:

    a. Net-positive outcomes
    b. Infinite resource extraction
    c. Randomness
    d. Market collapse

10. Memory ecologies model:

    a. Retention patterns
    b. Radio frequencies
    c. Algebraic systems
    d. Server cooling

11. Circadian modeling predicts:

    a. Optimal engagement windows
    b. Mountain altitudes
    c. Rocket fuel efficiency
    d. Genetic disorders

12. Evolutionary intelligence supports:

    a. Long-term trend modeling
    b. Tree cutting
    c. Cement mixing
    d. GPS tracking

13. Bioacoustics can detect:

    a. Emotional states
    b. Ocean salinity
    c. Atomic mass
    d. Steel thickness

14. Movement ecology maps:

    a. Retail navigation
    b. Fashion colours
    c. DNA sequencing
    d. Random numbers

15. Non-human communication inspires:

    a. UX vibration patterns
    b. Snowfall
    c. Volcano eruptions
    d. Chemical engineering

16. Social signalling models:

    a. Viral content
    b. Temperature
    c. Chemical purity
    d. Metal detectors

17. Entropy models predict:

    a. Attention decay
    b. Asteroid rotation
    c. Earthquakes
    d. Myopia

18. Pollination models explain:

    a. Innovation spread
    b. Sound insulation
    c. Rocket flight
    d. HVAC design

19. Carrying capacity applies to:

    a. Sustainable consumption
    b. Electric motors
    c. Crude oil
    d. Fiber optics

20. Superorganism theory helps analyze:

    a. Brand tribes
    b. Magnetism
    c. Steel strength
    d. Solar flares

Answers

1-a

2-a

3-a

4-a

5-a

6-a

7-a

8-a

9-a

10-a

11-a

12-a

13-a

14-a

15-a

16-a

17-a

18-a

19-a

20-a

Innovation in the Symbiocene is no longer technological first—it is ecological first, technological second.

09

Implementing Symbiocene AI

9.1 Symbiocene-inspired AI

Shifts the centre of innovation from:

- Control → Cooperation
- Extraction → Regeneration
- Domination → Interdependence
- Efficiency → Flourishing

Implementing such AI requires **a new blueprint**, not merely new algorithms.

This chapter gives a **roadmap** for how **industry + academia** can jointly build Symbiocene AI systems based on:

- More-than-human intelligence
- Eco-centric algorithms
- Regenerative design
- Multi-species ethics
- Ecosystem modeling
- Biological analogues

It includes:

- 5 industry projects
- 5 academic pathways
- Implementation frameworks

- Collaboration models
- 3-level governance
- Demonstration sandboxes
- Proof-of-concept planning
- Measurement & KPIs

9.2 What Makes Symbiocene AI Implementation Different?

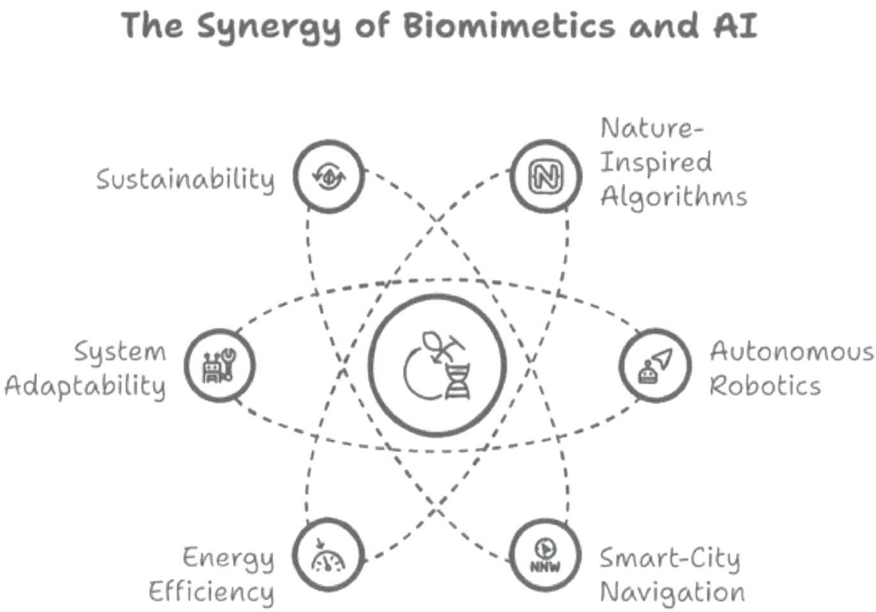

Figure 104: *Biomimetics and AI*

Traditional AI projects:

- Map human behavior
- Optimize for human-centric outcomes
- Maximize profits or efficiency
- Are extractive or predictive

Symbiocene AI projects:

- Model *non-human* intelligence
- Optimize *ecosystem-wide* well-being

- Balance community, environment, and business
- Are regenerative, adaptive, and ethical
- Use ecological metaphors as computational logic

This requires:

- New datasets
- New models
- New governance
- New design principles
- New partnerships

This chapter details **how**.

9.3 Symbiocene AI Implementation Megastructure

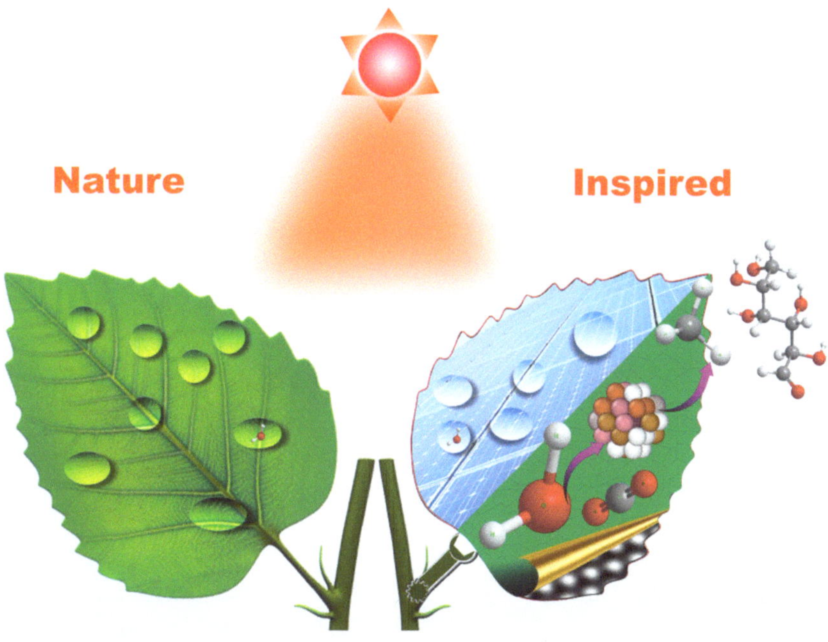

Figure 105: *Nature-Inspired*

The 5 Megastructures

Every Symbiocene AI project is built on 5 pillars:

1. Biological Inspiration Layer

Identify the natural process to model:

- Fungal routing
- Bee collaboration
- Ecosystem resilience
- Plant signalling
- Animal emotion patterns

2. Computational Translation Layer

Convert biological inspiration into:

- Algorithms
- Architectures
- Behavioral rules
- Mathematical functions

3. Human–Ecological Interface Layer

Design experiences that embed:

- Empathy
- Regeneration
- Mutual value

4. Multi-Stakeholder Collaboration Layer

Connect:

- Industry
- Academia
- Ecologists
- Designers
- Data scientists
- Indigenous knowledge holders

5. Planetary Alignment Layer

Ensure projects:

- Reduce ecological harm
- Enhance community well-being
- Respect planetary boundaries

9.4 Table: Biological System → AI Translation → Consumer Application

Biological System	AI Translation	Industry Use Case
Mycelium networks	Graph routing + weak-signal detection	Loyalty, churn sensing
Bee colonies	Multi-agent decision flows	Marketing resource optimization
Coral reefs	Layered community systems	Community engagement
Plant electrophysiology	Micro-signal modeling	Micro-engagement emotion detection
Ocean currents	Deep trend analysis	Trend forecasting
Ecosystem resilience	Stability modeling	Market collapse prediction

This table becomes the **foundation** for selecting project directions.

9.5 Ten Principles of Symbiocene Implementation

Principle 1—Regeneration Over Optimization

AI should leave systems healthier than it found them.

Principle 2—Multi-Species Intelligence

Models integrate nature's strategies, not only human logic.

Principle 3—Ecosystem Thinking

Every consumer action affects the whole environment.

Principle 4—Non-Extraction

Design must minimize cognitive, emotional, and ecological exploitation.

Principle 5—Co-Evolution

AI evolves with communities, not ahead of them.

Principle 6—Multi-Outcome Value

Success is measured across:

- Business outcomes
- Environmental impact
- Emotional flourishing
- Community well-being

Principle 7—Adaptive Ethics

Ethical models evolve based on real outcomes.

Principle 8—Locality Awareness

Systems align with local ecology & culture data.

Principle 9—Distributed Gains

Value is shared with users & stakeholders.

Principle 10—Stewardship

AI acts as a planetary steward, not a manipulator.

9.6 Industry Implementation Blueprint (High-Level)

Phase 1—Inspiration Scoping (2–6 weeks)

- Choose a biological analogue
- Map business use cases
- Identify data sources

Phase 2—Ecological Translation (4–8 weeks)

- Biomimicry mapping
- Algorithmic frameworks
- Preliminary mathematical designs

Phase 3—Experience Architecture (4–12 weeks)

- UX, engagement flows
- Ecological value pathways
- Regenerative interaction design

Phase 4—Prototype Build (2–4 months)

- Build minimal viable model (MVM)
- Internal testing
- Data calibration

Phase 5—Ecosystem Pilot (3–6 months)

- Launch in controlled environments
- Gather multi-level impact data

Phase 6—Regenerative Scaling (6–18 months)

- Expand to wider markets
- Add complexity layers
- Multi-stakeholder governance

This blueprint will be used for all five major industry project ideas.

9.7 Industry Project Idea #1 (Expanded Blueprint)

Mycelium-Inspired Loyalty & Customer Well-Being Network

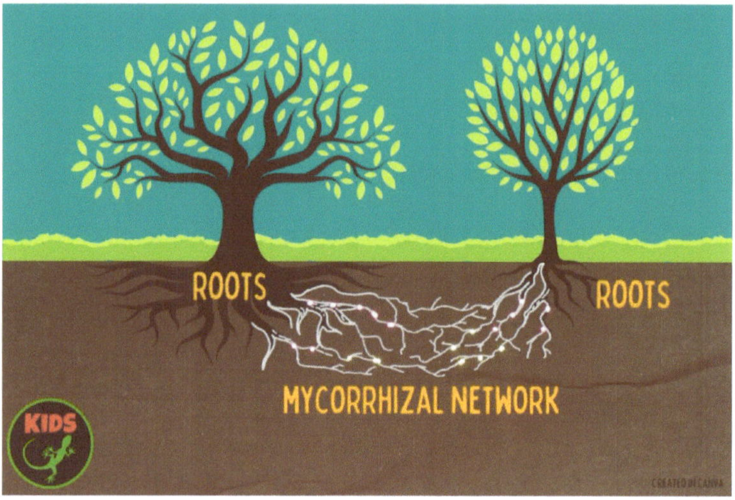

Figure 106: *Mycelium-Inspired Loyalty*

Biological Analogue:

Mycelial intelligence:

- decentralized
- adaptive
- resource-distributing
- stress-detecting

Problem:

Traditional loyalty is:

- transactional
- repetitive
- emotion-blind

Symbiocene Solution:

A loyalty network that:

- distributes rewards to at-risk customers
- supports vulnerable communities

- shares value across clusters
- balances ecosystem health

Technical Architecture:

- Graph neural networks
- Weak-signal anomaly detection
- Dynamic reward routing

Expected Impact:

✓ Lower churn

✓ Higher community belonging

✓ Regenerative brand ecosystems

9.8 Industry Project Idea #2 (Expanded Blueprint)

Bee-Colony-Inspired Autonomous Marketing Resource Planner

Figure 107: *Bee colony*

Biological Analogue:

Bee foraging:

- scouts explore
- foragers collect
- colony self-organizes

Industry Need:

Marketing budgets are misallocated due to:

- delayed feedback
- centralization
- rigid planning

Symbiocene AI Model:

A self-organizing budget allocator that:

- automatically adapts to channel performance
- assigns "scout agents" to new channels
- evolves strategies over time

Tech Stack:

- Multi-agent reinforcement learning
- Evolutionary optimization
- Real-time consensus algorithms

Impact:

✓ Lower waste

✓ Higher ROI

✓ Organic adaptation

✓ Zero micromanagement

9.9 Industry Project Idea #3 (Expanded Blueprint)

Ocean-Current Trend Forecasting Engine

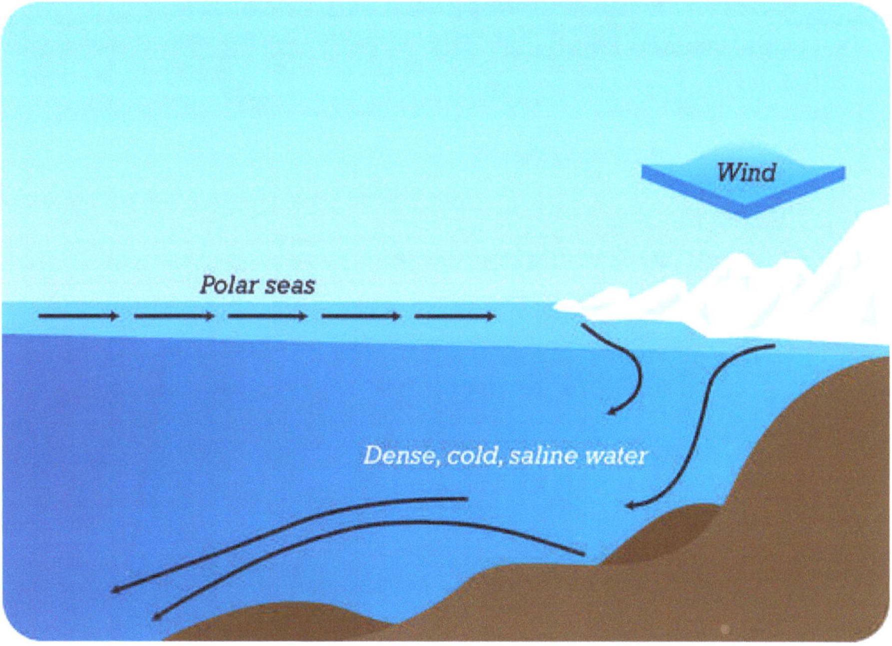

Figure 108: *Ocean-Current Trend Forecasting Engine*

Biological Inspiration:

Ocean systems:

- deep currents
- thermoclines
- upwelling events

Industry Challenge:

Most trend forecasting is shallow:

- surface sentiment
- influencer hot-takes
- short-term virality

Symbiocene Approach:

Detect deeper cultural patterns using:

- drift modeling
- deep-time sentiment mapping
- multi-layered trend currents

AI Techniques:

- Diffusion models
- Hidden Markov Models
- Stochastic drift equations

Impact:

✓ Early detection of long-term shifts

✓ Strategic foresight

✓ Reduced marketing volatility

9.10 Industry Project Idea #4 (Expanded Blueprint)

Plant-Signal Emotional Micro-Engagement Engine

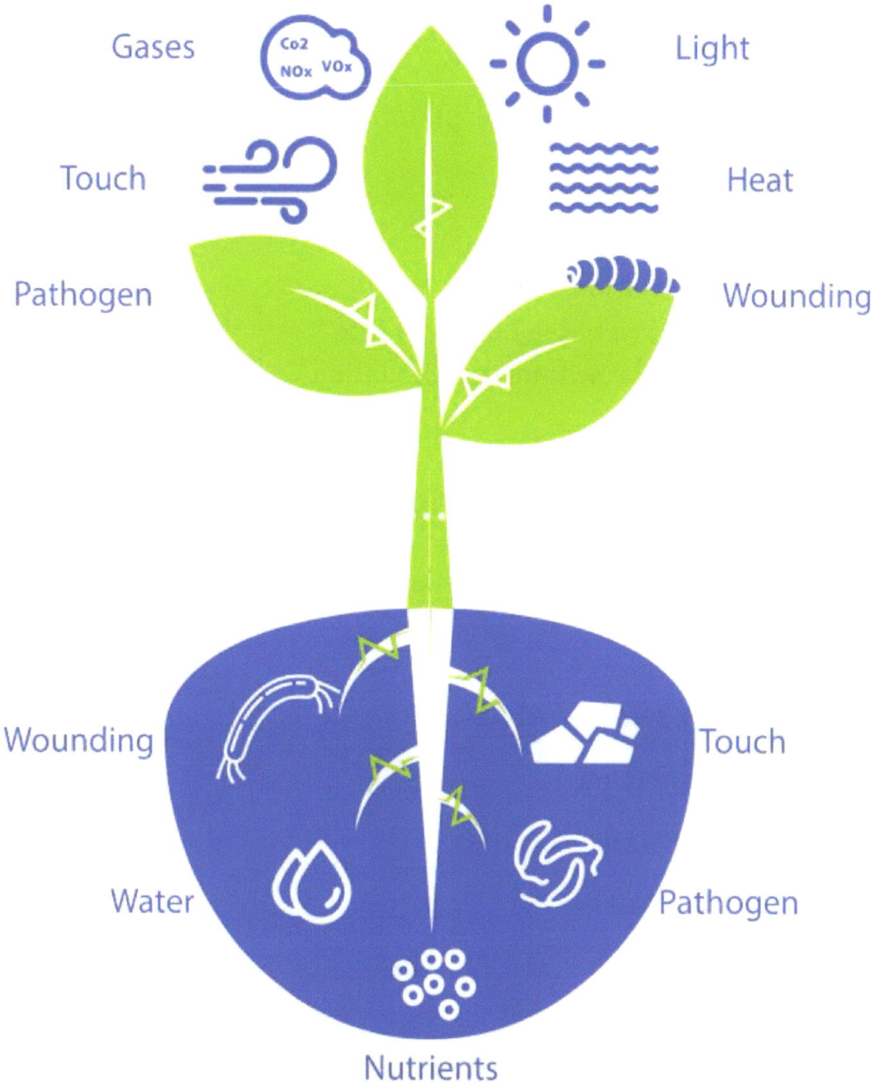

Figure 109: *Plant-Signal Emotional Micro-Engagement Engine*

Biological Analogue:

Plants send:

- electrical pulses
- chemical cues
- micro-stress signals

Symbiocene AI Application:

A passive emotional state interpreter.

Features:

- detect micro-engagement
- identify emotional fatigue
- predict churn based on subtle cues
- adapt content without manipulation

Tech Stack:

- Signal processing
- Micro-behavioral analytics
- Emotional tropism modeling

Impact:

✓ Emotionally sensitive AI

✓ Early risk detection

✓ Non-invasive personalization

9.11 Industry Project Idea #5 (Expanded Blueprint)

Ecosystem Resilience Engine for Market Stability

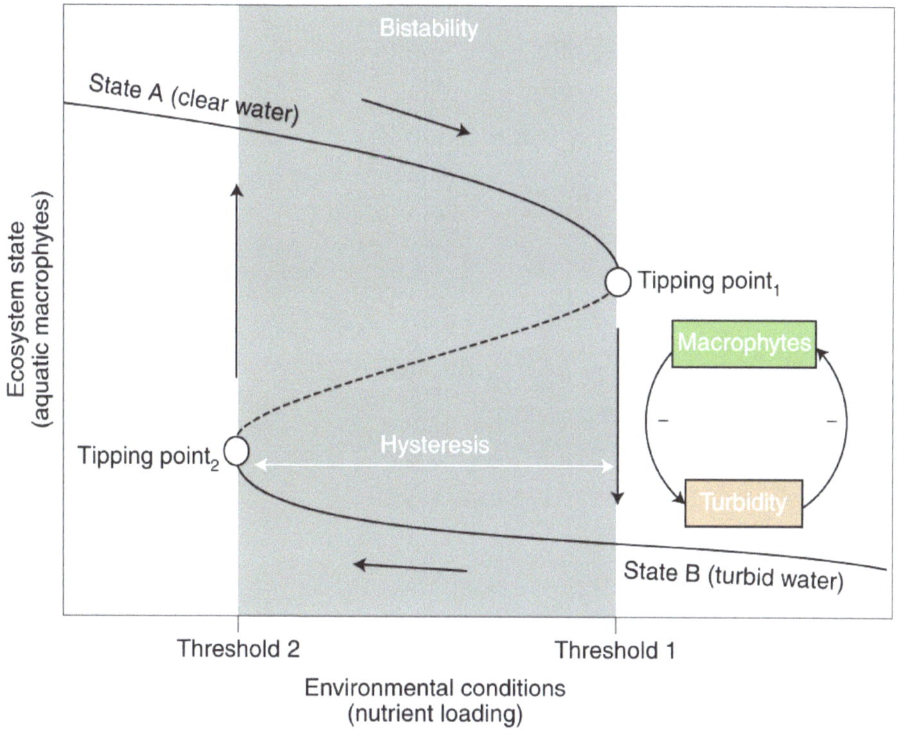

Figure 110: *Ecosystem Resilience Engine for Market Stability*

Biological Inspiration:

Forests, coral reefs, and grasslands use **resilience loops** to:

- prevent collapse
- buffer disturbances
- regenerate after damage

Industry Problem:

Markets collapse without warning:

- A sudden negative trend
- Competitor disruption
- Consumer backlash
- Social media outrage
- Micro-community fragmentation

Symbiocene Solution:

A digital engine that:

- Measures ecosystem health
- Predicts collapse or fragmentation
- Detects tipping points
- Models stability
- Suggests regenerative interventions

AI Techniques:

- Systems dynamics models
- Differential equations
- Network resilience analysis
- Early warning signals (EWS) detection

Outcome:

✓ Industry gains planetary-scale foresight

✓ Markets operate more sustainably

✓ Business planning becomes stability-focused

9.12 Industry Implementation Canvas (10 Dimensions)

This canvas provides a **unified framework** for planning any Symbiocene AI project.

Dimension	Questions to Answer	Examples
1. Biological Inspiration	Which species/system are we modeling?	Bees, fungi, coral reefs
2. Data Sources	What nature-equivalent data do we need?	Weak signals, flows, pulses
3. AI Methods	Which biomimetic algorithms apply?	Swarm RL, GNNs
4. Ecosystem Impact	How does this affect consumer well-being?	Emotional health
5. Community Role	What value flows to the community?	Loyalty, co-creation
6. Planetary Alignment	Does it respect ecological limits?	Net-positive outcomes
7. Ethical Design	How do we prevent manipulation?	Non-extractive personalization
8. Governance	Who oversees project evolution?	Multi-stakeholder boards
9. Metrics	What are the success KPIs?	Flourishing scores
10. Regeneration	How does the project renew itself?	Feedback loops

This canvas becomes the standard playbook for execution.

9.13 Industry Readiness Levels (TRLs) for Symbiocene AI

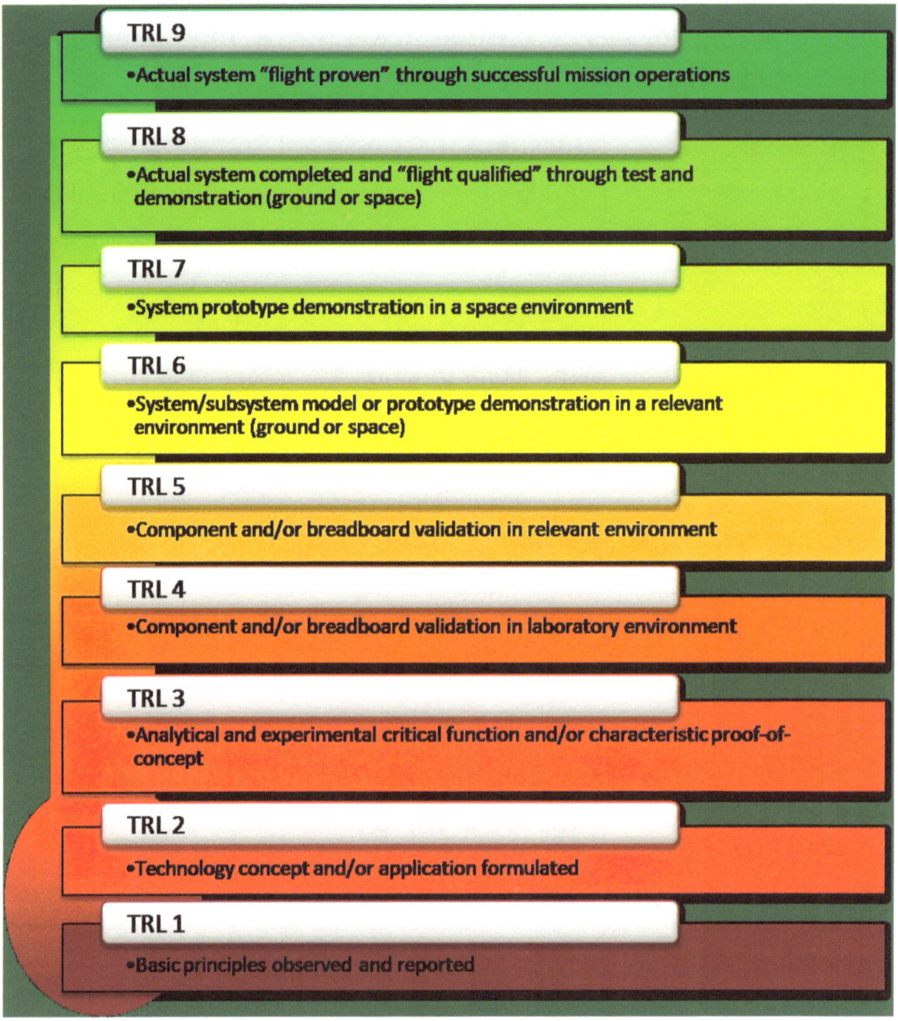

Figure 111: *Industry Readiness Levels (TRL1 to TRL9)*

Symbiocene AI requires a unique maturity model.

TRL 1—Conceptualization

The biological analogue is chosen.

TRL 2—Computational Mapping

Biological processes → algorithms.

TRL 3—Prototype AI Models

Early experiments & simulations.

TRL 4—Controlled Pilot

Testing in limited, ethical environments.

TRL 5—Ecological Scaling

Including community health metrics.

TRL 6—Industry Standardization

Becoming mainstream practice.

TRL 7—Multi-Sector Integration

Cross-industry adoption.

TRL 8—Planetary Systems Integration

Symbiocene AI embedded into global sustainability networks.

TRL 9—Regenerative Intelligence Ecosystems

Self-healing, evolving AI.

9.14 Example Workflow: How a Symbiocene AI Project Moves Through TRLs

Step 1: Inspiration Identification

Team studies ants → identifies "pheromone trails" as engagement analogues.

Step 2: Computational Translation

Use Ant Colony Optimization (ACO).

Step 3: Prototype

Small-scale journey optimizer.

Step 4: Pilot

Test on a 5% user segment.

Step 5: Evaluate Regeneration

Does it reduce emotional friction?
Does it improve well-being?

Step 6: Expand

Roll out system-wide.

Step 7: Regulatory Integration

Align with sustainability policies.

Step 8: Multi-sector scaling

Apply model to retail, health, finance.

Step 9: Regeneratively Evolve

System improves autonomously.

9.15 Academia–Industry Collaboration Structures

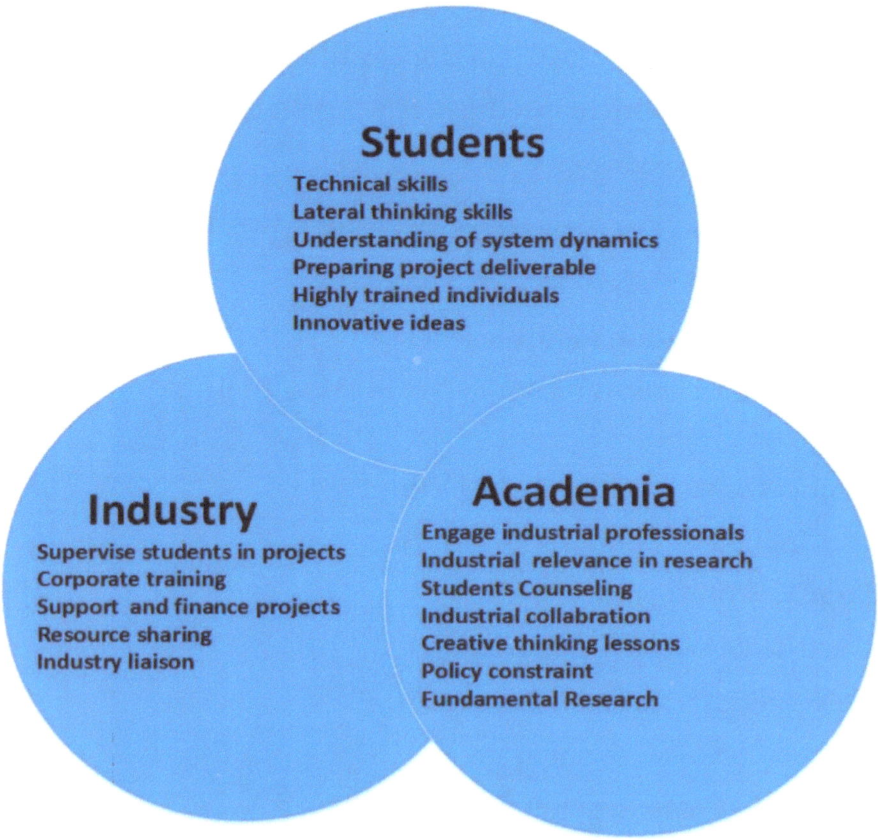

Figure 112: *Academia–Industry Collaboration*

1. Symbiocene Innovation Labs (SILs)

Co-funded by:

- Corporations
- Universities
- Philanthropic foundations

Focus:

- Biomimicry
- Environmental sensing
- AI-for-regeneration

2. Co-Advised PhD Programs

Students split time between:

- corporate AI teams
- university labs

3. Shared Datasets

Including:

- plant electrophysiology
- fungal network mapping
- social ecology patterns

4. Living Laboratories

Use:

- campuses
- retail stores
- smart cities

as test environments.

5. Research Fellowships

Long-term placements aligned with Symbiocene AI.

9.16 Academic Pathway #1

Multi-Species Data Acquisition & Translation Research**

Research Objective:

Create the **world's first academic repository** of:

- plant signals
- animal group behaviors
- fungal communication pulses
- environmental data patterns

Core Activities:

- Field studies
- Bio-logging
- AI-assisted observation
- Bioacoustics data collection

Outputs:

- Open datasets
- Bio-inspired algorithm libraries
- Research papers
- Pipeline tools

A crucial foundation for all future Symbiocene AI systems.

9.17 Academic Pathway #2

Eco-Behavioral Consumer Science

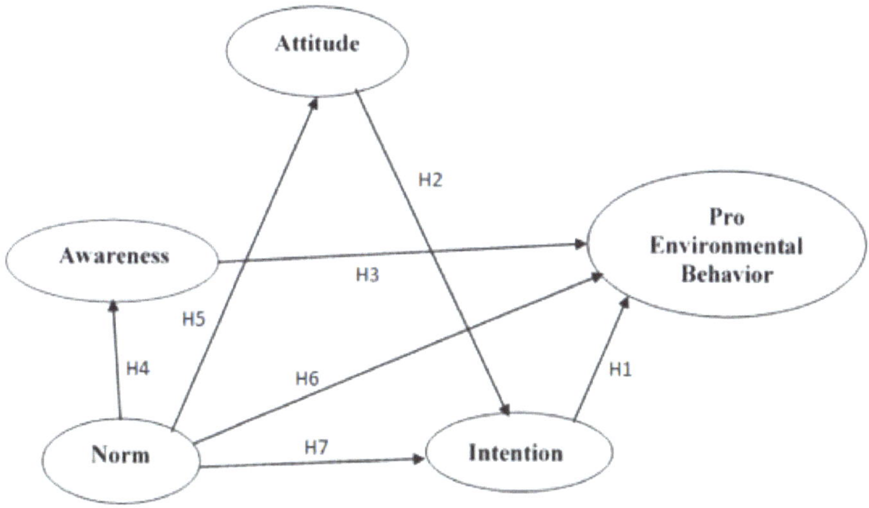

Figure 113: *Eco-Behavioral Consumer Science*

Emerging Research Questions:

1. What ecological metaphors best represent consumer journey dynamics?
2. Do consumers behave like species in a forest or shoals in the sea?
3. How do environmental conditions shape digital behavior?
4. Can ecological stress mapping predict churn or dissatisfaction?

Expected Outcomes:

- Theoretical breakthroughs
- Doctoral dissertations
- New empirical models
- Cross-domain predictive frameworks

This becomes a new branch of marketing science.

9.18 Academic Pathway #3

Regenerative Economics & AI Value Systems**

Traditional economics:

- focuses on extraction
- maximizes consumption
- ignores ecological cost

Regenerative economics:

- is circular
- replenishes resources
- operates within planetary boundaries

Academic Work Includes:

- Designing regenerative value loops
- Modeling consumer flourishing
- Creating ecological KPIs
- Studying multi-species value systems

Output:

A new theoretical foundation for sustainable marketing.

9.19 Academic Pathway #4

Symbiocene AI Governance & Ethics

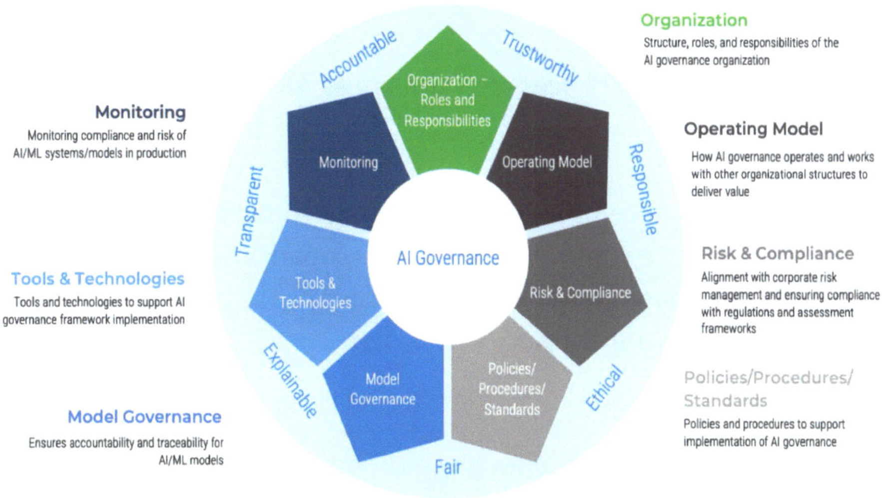

Figure 114: *AI Governance Framework*

Focus:

- AI that protects ecosystems
- Preventing algorithmic harm
- Ensuring emotional well-being
- Embedding multi-species justice

Key Research Questions:

1. What are the moral obligations of AI toward ecosystems?
2. Should AI optimize only for human outcomes?
3. How do we prevent harm from predictive manipulation?
4. How do we re-define consent in ecological AI systems?

Outputs:

- Policy frameworks
- AI ethics curricula
- Regulatory models
- Industry charters

9.20 Academic Pathway #5

Evolutionary, Swarm & Biomimetic Algorithms for Business Systems

Objective:

Translate biological processes → business AI.

Research Themes:

- Multi-agent reinforcement learning from ants
- Evolutionary optimization for personalization
- Swarm search for content discovery
- Fungal routing for network design

Outputs:

- Open-source algorithm libraries
- Benchmark datasets
- Cross-disciplinary science
- Applied AI frameworks

9.21 The Seven Symbiocene AI Design Principles for Industry

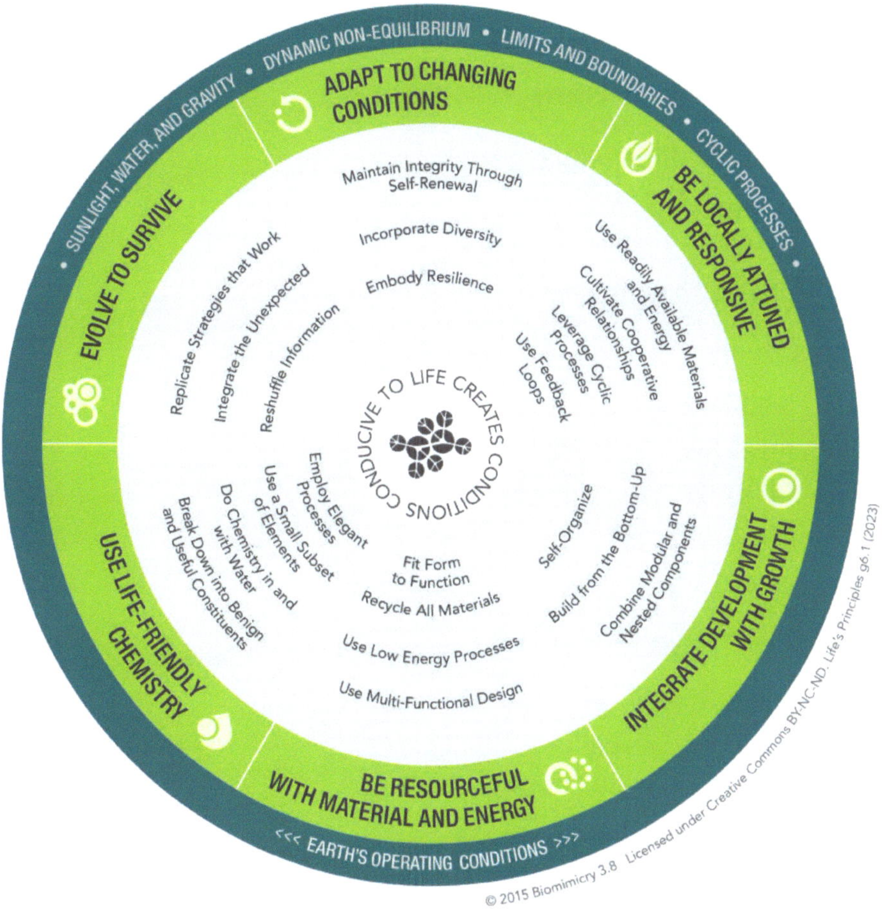

Figure 115: *Symbiocene AI Design Principles for Industry*

Every Symbiocene AI system must follow **seven design principles** to ensure ecological, emotional, and social harmony.

1. Design for Mutual Benefit (Mutualism)

People → benefit
Brands → benefit
Planet → benefit

No system should:

- drain user emotion
- exploit cognitive biases
- degrade ecosystems

2. Design for Flourishing, Not Addiction

Instead of maximizing:

- screen time
- scrolling
- attention capture

Symbiocene systems maximize:

- well-being
- meaning
- fulfilment
- community health

3. Design for Ecological Transparency

The system must reveal:

- why it made decisions
- ecological impacts
- emotional implications

4. Design for Interdependence

Systems must:

- incorporate networks
- account for community dynamics
- model ecological relationships

5. Design for Regeneration

Each interaction should:

- strengthen user confidence
- enhance community trust
- reduce emotional fatigue

6. Design for Adaptability

Like ecosystems, systems must:

- evolve
- diversify
- change with context

7. Design for Stewardship

AI should act as a *guardian* of:

- user well-being
- community ecosystems
- emotional health
- environmental boundaries

This is the ethical backbone of Symbiocene AI.

9.22 The Symbiocene AI Technology Stack (SATS)

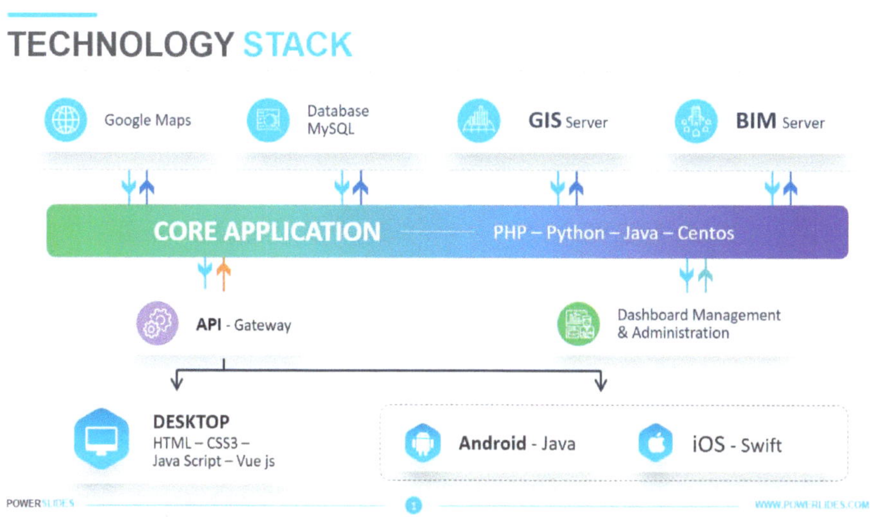

Figure 116: *Symbiocene AI Technology Stack*

The SATS framework helps organizations understand the layers necessary for ecological AI implementation.

Layer 1—Nature-Inspired Behavioral Models

From:

- swarms
- fungal networks
- ecosystems
- plant signalling
- animal cognition

Provides the logic.

Layer 2—Ecological Data Infrastructure

Including:

- environmental sensors
- micro-engagement detectors
- community network analyses
- emotional ecology mapping

Layer 3—Biomimetic AI Engines

Algorithms such as:

- swarm RL
- evolutionary neural nets
- ecological forecasting systems
- multi-agent behavioral models

Layer 4—Regenerative Experience Layer

UX systems that:

- support autonomy
- lower friction
- restore emotional energy

Layer 5—Ecosystem Governance Layer

AI + human oversight systems for:

- emotional safety
- ecological thresholds
- community health

9.23 Operational Ecosystem Model (OEM) for Symbiocene AI

The OEM defines the operational structure for deploying and maintaining Symbiocene AI.

1. Ecosystem Actors

- consumers
- brand managers
- data scientists
- ecologists
- community representatives
- policy specialists

2. Resource Flows

What flows across the system?

- emotional energy
- attention
- value
- trust
- ecological impact
- cultural influence

3. Feedback Loops

Continuous loops include:

- community sentiment → system adaptation
- user behavior → regenerative reinforcement
- ecosystem stress → algorithmic intervention

4. System Boundaries

Set rules around:

- privacy
- consent
- ecological harm prevention
- emotional safety

5. Regenerative Outputs

The system outputs:

- community uplift
- emotional flourishing
- sustainable consumption
- ecological awareness

This model operationalizes Symbiocene thinking.

9.24 The 3-Level Ecosystem Governance Model

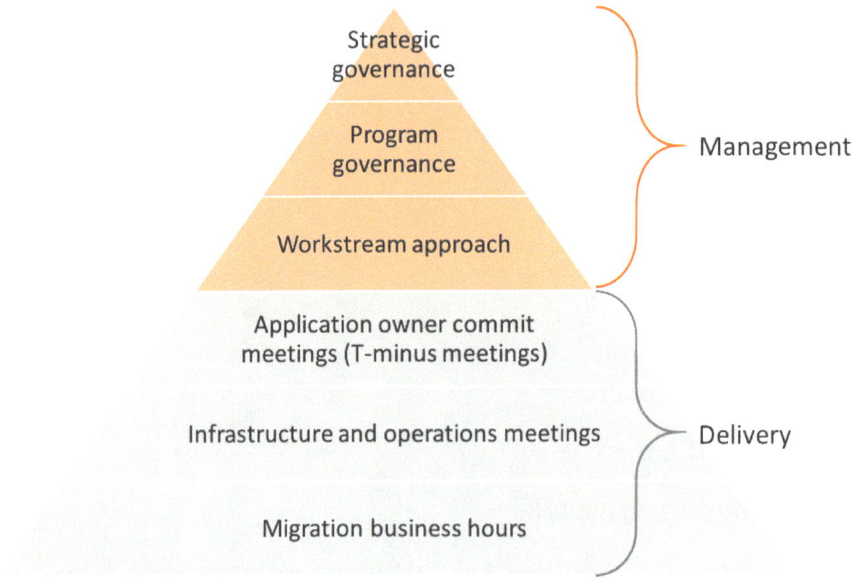

Figure 117: *3-Level Ecosystem Governance Model*

Symbiocene AI requires a **novel governance structure**, unlike traditional AI oversight.

LEVEL 1—Technical Governance

Focused on:

- algorithm accuracy
- fairness
- transparency

Managed by:

- data scientists
- AI engineers

LEVEL 2—Ecological Governance

Ensures:

- emotional well-being
- sustainability
- non-extraction
- ecological alignment

Managed by:

- ecologists
- sustainability leaders
- emotional well-being researchers

LEVEL 3—Planetary Governance

Ensures alignment with:

- planetary boundaries
- biodiversity
- climate commitments

Managed by:

- policymakers
- NGOs
- global consortiums

This ensures Symbiocene AI is safe across multiple dimensions.

9.25 Symbiocene AI Workflow Diagram

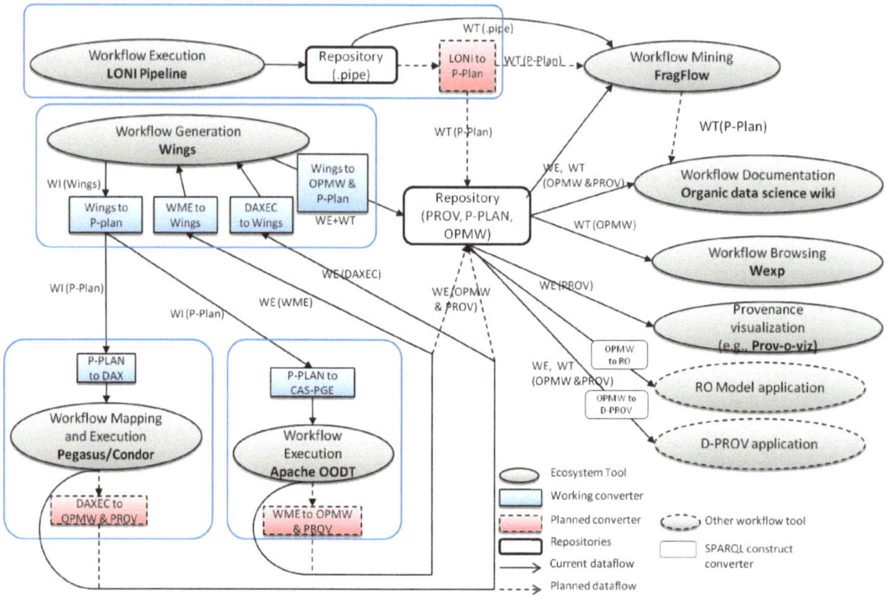

Figure 118: *Symbiocene AI Workflow Diagram*

Workflow Steps:

1. Observe Nature
2. Extract Principles
3. Abstract Computational Logic
4. Build AI Engine
5. Design Regenerative UX Layer
6. Run Ecosystem Simulation Tests
7. Deploy to Controlled Environments
8. Gather Ecological & Emotional Signals
9. Iterate
10. Scale
11. Govern

This flow ensures no harmful or extractive AI reaches users.

9.26 The Consumer–Ecosystem Interaction Map

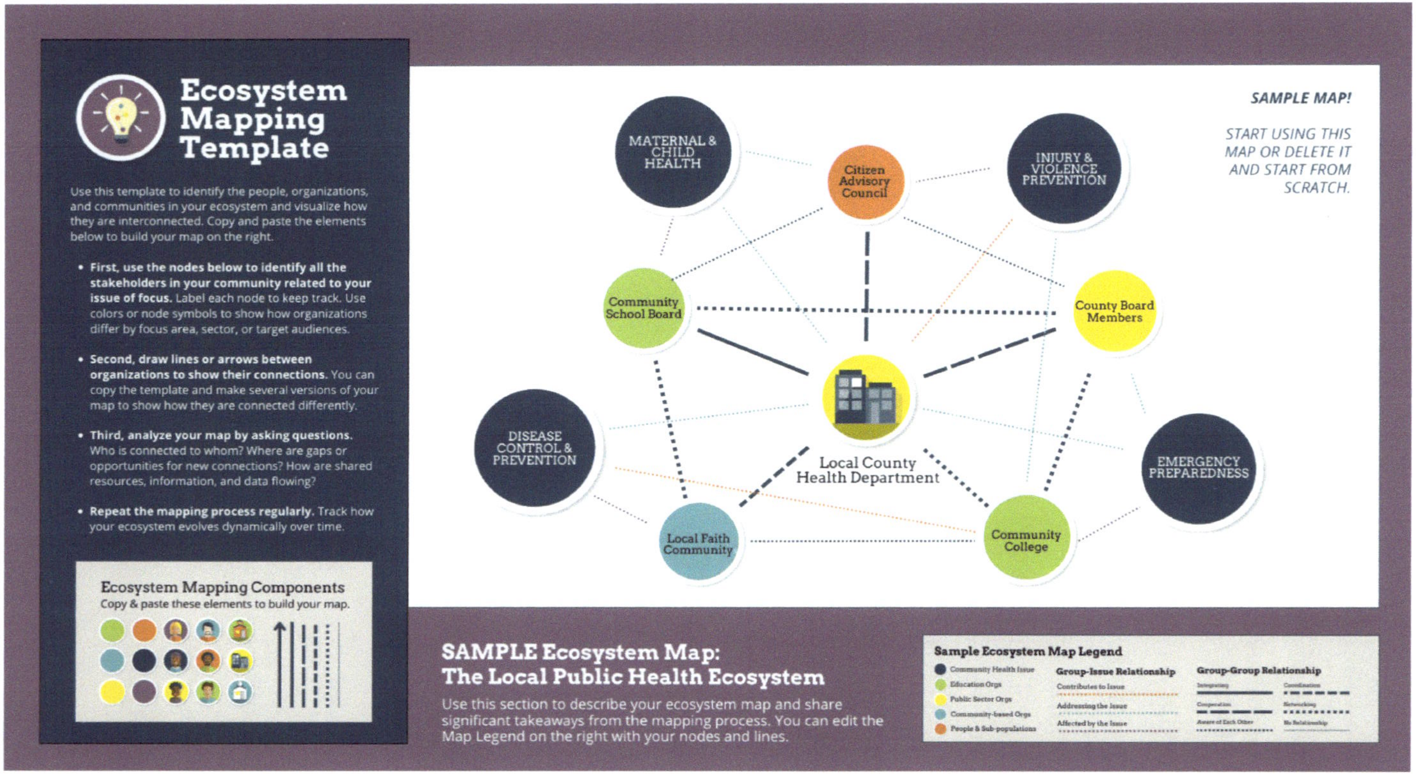

Figure 119: *Consumer–Ecosystem Interaction Map*

This map explains how consumers interact with Symbiocene AI systems.

1. Individual Level

- emotional state
- cognitive load
- micro-engagement
- personal values

2. Community Level

- shared identity
- social sentiment
- peer influence
- collective behavior patterns

3. Ecosystem Level

- platform health
- content ecology
- value flows
- system stability

4. Planetary Level

- carbon impact
- resource footprint
- environmental responsibility
- long-term sustainability

This multi-layer interaction map is key for inclusive, holistic AI design.

9.27 Blueprint for Cross-Disciplinary Teams

Symbiocene AI projects cannot be built by AI engineers alone.

Team Makeup:

1. AI Scientists

- ML specialists
- deep learning architects
- reinforcement learning engineers

2. Ecologists

- understand animal, plant, fungal systems
- translate ecological dynamics

3. Cognitive Scientists

- map human emotional tendencies
- prevent harm

4. Behavioral Economists

- understand choice patterns
- build non-manipulative designs

5. UX Designers

- design regenerative interactions
- reduce emotional friction

6. Ethicists

- ensure multi-species justice
- review ecological impact

7. Community Representatives

- ensure cultural alignment
- provide lived experience

8. Indigenous Knowledge Holders

- bring traditional ecological wisdom
- ensure multicultural perspectives

This combination is non-negotiable for Symbiocene systems.

9.28 The 6-R Model of Regenerative Experience Design (RXD)

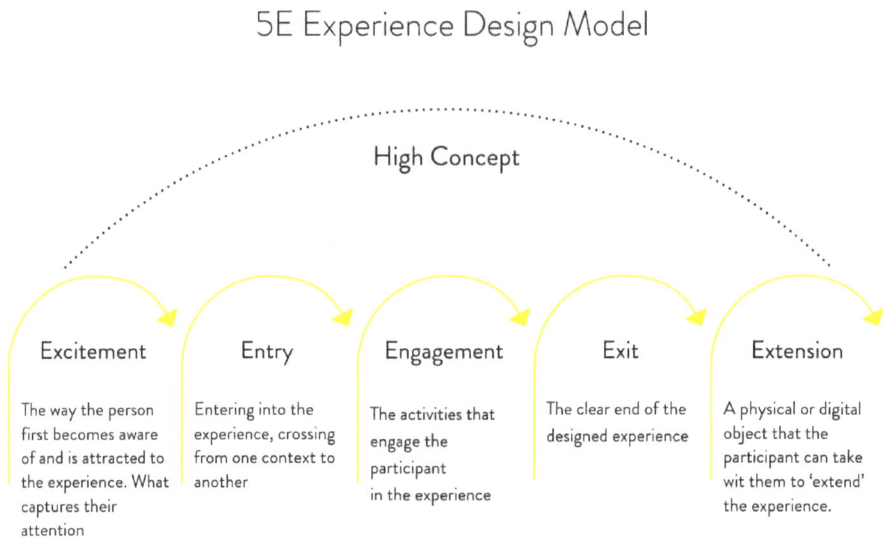

Figure 120: *6-R Model of Regenerative Experience Design*

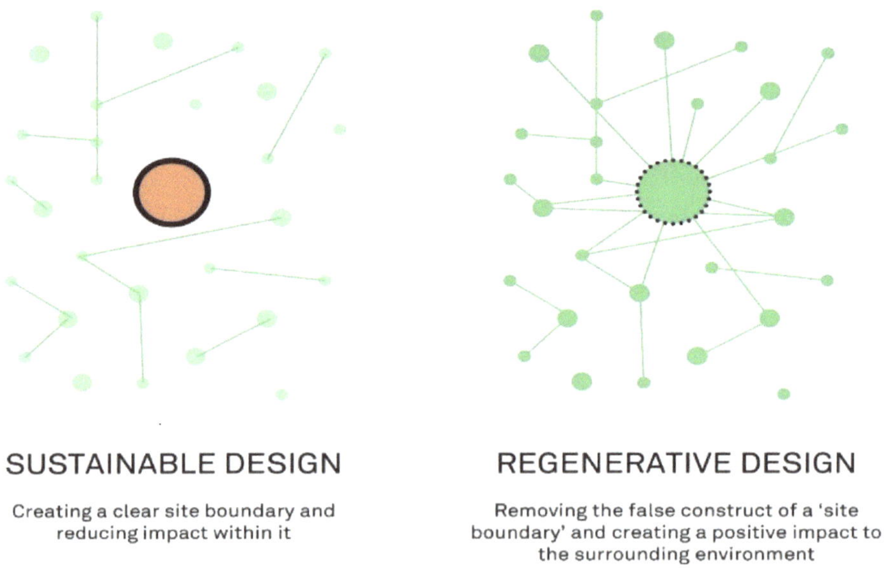

Figure 121: *6-R Model of Regenerative Experience Design*

Every user interaction must follow the "6-R" criteria:

1. Reduce Harm

UI avoids:

- overstimulation
- addictive loops
- cognitive overload

2. Restore Capacity

Interaction replenishes:

- focus
- clarity
- emotional balance

3. Reconnect to Meaning

UI nudges towards:

- purposeful choices
- value-based decisions

4. Regulate Stress

Experience reduces:

- friction
- anxiety
- overwhelm

5. Rebalance Ecosystems

Promotes:

- community harmony
- fair participation

6. Regenerate Well-Being

Provides:

- psychological nourishment
- long-term satisfaction

This is the emotional philosophy of Symbiocene UX.

9.29 The Symbiocene KPI Dashboard (Prototype)

This dashboard contains ecological + emotional + technological KPIs.

KPI Categories:

1. **Emotional Health KPIs**
    - fatigue score
    - frustration index
    - emotional recovery rate
2. **Community KPIs**
    - harmony score
    - polarization risk
    - collaborative engagement
3. **Ecosystem KPIs**
    - churn prediction
    - stability index
    - value flow balance
4. **Environmental KPIs**
    - carbon impact
    - sustainable consumption index

5. **Ethical KPIs**
    - autonomy protection
    - consent integrity
6. **Regeneration KPIs**
    - well-being uplift
    - community growth rate

This dashboard is standard for all Symbiocene AI deployments.

9.30 The Symbiocene Algorithmic Safety Matrix

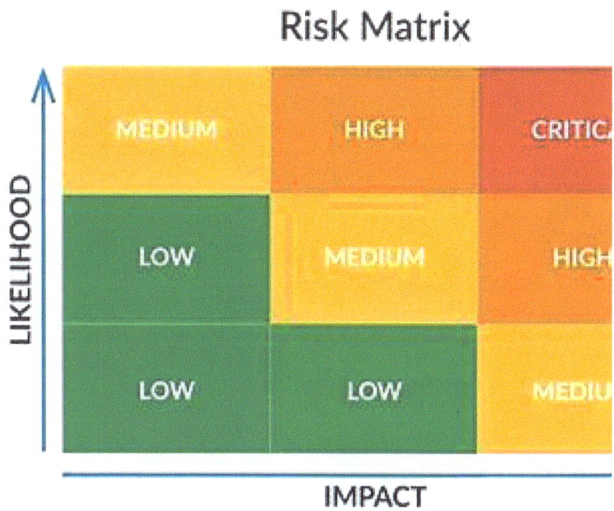

Figure 122: *Symbiocene Algorithmic Safety Matrix*

The matrix assesses:

- safety
- ecological impact
- emotional health
- community stability

Four Quadrants:

Quadrant	**Description**	**Acceptability**
Q1—Regenerative	Improves well-being & ecology	Fully acceptable
Q2—Neutral	Neither harms nor helps ecology	Conditional
Q3—Extractive	Drains attention/emotion	Prohibited
Q4—Harmful	Damages ecosystems or communities	Unacceptable

Every AI system must be tested across all four quadrants before release.

9.31 The Symbiocene Data Architecture (SDA)

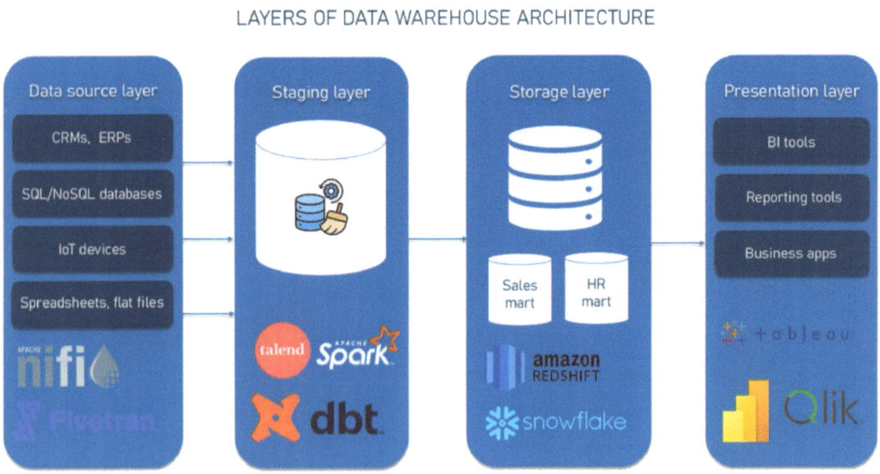

Figure 123: *The Symbiocene Data Architecture (SDA)*

Symbiocene AI requires a **new type of data architecture** that blends:

- ecological data
- emotional data
- behavioral data

- environmental data
- community dynamics

Traditional databases cannot capture:

- subtle micro-signals
- multi-species analogues
- ecological relationships
- regeneration loops

Thus, we introduce the SDA framework.

Layer 1—Sensorial Layer

Captures micro-signals:

- micro-engagement
- pauses
- hesitation
- frustration
- environmental conditions

Equivalent to:

- plant electrophysiology
- animal bioacoustics
- fungal signal pulses

Layer 2—Contextual Layer

Captures:

- location
- environmental quality
- device state
- emotional context

9.32 Symbiocene Data Architecture (SDA)—Layer 2 & 3

Layer 2—Contextual Ecology Layer

Just as ecosystems change with:

- humidity
- light
- temperature
- stress

Consumers change with digital context:

- time of day
- device conditions
- emotional state
- social climate
- environmental triggers

This layer captures:

- cognitive load
- situational stress
- emotional context
- environmental background (noise, light, weather)
- platform micro-environment

It mirrors **ecological situational awareness**.

Layer 3—Community & Network Layer

Inspired by:

- ant colony cooperation
- bee hive communication
- coral reef interdependence

This layer captures:

- group influence patterns
- micro-community sentiment
- cluster migrations
- influencer role shifts
- network cohesion/fragmentation

It transforms consumer behavior from "individual" → **ecosystemic**.

9.33 SDA Layers 4–6: Bringing Ecology Into AI

Layer 4—Ecological State Layer

Mirrors:

- ecosystem stress
- biodiversity health
- resilience scores

Digitally, this layer measures:

- emotional ecosystem stability
- value distribution fairness
- community trust
- content toxicity
- attention pollution

This replaces simple metrics like "CTR" with **ecosystem well-being metrics**.

Layer 5—Regenerative Intelligence Layer

This is where the AI:

- learns
- adapts
- evolves
- self-regulates

Using:

- evolutionary algorithms
- multi-agent reinforcement learning
- ecological feedback loops
- stability modeling

This layer ensures:

- no over-optimization
- no manipulation
- no extractive logic

The AI behaves like a **living system**.

Layer 6—Planetary Impact Layer

Measures:

- carbon impact of engagement
- sustainable consumption patterns
- long-term ecological footprint
- planetary boundary alignment

This ensures AI aligns with:

- climate science
- ecological ethics
- intergenerational fairness

9.34 Diagram: Symbiocene Data Architecture (SDA)

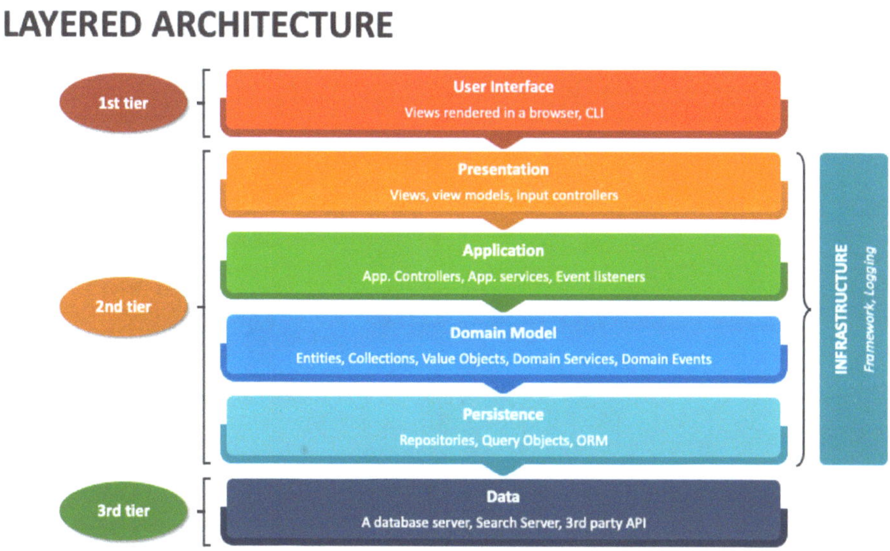

Figure 124: *The Symbiocene Data Architecture (SDA)*

SDA STACK OVERVIEW

1. Micro-Signal Layer
2. Contextual Ecology Layer
3. Community Dynamics Layer
4. Ecological State Layer
5. Regenerative Intelligence Layer
6. Planetary Impact Layer

This layered architecture forms the backbone of all future Symbiocene AI deployments.

9.35 Implementing SDA in Industry: 7-Step Execution Framework

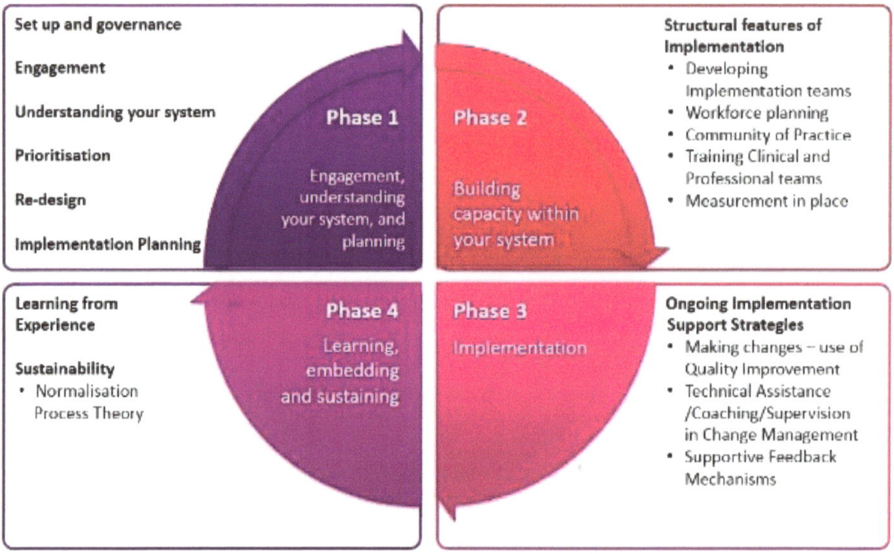

Figure 125: *Implementing SDA in Industry*

Step 1—Ecological Data Mapping

Identify what nature-inspired signals the company should collect.

Step 2—Multi-Source Data Integration

Merge emotional, behavioral, environmental, and community datasets.

Step 3—Ecological Feature Engineering

Create features such as:

- emotional resilience score
- attention integrity index
- community harmony metric

Step 4—Regenerative Objective Functions

Replace accuracy + profit maximization with:

- well-being
- fairness
- sustainability
- ecosystem stability

Step 5—Ecological AI Model Training

Train models using:

- swarm optimization
- evolutionary selection
- ecological simulations

Step 6—Ethical & Planetary Validation

Check for:

- emotional safety
- ecological alignment
- community harmony

Step 7—Regenerative Deployment

Deploy with real-time feedback loops.

9.36 The Ecological KPI System (EKPIS)

Figure 126: *The Ecological KPI System*

Symbiocene AI requires a **completely new KPI paradigm**.

1. Emotional Ecology KPIs

- Emotional Recovery Rate (ERR)
- Cognitive Load Balance (CLB)
- Micro-Fatigue Score (MFS)

2. Community Ecosystem KPIs

- Harmony Index
- Trust Stability Curve
- Community Regeneration Score

3. Attention Ecology KPIs

- Attention Integrity Ratio (AIR)
- Overstimulation Risk Index

4. Sustainability KPIs

- Carbon per Engagement Unit
- Sustainable Consumption Score

5. Ethical KPIs

- Autonomy Preservation Rate
- Transparency Satisfaction Score

These metrics ensure AI supports human and planetary well-being.

9.37 The Symbiocene Systems Maturity Model (SSMM)

LEVEL 1—Awareness

Company understands Symbiocene concepts.

No implementation.

LEVEL 2—Experimentation

Small prototypes inspired by:

- swarms
- fungal routing
- plant signals

LEVEL 3—Integration

Symbiocene AI integrated into:

- loyalty
- engagement
- analytics

LEVEL 4—Transformation

Business transforms into a **regenerative ecosystem**.

LEVEL 5—Ecosystem Stewardship

Company becomes:

- ecological guardian
- regenerative leader
- global influence hub

This is the maturity roadmap.

9.38 The Symbiocene Risk Framework (SRF)

Impact →

Likelihood ↑	Negligible	Minor	Moderate	Significant	Severe
Very Likely	Low Med	Medium	Med Hi	High	High
Likely	Low	Low Med	Medium	Med Hi	High
Possible	Low	Low Med	Medium	Med Hi	Med Hi
Unlikely	Low	Low Med	Low Med	Medium	Med Hi
Very Unlikely	Low	Low	Low Med	Medium	Medium

Figure 127: *Symbiocene Risk Framework*

Symbiocene AI must analyze **five categories of risk**:

1. Emotional Exploitation Risk

Does the AI manipulate emotions?

2. Ecological Extraction Risk

Does the AI maximize behaviors that harm the planet?

3. Community Fragmentation Risk

Does the system produce:

- polarization
- toxicity
- community breakdown?

4. Autonomy Erosion Risk

Does the AI undermine:

- free choice
- user agency

5. Planetary Misalignment Risk

Do consumption patterns exceed:

- carbon thresholds?
- resource boundaries?

A Symbiocene system must stay in the LOW-RISK zone for all categories.

9.39 The 9 Ethical Rules for Symbiocene AI

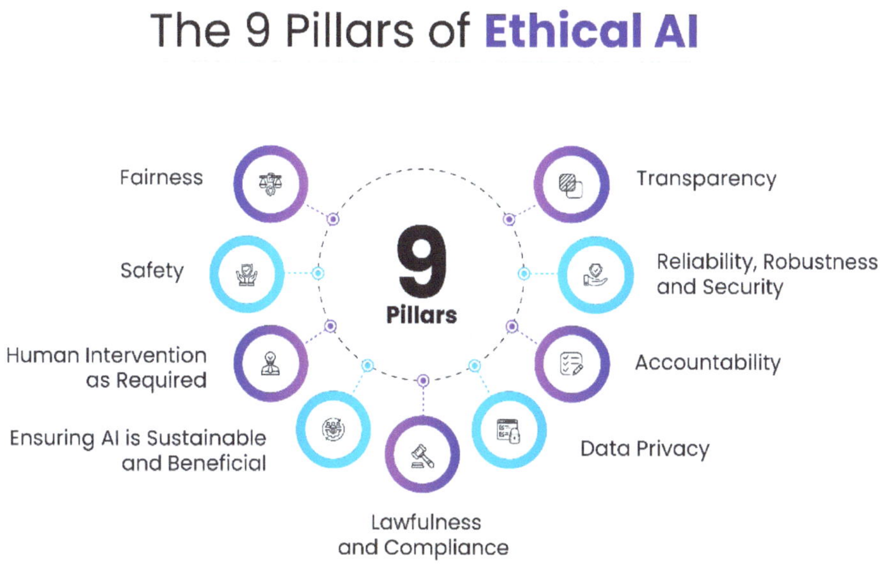

Figure 128: *Ethical Rules for Symbiocene AI*

1. Do No Ecological Harm
2. Do No Emotional Harm
3. Preserve Autonomy

4. Reduce Cognitive Load
5. Avoid Over-Optimization
6. Minimize Manipulation
7. Prioritize Community Well-Being
8. Design for Regeneration
9. Respect Planetary Boundaries
10. Ensure Value Reciprocity
11. Support Flourishing and Meaning
12. Evolve Ethically Over Time

These rules act as a **constitution** for Symbiocene AI systems.

9.40 The Symbiocene Ecosystem Simulator (SES)

SES is a simulation environment for AI–ecosystem testing, using:

1. Agent-Based Models

Simulate:

- users
- communities
- influencers
- brands

2. Emotional Ecology Maps

Capture:

- emotional signals
- community mood shifts
- stress propagation

3. Ecological Stress Tests

Test how the AI behaves under:

- viral content storms
- community polarization

- misinformation attacks
- trend shocks

4. Regenerative Cycle Validation

Confirm whether:

- the system heals itself
- the ecosystem stabilizes
- trust regenerates

SES is mandatory before deployment of Symbiocene AI.

9.41 Building a Real Symbiocene AI Project: Full Roadmap

This section combines everything from earlier parts into a **single implementable blueprint** that industry can start *tomorrow*.

PHASE 1—Ecological Inspiration & Translation (Month 0–2)

Teams identify which natural intelligence will inspire the model:

- **Fungal networks** → loyalty, retention
- **Bee swarms** → resource allocation
- **Plant signalling** → emotional detection
- **Marine ecosystems** → trend forecasting
- **Ecosystem resilience** → market stability

Deliverables:

- Biological principle documentation
- Ecological–AI translation matrix
- Problem framing

9.42 PHASE 2: Data Ecosystem & SDA Implementation (Month 2–4)

Teams construct the **Symbiocene Data Architecture (SDA)**:

- Micro-signal detection
- Emotional context mapping
- Community network analysis
- Ecological & sustainability indicators
- Planetary impact metrics

Required Data Types:

Data Type	Nature Analogue	Examples
Behavioral	Animal movement	click patterns, scroll behavior
Emotional	Plant signals	hesitation, micro-friction
Community	Coral/forest layers	cluster shifts, group sentiment
Ecological	Climate cycles	consumption phases
Planetary	Ecosystem balance	carbon impact per action

Deliverables:

- SDA 6-layer data model
- Data ingestion pipelines
- Context + community graphs

9.43 PHASE 3: Algorithmic Development & Ecosystem Modeling (Month 4–9)

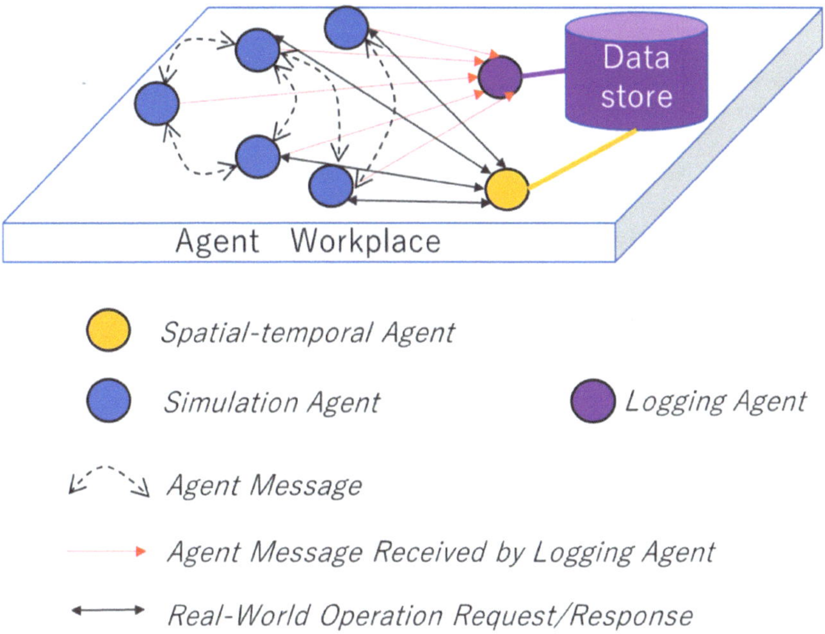

Figure 129: *Algorithmic Development & Ecosystem Modeling*

Models Used:

1. Multi-Agent Reinforcement Learning (MARL)

For:

- swarm systems
- resource allocation
- multi-channel optimization

2. Evolutionary Algorithms

For:

- personalization
- segmentation
- emergent strategy discovery

3. Graph Neural Networks (GNNs)

For:

- community mapping
- loyalty ecosystems
- value network modeling

4. Ecological Differential Equations

Used analogously to:

- predator–prey models
- resilience curves
- tipping point detection

5. Emotional Signal Models

Based on:

- HMM
- sequence modeling
- neural oscillation mapping

Deliverables:

- Functional prototype
- Agent-based simulation output
- Safety & regeneration metrics

9.44 PHASE 4: Regenerative Experience Architecture (Month 9–12)

This stage transforms the model into an **actual user experience**.

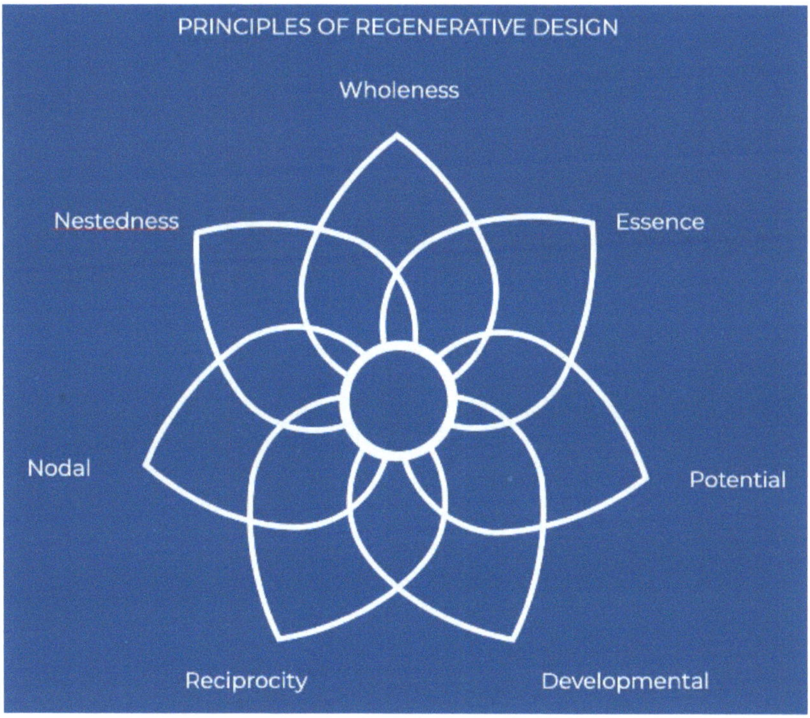

Figure 130: *Regenerative Experience Architecture*

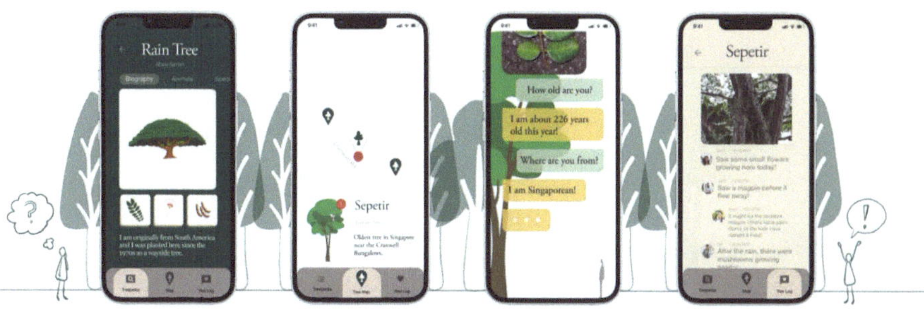

Figure 131: *Regenerative Experience Architecture*

Design Layers:

1. **Emotional restoration**
    - calming visual states
    - reduced overload
2. **Cognitive relief**
    - simplified journeys
    - friction reduction
3. **Regenerative content**
    - intention-based recommendations
    - healthier digital patterns
4. **Planet-aware nudges**
    - low carbon options
    - ethical consumption cues
5. **Community uplift mechanics**
    - collaborative loops
    - contribution-based rewards

Deliverables:

- Symbiocene UX Design System
- Emotional Ecology Interface Guide
- Beta interface & feedback

9.45 PHASE 5: Pilot Deployment in Digital Ecosystems (Month 12–18)

Pilot Environments:

- A retail brand's loyalty app
- A media platform

- An e-commerce interface
- A smart city dashboard
- A banking app for sustainable finance

Testing Criteria:

A. Emotional Ecology KPIs

- Cognitive Load Reduction
- Recovery Time
- Emotional Stability Index

B. Community KPIs

- Harmony Score
- Engagement Resilience
- Community Cohesion

C. Ecosystem KPIs

- Churn reduction
- Loyalty flow rates
- Multi-touchpoint resilience

D. Planetary KPIs

- Sustainable consumption shifts
- Carbon-conscious engagement patterns

Deliverables:

- Pilot report
- Model refinement loops
- Safety audit

9.46 PHASE 6: Regenerative Scaling & Ecosystem Integration (Month 18–24)

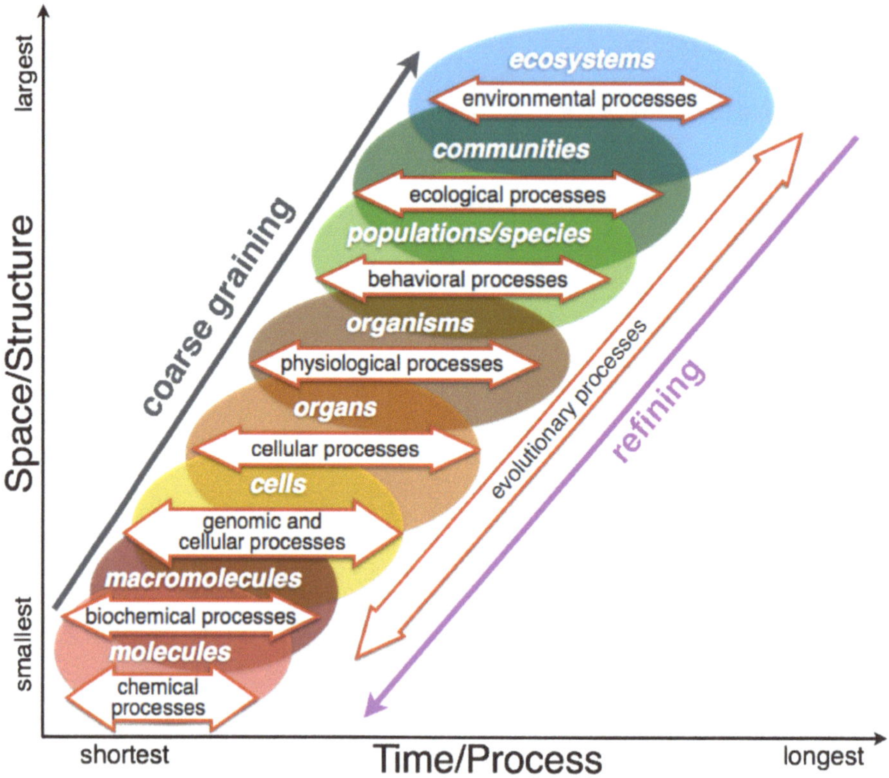

Figure 131: *Regenerative Scaling & Ecosystem Integration*

Scaling Principles:

1. **Slow, ecological scaling**

   Scaling must not destabilize the ecosystem.

2. **Feedback-based evolution**

   Continuous learning from:

   - emotional patterns
   - cultural shifts
   - ecological impacts

3. **Community co-governance**

   Users act as stakeholders.

4. **Planetary stewardship alignment**

   Carbon, biodiversity, and sustainability are integrated at the model level.

5. **Symbiotic economic loops**

   Value flows back into:

   - communities
   - environment

Deliverables:

- Full-scale rollout
- Governance charter
- Cross-industry partnerships

Project: Fungal-Network-Inspired Loyalty & Well-Being System

PROJECT OVERVIEW

Create a loyalty system inspired by **mycelium intelligence** that:

- detects early signs of customer dissatisfaction
- reallocates rewards to strengthen weak relationships
- distributes value fairly across communities
- reduces emotional friction
- regenerates trust

BUSINESS OUTCOME

- Reduce churn by 25–40%
- Increase loyalty by 20–30%
- Increase emotional well-being markers by 2×
- Build community-driven retention

DATA REQUIRED

- micro-behavior signals
- emotional friction patterns
- community network maps
- ecological consumption patterns

AI COMPONENTS

- GNN for loyalty graphs
- MARL for adaptive reward distribution
- Weak-signal anomaly detectors
- Emotional ecology models

ALGORITHMIC FLOW

1. Detect weak nodes (customers at risk)
2. Strengthen edges (relationships)

3. Redistribute nutrients (rewards)
4. Regenerate the network (loyalty cycles)

Solutions

1. Graph Neural Network (GNN)

For modeling:

- customer relationships
- community clusters
- resilience patterns

Mathematical Form:

$$H^{(k+1)} = \sigma(AH^{(k)}W^{(k)})$$

2. Multi-Agent Reinforcement Learning (MARL)

For resource allocation.

Each agent maximizes:

$$R = \alpha L + \beta E + \gamma S$$

Where:

- **L** = loyalty uplift
- **E** = emotional well-being
- **S** = sustainability impact

3. Signal-Processing for Emotional Micro-Patterns

Using:

- FFT
- HMM
- LSTM
- Wavelet transforms

For detecting:

- micro-stress
- hesitation
- emotional fatigue

4. Ecological Forecasting Models

Based on:

- Lotka–Volterra equations
- resilience curves
- tipping point analysis

Used for:

- churn prediction
- market collapse risk

5. Regenerative Optimization

Objective:

$$max\ (CFI + ESS + EWBM)$$

Where:

- CFI = Community Flourishing Index
- ESS = Ecosystem Stability Score
- EWBM = Emotional Well-Being Metric

MCQs

1. Which Symbiocene layer detects micro-emotional signals?

    A. Community layer
    B. Sensory micro-signal layer
    C. Regenerative layer
    D. Ecology layer

2. MARL is used because Symbiocene AI requires:

    A. Linear optimization
    B. Isolated agent decisions
    C. Multi-agent cooperation
    D. Static modeling

3. Fungal networks inspire which feature?

    A. Journey simplification
    B. Adaptive reward routing
    C. Push notifications
    D. Price optimization

4. Which KPI measures emotional ecosystem health?

    A. CTR
    B. Recovery Time
    C. CAC
    D. ROAS

5. The purpose of ecological simulations is:

    A. UI testing
    B. Predict ecosystem behavior
    C. Improve GPU usage
    D. Train text models

6. “Regenerative optimization” maximizes:

    A. Profit
    B. Engagement
    C. Well-being + stability
    D. Display time

7. The planetary layer measures:

    A. Carbon impact
    B. Likes
    C. Scroll depth
    D. Session time

8. Bee colony intelligence contributes to:

    A. Deepfake generation
    B. Autonomous resource allocation
    C. CAPTCHA solving
    D. UI coloring

9. Lotka–Volterra models are used for:

    A. Trend virality
    B. Search ranking
    C. Ecosystem stability
    D. UI animation

10. A fungal-inspired system prioritizes:

    A. Competition
    B. Extraction
    C. Cooperation
    D. More ads

11. GNNs are best for:

    A. Single-user sequences
    B. Grid images
    C. Networked relationships
    D. Audio files

12. Emotional micro-patterns can be detected with:

    A. SQL
    B. FFT
    C. JPEG
    D. PNG

13. The Symbiocene principle “Do No Harm” refers to:

    A. Data size
    B. Ecological & emotional protection
    C. Maximizing impressions
    D. Promoting impulse buying

14. Ecological KPIs track:

    A. Stock market
    B. Churn prediction
    C. Page load time
    D. Email clicks

15. Biomimicry translation requires:

    A. UX designers only
    B. Ecologists + AI experts
    C. Accountants
    D. Hardware engineers

16. A regenerative UX reduces:

    A. Emotional friction
    B. Session time
    C. Battery usage
    D. Transactions

17. Community harmony score measures:

    A. Revenue
    B. Polarization
    C. Discounts
    D. Taxes

18. A multi-species intelligence view means:

    A. AI ignores humans
    B. AI models nature + humans
    C. Only insects matter
    D. Plants run AI

19. Ecological constraints ensure:

    A. Data privacy only
    B. Carbon & sustainability alignment
    C. More ads
    D. UI reload speed

20. Symbiocene scaling requires:

    A. Rapid expansion
    B. Slow ecological scaling
    C. Unlimited notifications
    D. Personalized ads

Answers

1-B

2-C

3-B

4-B

5-B

6-C

7-A

8-B

9-C

10-C

11-C

12-B

13-B

14-B

15-B

16-A

17-B

18-B

19-B

20-B

References

Crutzen, P.J. (2002) 'Geology of mankind', Nature, 415(6867), pp. 23–23.

Steffen, W., Crutzen, P.J. and McNeill, J.R. (2007) 'The Anthropocene', Ambio, 36(8), pp. 614–621.

Steffen, W. et al. (2015) 'Planetary boundaries', *Science*, 347(6223), p. 1259855.

Hamilton, C., Bonneuil, C. and Gemenne, F. (2015) *The Anthropocene and the Global Environmental Crisis*. London: Routledge.

Haraway, D. (2016) *Staying with the Trouble: Making Kin in the Chthulucene*. Durham: Duke University Press.

Moore, J.W. (2016) *Anthropocene or Capitalocene? Nature, History, and the Crisis of Capitalism*. Oakland: PM Press.

Latour, B. (2017) *Facing Gaia: Eight Lectures on the New Climatic Regime*. Cambridge: Polity Press.

Rockström, J. et al. (2009) 'A safe operating space for humanity', *Nature*, 461, pp. 472–475.

Albrecht, G. (2019) *Earth Emotions: New Words for a New World*. Ithaca: Cornell University Press.

Albrecht, G. (2020) 'The Symbiocene', *Sustainability*, 12(5), pp. 1–15.

Wahl, D.C. (2016) *Designing Regenerative Cultures*. Axminster: Triarchy Press.

Raworth, K. (2017) *Doughnut Economics: Seven Ways to Think Like a 21st-Century Economist*. London: Random House.

Capra, F. and Luisi, P.L. (2014) *The Systems View of Life*. Cambridge: Cambridge University Press.

Lovelock, J. (2006) *The Revenge of Gaia*. London: Penguin.

Meadows, D.H. (2008) *Thinking in Systems*. White River Junction: Chelsea Green.

Holland, J.H. (2014) *Complexity: A Very Short Introduction*. Oxford: Oxford University Press.

Kauffman, S. (1995) *At Home in the Universe*. Oxford: Oxford University Press.

Barabási, A.-L. (2016) *Network Science*. Cambridge: Cambridge University Press.

Mitchell, M. (2009) *Complexity: A Guided Tour*. Oxford: Oxford University Press.

Russell, S. and Norvig, P. (2021) *Artificial Intelligence: A Modern Approach*. 4th edn. Harlow: Pearson.

Turing, A.M. (1950) 'Computing machinery and intelligence', *Mind*, 59(236), pp. 433–460.

McCarthy, J. et al. (1955) *A Proposal for the Dartmouth Summer Research Project on Artificial Intelligence*.

Goodfellow, I., Bengio, Y. and Courville, A. (2016) *Deep Learning*. Cambridge, MA: MIT Press.

Sutton, R.S. and Barto, A.G. (2018) *Reinforcement Learning: An Introduction*. Cambridge, MA: MIT Press.

Bostrom, N. (2014) *Superintelligence: Paths, Dangers, Strategies*. Oxford: Oxford University Press.

Floridi, L. (2019) *The Logic of Information*. Oxford: Oxford University Press.

Crawford, K. (2021) *Atlas of AI*. New Haven: Yale University Press.

Benjamin, R. (2019) *Race After Technology*. Cambridge: Polity Press.

Mittelstadt, B. et al. (2016) 'The ethics of algorithms', *Big Data & Society*, 3(2).

Bonabeau, E., Dorigo, M. and Theraulaz, G. (1999) *Swarm Intelligence*. Oxford: Oxford University Press.

Dorigo, M. and Stützle, T. (2004) *Ant Colony Optimization*. Cambridge, MA: MIT Press.

Holland, O. and Melhuish, C. (1999) 'Stigmergy, self-organization and sorting in collective robotics', *Artificial Life*, 5(2), pp. 173–202.

Ball, P. (2001) *The Self-Made Tapestry*. Oxford: Oxford University Press.

Camazine, S. et al. (2003) *Self-Organization in Biological Systems*. Princeton: Princeton University Press.

Simard, S. (2021) *Finding the Mother Tree*. New York: Knopf.

Wohlleben, P. (2016) *The Hidden Life of Trees*. Vancouver: Greystone.

Sheldrake, M. (2020) *Entangled Life*. London: Bodley Head.

Tero, A. et al. (2010) 'Rules for biologically inspired adaptive network design', *Science*, 327(5964), pp. 439–442.

Wiener, N. (1948) *Cybernetics*. Cambridge, MA: MIT Press.

Ashby, W.R. (1956) *An Introduction to Cybernetics*. London: Chapman & Hall.

Beer, S. (1972) *Brain of the Firm*. London: Penguin.

Braidotti, R. (2013) *The Posthuman*. Cambridge: Polity Press.

Bennett, J. (2010) *Vibrant Matter*. Durham: Duke University Press.

Morton, T. (2013) *Hyperobjects*. Minneapolis: University of Minnesota Press.

Deleuze, G. and Guattari, F. (1987) *A Thousand Plateaus*. Minneapolis: University of Minnesota Press.

Rolnick, D. et al. (2019) 'Tackling climate change with machine learning', *arXiv preprint*.

Vinuesa, R. et al. (2020) 'The role of AI in achieving the Sustainable Development Goals', *Nature Communications*, 11, p. 233.

Van Wynsberghe, A. (2021) *AI Ethics*. London: Routledge.

Luhmann, N. (1995) *Social Systems*. Stanford: Stanford University Press.

Castells, M. (2010) *The Rise of the Network Society*. Oxford: Wiley-Blackwell.

Benkler, Y. (2006) *The Wealth of Networks*. New Haven: Yale University Press.

Toffler, A. (1970) *Future Shock*. New York: Random House.

Kurzweil, R. (2005) *The Singularity Is Near*. New York: Viking.

Dunne, A. and Raby, F. (2013) *Speculative Everything*. Cambridge, MA: MIT Press.

Kimmerer, R.W. (2013) *Braiding Sweetgrass*. Minneapolis: Milkweed Editions.

Escobar, A. (2018) *Designs for the Pluriverse*. Durham: Duke University Press.

Ostrom, E. (1990) *Governing the Commons*. Cambridge: Cambridge University Press.

Dennett, D.C. (1991) *Consciousness Explained*. Boston: Little, Brown.

Chalmers, D. (1996) *The Conscious Mind*. Oxford: Oxford University Press.

Friston, K. (2010) 'The free-energy principle', *Nature Reviews Neuroscience*, 11(2), pp. 127–138.

Benyus, J.M. (1997) *Biomimicry*. New York: HarperCollins.

Zuboff, S. (2019) *The Age of Surveillance Capitalism*. London: Profile Books.

Maturana, H. and Varela, F. (1980) *Autopoiesis and Cognition*. Dordrecht: Reidel.

Bateson, G. (1972) *Steps to an Ecology of Mind*. New York: Ballantine.

Tegmark, M. (2017) *Life 3.0*. New York: Knopf.

UNESCO (2022) *Recommendation on the Ethics of Artificial Intelligence*. Paris: UNESCO.

Capra, F. (1996) *The Web of Life*. New York: Anchor Books.

Latour, B. (2018) *Down to Earth*. Cambridge: Polity Press.

Index

www.ingramcontent.com/pod-product-compliance
Lightning Source LLC
LaVergne TN
LVHW051127210926
848482LV00001B/5